ANIMAL PHILOSOPHY

ANIMAL PHILOSOPHY:

ESSENTIAL READINGS IN CONTINENTAL THOUGHT

EDITED BY

Matthew Calarco and Peter Atterton

continuum

Continuum
The Tower Building, 11 York Road, London SE1 7NX
80 Maiden Lane, Suite 704, New York, NY 10038

www.continuumbooks.com

First published 2004
Reprinted 2005, 2006

British Library Cataloguing-in-Publication Data
A catalogue record for this book is available from the British Library.

ISBN   0-8264-6413-0
       0-8264-6414-9

Typeset by Fakenham Photosetting Limited, Fakenham, Norfolk.
Printed and bound by Biddles Ltd, King's Lynn, Norfolk.

CONTENTS

ACKNOWLEDGMENTS

We thank the copyright holders for granting permission to reproduce all or portions of the following material:

Martin Heidegger, *The Fundamental Concepts of Metaphysics: World, Finitude, Solitude*, trans. William McNeill and Nicholas Walker (Bloomington: Indiana University Press, 1995).

Georges Bataille, *Theory of Religion*, trans. Robert Hurley (New York: Zone Books, 1992).

Emmanuel Levinas, "The Name of a Dog, or Natural Rights," in *Difficult Freedom: Essays on Judaism*, trans. Seàn Hand (Baltimore: Johns Hopkins University Press, 1990).

Michel Foucault, *Madness and Civilization*, trans. Richard Howard (New York: Vintage, 1973).

Gilles Deleuze and Félix Guattari, *A Thousand Plateaus: Capitalism and Schizophrenia*, trans. Brian Massumi (London: The Athlone Press, 1988).

Gilles Deleuze and Félix Guattari, *Kafka: Toward a Minor Literature*, trans. Dana Polan (Minneapolis: University of Minnesota Press, 1986).

Jacques Derrida, "The Animal That Therefore I Am (More to Follow)," trans. David Wills, *Critical Inquiry*, 28 (Winter 2002). © The University of Chicago.

Luc Ferry, *The New Ecological Order*, trans. Carol Volk (Chicago: University of Chicago Press, 1995). © The University of Chicago.

Hélène Cixous, *Three Steps on the Ladder of Writing*, trans. Sarah Cornell and Susan Sellers (New York: Columbia University Press, 1993).

Matthew Calarco wishes to thank Nicole Garrett for her emotional and intellectual support in the completion of this volume. Peter Atterton would like to thank Gabriella Burden for her helpful contribution.

CONTRIBUTORS

Peter Atterton is Lecturer in Philosophy at the University of Cal
Diego.

Matthew Calarco is Assistant Professor of Philosophy at Sweet Bria

Verena Conley is Professor at French at Miami University, Ohio,
Professor of History and Literature at Harvard University.

Luce Irigaray is Director of Research at the Centre National de
Scientifique in Paris, France.

Alphonso Lingis is Professor of Philosophy at Penn State Univer

Jill Marsden is Lecturer in Philosophy at Bolton Institute.

Clare Palmer is Senior Lecturer in Philosophy at Lancaster Uni

Stephen David Ross is Professor of Philosophy, Interpretation, a
Professor of Philosophy and Comparative Literature at Bingha

James Urpeth is Lecturer in Philosophy at the University of C

David Wood is Chair and Professor in the Department
Vanderbilt University.

PREFACE

Peter Singer

Throughout Western civilization, nonhuman animals have been seen as beings of no ethical significance, or at best, of very minor significance. Aristotle thought that animals exist for the sake of more rational humans, to provide them with food and clothing. St. Paul asked "Doth God care for oxen?" but it was a rhetorical question – he assumed that the answer was obviously no. Later Christian thinkers like Augustine and Aquinas reinforced this view, denying that the suffering of animals is any reason, in itself, for not harming them. (The only reason they offered for not being cruel to animals was that it may lead to cruelty to humans; the animals themselves were of no account.)

Most Western philosophers accepted this attitude. Descartes even denied that animals can suffer. Kant thought only rational beings can be ends in themselves, and animals are mere means. But there were exceptions. Montaigne challenged human arrogance, and Hume thought we owed "gentle usage," although not justice, to animals. The strongest dissent to the dominant view came from the British utilitarian writers, Bentham, Mill, and Sidgwick, each of whom insisted that the suffering of animals mattered in itself. Bentham went so far as to look forward to the day when animals will be recognized as having rights. But even the classical utilitarians relegated their comments on animals to the margins of their philosophical writings. Their thinking was influential in leading to laws that sought to prohibit gross acts of cruelty to animals, but it did not lead to reconsideration of the assumption of the priority of human interests when they conflict with the interests of animals.

Over the past 30 years, however, something new has happened. Philosophers from a variety of ethical traditions have mounted a strong challenge to the traditional view of the status of nonhuman animals. They have argued that the interests of animals deserve equal consideration with the similar interests of humans, or that animals have rights. They have sought to bridge the ethical gap that has hitherto been perceived to exist between members of our own species and members of other species. They reject the assumption of the priority of human interests as "speciesism." By using that term, they make an analogy between our attitudes toward other species and the earlier, now discredited, attitudes of European racists toward members of other races. As a consequence, they argue that we need to alter radically our practices regarding animals, including our practice of routinely raising them for food.

One way of gauging the extent to which this issue has become more prominent is to look at Charles Magel's comprehensive bibliography of writings on the moral status of animals. Magel found only 94 works on that subject in the first 1,970 years of the Christian era, but 240 works in the next 18 years, up to the date when he completed his work.[1] The tally now would probably be in the thousands. Although most of these writers have been in what is often referred to as the "Anglo-American tradition," the debate is not limited to the English-speaking world, or even to Western cultures. Leading works on animals and ethics have been translated into, and discussed in, most of the world's major languages, including Japanese, Chinese, and Korean. For those who think that philosophy follows trends rather than instigating them, it is significant to note that in this instance it was the other way round. The philosophical arguments came first; the movement followed. As James Jasper and Dorothy Nelkin observed in *The Animal Rights Crusade*, "Philosophers served as midwives of the animal rights movement in the late 1970s."[2] This movement has had a significant impact in changing both popular attitudes and practices regarding the treatment of animals.[3]

How much of this philosophical impetus that gave rise to a practical challenge to the way we think about nonhuman animals came from writers in the philosophical traditions of Continental Europe, from such thinkers as Heidegger, Foucault, Levinas, and Deleuze, or those who take the work of these thinkers as setting a framework for their own thought? The answer is, as far as I can judge, none – and that is a judgment that is largely confirmed by a reading of the selections that follow. Thus for me the most significant question raised by this volume is why such an extensive body of thought should have failed to grapple with the issue of how we treat animals. What does this failure say about the much-vaunted critical stance that these thinkers are said to take to prevailing assumptions and social institutions?

Of course, it is possible to ask the same question of philosophy in the Anglo-American tradition before the 1970s, and some of the possible answers are common to all philosophical traditions. Just as it was convenient for the slave traders and slave owners to believe that they were justified in treating people of African descent as property, so too it is convenient for humans to believe that they are justified in treating animals as things that can be owned, and to deny that they have interests that give rise to moral claims upon us. But there are other, more specific factors involved in the failure of the Continental tradition to challenge orthodoxy regarding animals, even when philosophers outside that tradition were actively engaged in debating the issue. The deficiencies of the various thinkers in the Continental tradition in respect to their treatment of animals are illuminatingly explored in the commentaries that follow the selections in this volume. From pondering these deficiencies, we may learn more about the limitations of our own thinking when we consider beings who are not members of our own species. We may also be led to reflect on the importance, in addressing ethical issues, of going beyond the culture in which we live, of questioning widespread assumptions, and of refusing to accept vague rhetorical formulations that appear profound but do more to camouflage weaknesses in reasoning than to hold them up for critical scrutiny.

Yet it would be wrong to end on this negative note. Several of the commentaries that follow point to the positive potential that lies in the work of some thinkers in the Continental tradition. Just as it is possible to argue that the premises of Anglo-American thinkers who oppose racism and sexism carry logical implications that also challenge the way we treat nonhuman animals, so too the ideas of thinkers in the Continental tradition may point beyond the conclusions that they themselves have reached. Some of the thinkers whose selections appear in this book have unwittingly provided a philosophical framework that cannot, while remaining true to itself, be limited to upholding the special moral status of members of our own species. If this volume triggers a new debate about the real implications for our relations with nonhuman animals of the work of writers in the Continental tradition, it will have served a valuable purpose.

EDITORS' INTRODUCTION: THE ANIMAL QUESTION IN CONTINENTAL PHILOSOPHY

Matthew Calarco and Peter Atterton

The sight of man now fatigues. – What is present day Nihilism if not that? – We are tired of man. (Nietzsche)

It is perhaps with a certain amount of incredulity and astonishment that we learn that Continental philosophy has only rarely given serious attention to the animal question. For the most part it has spoken about human beings – and little else. The general neglect of the animal question is puzzling not only because Continental philosophy has displayed a tremendous reluctance to embrace traditional humanism and anthropological discourse, but also because of the tremendous reception it has given a thinker as seemingly pro-animal as Nietzsche. We now have stronger reasons than ever before for rejecting a certain conception of what it is to be human, but we seem to be hardly any closer to a post-metaphysical thinking regarding the animal. You might say that Continental philosophy has had an easier time denouncing what Descartes or Kant said about the human than it has criticizing what they said about the animal, an observation that naturally leads one to question whether the humanism it rejects is really quite so defunct after all. The "end of humanism," the "ends of man," the "end of philosophy," the "death of the author," the "death of God," the "death of man" – these apocalyptic shibboleths are becoming self-defeating utterances amid a discourse that has said hardly anything about animals in comparison.

We can only speculate why Continental philosophers have generally not had more to say about the traditional other of man – animals. One might perhaps attempt to account for the grossness of the discrepancy between man-talk and animal-talk by evoking the seemingly insurmountable difficulties of escaping metaphysical discourse itself. It is an established part of Heideggerian lore that the philosopher who seeks to go beyond metaphysics is destined to find herself all the more firmly rooted within it. Does not the discourse on the animal as such presuppose a distinction be made between animals and humans, thereby reaffirming the hegemony of humanism according to the familiar logic of negation? Would it not be better to eschew speaking of an *opposition* between the human and the animal altogether? The editors of this book are sympathetic with that strategy out of respect for such thinkers as radical as Darwin, Nietzsche, and Freud. However, while it is true biologically speaking that human beings are animals, the distinction is one that nearly every thinker in this volume – again with the possible exception of Nietzsche – maintains in some degree or other. What they mean by the distinction, and whether they are indeed right to make it on *philosophical* grounds is not up to us to say. We are here simply concerned to underscore the fact that much of what goes by the name Continental philosophy has been an uncritical devotee of the very distinction that has been called into question elsewhere. And not just in biology.

This volume was in many ways inspired by tremendous advances the Anglo-American philosophical tradition has made regarding the animal question over the last thirty years or so, from Peter Singer's and Tom Regan's writings on animal ethics through to the debates surrounding animal cognition. It seemed to the editors that Continental philosophy has lagged behind its Anglo-American neighbor on precisely these issues, despite its tendency to see itself in many ways as the more avant-garde, more radical, more politically engaged, and less philosophically naïve of the two. At the same time, it also appeared to us that Continental philosophy is perhaps better placed than is Anglo-American philosophy to accommodate the animal question owing to its more sophisticated understanding of the role of history in philosophical discourse, a historicism that has enabled it to make significant advances in other fields, from feminism to psychoanalysis, and from cultural studies to critical race theory. If much of that success is due to its far-reaching and profound critique of the virile Western humanistic subject, then the same results might be expected in the area of animal philosophy – and for many of the same reasons and arguments.

This book is not about animal liberation or animal rights; it presents no single or unified moral vision regarding animals. One will be disappointed if one turns its motley pages in the hope of discovering an argument why we should or should not eat animals. Derrida's description of the Western philosophical tradition as "carno-phallogocentric" in "'Eating Well'" (1991) is one of the few occasions when a major figure in Continental philosophy has intervened in the debate concerning animal suffering or "sacrifice" (something Derrida addresses again in "The Animal That Therefore I Am," an abridgement of which is reprinted here), though it is not altogether easy to assimilate the mistreatment of animals to logocentrism and/or man's technological will to power that has come under attack by Continental philosophy for half a century. The mistreatment of animals could perhaps be viewed as a necessary consequence of a humanism that has always sought to elevate the human at the expense of animals, but that only makes it all the more puzzling why much of Continental philosophy, in its ostensible rejection of humanism, should have been so unconcerned to call such chauvinism into question. Heidegger's work on the animal in *The Fundamental Concepts of Metaphysics* is just such a case in point. Not only does Heidegger conspicuously miss the opportunity to challenge the technological drive behind the practice of vivisection, whose scientific results he uncharacteristically allows to stand as evidence for his own conclusions, he clearly struggles to free himself from the prejudices of the very discourse he was among the first to expose. While he clearly intended to maintain the human/animal distinction in a way that was no longer integral to humanism, he seems to have been unable to carry out those intentions. This is especially significant when we consider the seminal influence of Heidegger on Continental philosophy, and even perhaps explains why so many of his followers have not dared to tread where less clay feet have stumbled.

Heidegger's failure to think through the animal question – a failure acknowledged by Heidegger himself – is perhaps the inevitable outcome of a philosophy that presents animals as separated from humans by an "abyss of essence."[1] Indeed, it is perhaps no exaggeration to say that philosophy in general has never quite known what to do with animals or where to place them on the conceptual map. From the moment Aristotle first defined man as a rational (or linguistic) animal, it was assumed that man was more *rational* than he was animal, leading many humanistic philosophers to dispense with the predicate animal altogether, and to speak of man simply as a "rational being as such." This was made all the easier by the biblical story of man being made in the image of god and having dominion over the animals. However, with the "death of god" and modern evolutionary biology, philosophers are gradually discovering the conceptual resources to call into question the traditional privilege enjoyed by the human. While science is assuredly leading the way here, philosophy, especially in the Continental tradition, still has some way to go, which explains why we have felt the need to publish a book like this. The selections we have chosen are not exhaustive, but they are exemplary; they constitute an accurate representation of the views of the thinkers behind them, and constitute in every case their most sustained treatments of the animal topic. They set out the terms of the debate in a way that is most likely to be useful for scholars and students working in the field of Continental philosophy and/or coming to the animal question for the first time. They open up new vistas for research even if they often turn out to be cul-de-sacs for the thinkers themselves.

It is admittedly not an easy task to survey a whole field in relation to a specific question – the animal question – and we have refrained from attempting to do so in the present volume. Our choice of which thinkers to include was determined by their current stature in Continental philosophy, and the novelty of their approach to the question at hand. Each of the readings is thoroughly original – or about as original as can be in the context of a discourse that everywhere puts into question the traditional authorial pretense to say something "new." The quality of originality about each of the readings is what prompted us to provide a critical commentary by distinguished scholars in the field following each reading. We felt that it would be helpful to the reader if he or she were also supplied with an interpretative framework and critical perspective to guide him or her on the way. The exception here is Luce Irigaray's article "Animal Compassion," which was especially commissioned for this book, and thus intended to speak for itself. It appears here for the first time.

Our first chapter consists of a number of key passages from Friedrich Nietzsche (1844–1900). Nietzsche is perhaps the thinker in the tradition most inclined to erase the sharp line that is usually drawn between humans and animals, though just as often we find him redrawing it – sometimes even at the same time. Thus we read in *The Antichrist*: "We no longer derive man from 'the spirit' or 'the deity'; we have placed him back among the animals. We consider him the strongest because he is the most cunning: his spirituality is a consequence of this."[2] Nietzsche goes on to make it clear, however, that such strength and cunning does not make man the crown of creation; on the contrary, "man is the most bungled of the animals, the sickliest, and not one has strayed more dangerously from its instincts."[3] For Nietzsche, health and vitality consist in following one's animal instincts as an antidote to a millennial training in Christianity in which those instincts are subordinated to morality or suppressed. This explains why Nietzsche should write, acerbically, "regarding Christians, a well known theory of descent [from the apes] becomes a mere compliment."[4] Alphonso Lingis shows just how entrenched Nietzsche's philosophy is in zoology and modern scientific ethology. According to Lingis, Nietzsche's philosophy does not merely designate animal species as allegories of human virtues or vices. "It is not Zarathustra's pride and wisdom that Nietzsche attributes to the eagle and serpent, but the eagle's pride and serpent's wisdom that he attributes to Zarathustra." Everything that Nietzsche evaluates positively in human beings – strength, nobility, independence – stems from the sound instincts and vital energy of solitary animals such as tigers and eagles; whereas everything he deprecates – weakness, servility, and dependence – consists in the adoption of feelings and behavioral traits of gregarious and domestic animals such as cattle and sheep. Lingis goes on to explain how according to Nietzsche nature has set itself the paradoxical task in the case of man of selectively "breeding" an animal that has "the right to make promises" – an animal that has enough self-constancy and unassailable will to stand above the deceptions of Christian moralism and the corruption of Western nihilism. Lingis likens this breeding to the cultivation of a healthiness that resembles Nietzsche's own, despite his physical afflictions, and which enabled him to overcome the ailments of his generation "like the lotus rising to flower over stagnant waters." For once the botanical no longer assumes the repose of plants; call it *physis*.

Throughout his writings, Martin Heidegger (1889–1976) consistently rejects the kind of reversal of values associated with the human/animal distinction that we find in Nietzsche. Confronted with the Nietzschean and Rilkean attempt to valorize animal over human existence, Heidegger sarcastically asks: "Are we then supposed to turn into 'animals'?"[5] But Heidegger does not wish simply to revert to the humanist gesture of placing human existence above animal life. Rather his task consists in trying to rethink the essence of the human independently of the Western metaphysical tradition and the timeworn idea that human beings are merely animals endowed with a capacity that other animals lack, namely, reason. This involves rethinking both the essence of human beings in distinction from the essence of animal life, a project undertaken in his 1929–30 Freiburg lecture course, *The Fundamental Concepts of Metaphysics*. In this work, the distinction between humans and animals is rethought in terms of their different relations to "world." Heidegger argues that animals are "poor in world," by which he means that they are unable to grasp other beings *as such*. Not that they are simply like stones, which, according to Heidegger, are *completely* without world. Animals are indeed open to other beings, but unlike human beings, who are said to be "world-forming," they are altogether unable to encounter other beings within a meaningful context that allows the being of those beings to be grasped and understood. These radically diverging world relations lead Heidegger to argue that all continuist notions of the human/animal distinction must be replaced by a thought that starts out from the essential differences and abyssal ruptures between human beings and animals. For Heidegger, it is only by attending to these essential differences that we can recover the essence and the dignity of the human in its role of keeping watch over and shepherding the being of beings. In his discussion of Heidegger's analysis, Matthew Calarco underscores Heidegger's attempt to understand the animal's relation to world on the animal's own terms rather than from the perspective of the human. Although Heidegger ultimately fails to carry through on his ambitions, Calarco notes that Heidegger's radically non-anthropocentric stance is essential for understanding recent poststructuralist thought about animal life à la Jacques Derrida, Giorgio Agamben, and Jean-Luc Nancy. The chief limit in Heidegger's thought, as Calarco presents it, consists in Heidegger's reliance on oppositional distinctions between human beings and animals. Despite Heidegger's insightful critique of metaphysical humanism, he is ultimately unable to overcome the anthropocentrism of the metaphysical tradition, which consistently defines animals in opposition to and by measure of the human. In order to present an effective alternative to metaphysical definitions of human beings and other animals, this anthropocentric dogma is precisely what needs to be addressed.

In "Animality," the first chapter of *Theory of Religion*, Georges Bataille (1897–1962) treats the problem of immanence through an examination of animality. In contrast to transcendence, which designates the relation of knowledge between a subject and object, "immanence" means a state of continuity between beings whose isolation and separation from each other has disappeared. Bataille sees the paradigm of this relation in the situation of one animal devouring another. He does not claim that there is no difference between the eater and the eaten; rather there is no "discernible" difference between them such as requires the use of concepts and dialectical intermediaries. Bataille is aware that what he wants to say here about animality is constrained by philosophical discourse that reduces everything to subjective experience and consciousness. He insists that "Nothing . . . is more closed to us than this animal life from which we are descended." Nevertheless, although it is not possible to describe such a phenomenon literally, we are able to speak of it figuratively and poetically. In her commentary, Jill Marsden suggests that Bataille's own poetical formulation "the animal is in the world like water in water" is just such an attempt to communicate the immanence of animality that lies at the limits of language and on the other side of knowledge. Linking Bataille's work on eroticism with his reflections on animality, Marsden underscores the fact that "The dissolution of boundaries in poetic and erotic activity is not a reduction of difference to sameness, which would be to understand difference conceptually," but a dissolution of identity thinking altogether. This perhaps begs the question of the practical implications of Bataille's account. However, Marsden argues that one seeks in vain for an explicit analysis of the correct treatment of animals from Bataille. The reason for this is that the question is "profane." It erroneously assumes "that animals are available for our appropriation," thereby presupposing that the identity of the farmer and of the animal are separate and intact, rather than coterminous with each other. Marsden ends her commentary by asking whether "Bataille's frequent references to the dumb passivity of the animal might be regarded as evidence of the most blatant speciesism." Her answer is that they do not. This is not because Bataille recognizes the animal as an equal, which is not true. Indeed, it is the very failure of recognition between human and animal – and thus the failure to reduce animality to what Marsden dubs "paradigms of humanist thought" – that an immanent connection between human and animal is forged. What might thus be considered a failure of recognition between species attests to their radical heterogeneity and leads to "the re-intensification of anguish, dread, and utter loss." This is not something to be avoided from Bataille's point of view, but celebrated. It is contact with the sacred, and thus subjectivity transcended in immanence.

Emmanuel Levinas (1906–95) is widely regarded as the most original ethical philosopher in the twentieth-century Continental tradition. Although Levinas's ethical philosophy is grounded in a responsibility for the other who is unknowable and incomprehensible, it is clear that by the term "other" Levinas has in mind the human other, whose face is the face of destitution and distress. This explains why Levinas had so little to say about *animal* suffering and about the relation between animals and ethics in general. Indeed, the tenor of his writing suggests that animals, much like plants and material objects, are encountered phenomenologically as little more than mere things, and thus offer little resistance to the *libido dominandi* of the human subject in its natural state. There are, however, a few occasions when Levinas complicates this picture somewhat. The two excerpts reprinted here, "The Name of a Dog, or Natural Rights" (1974) and a portion of the interview "The Paradox of Morality" (1986), are the best examples of this. In them, Levinas suggests the possibility that animals are capable of certain forms of ethical agency; he acknowledges that some animals do indeed have a face; and he admits that the ethical extends beyond human beings to other life forms. However, as Peter Atterton notes in his analysis, these kinds of extensional gestures are nearly always accompanied by exclusionary ones whereby Levinas reestablishes the traditional priority accorded to the human in ethical matters. Atterton argues that in order to overcome this kind of human chauvinism we should concern ourselves less with the task of establishing an essential identity or difference between human beings and animals, and more with thinking through the ways in which Levinas's ethical theory already implies responsibility toward the other who suffers – be it animal or human – even if Levinas himself was clearly unable or unwilling to draw the full implications of his own thinking.

Michel Foucault (1926–84) presents his reflections on animality in *Madness and Civilization*, a work in which he plots the course of the history of madness from the end of the Middle Ages to the beginning of modernity. Foucault argues that at the beginning of the Renaissance the mad were likened to animals whose fascinating qualities made them potential sources of religious revelation and esoteric learning. This was to change in the classical age (roughly from 1650 to 1800), when madness was essentially divested of spiritual and pedagogic value, and considered a social menace. Whereas animality once had value as the sign of the extra-worldly, it now was simply identified with "madness, without relation to anything but itself: his madness in a state of nature." The mad were considered wild beasts, untamed, and frenzied, who had abdicated their humanity and delivered themselves over to "unreason" (*déraison*) (including sexual promiscuity, social deviancy, atheism, heresy, and idleness). They had chosen to live like animals, and thus they would be treated as such. Throughout the classical age, they were subjected to harsh disciplinary "training," including being confined in cages and sleeping on beds of straw. In her essay, Clare Palmer shows how, according to Foucault, our conception of animality in history has changed no less than our views of madness. Animality is a "constructed category" that is determined differently in different periods. Palmer finds a common thread that runs through Foucault's representations of animality from one epoch to the next, namely, unreason and emotion. Whether it be the possibility of revelation from sources other than reason, the power of the raging passions, or the potential to stimulate works of genius, these various ways of understanding animals have a positive meaning for Foucault. In the spirit of Foucault's later genealogical project, Palmer inquires into the power–knowledge interests that are implicated in presenting the animal in these terms. She closes with a discussion of an alternative conception of the reason/animal-madness binary, where "the relationship between reason and animality is one whose terms do not necessarily exclude the other, that is, a discourse where some aspects, at least, of 'being animal' overlap with some aspects, at least, of reason." This is a more scientific alternative that Foucault for the most part ignores, leading Palmer to conclude that "Foucault's discourse of animality is thus largely symbolic and imaginative, and has little or no contact with animals understood as living biological organisms."

Gilles Deleuze (1925–95) and Félix Guattari (1930–92) are not particularly fond of pets, nor are they interested in animality per se. Rather they are interested in what they call "becoming-animal," a theme they have discussed at length in *Kafka: Toward a Minor Literature* and *A Thousand Plateaus*. Becoming-animal does not mean imitation and should not be thought of as identification with an animal; it is not a psychoanalytic regression, or an evolutionary progression. All these ways of relating to the animal attribute to it a fixed identity that lies beyond becoming and change. For Deleuze and Guattari, on the contrary, animals serve to rupture notions of identity and sameness. Becoming-animal is precisely the way in which Parmenidean monism is overcome "in reality," which means to say that the animal is the very *mode* in which becoming is possible. Like the revolutionary schizophrenic discussed in the first volume of *Capitalism and Schizophrenia*, animality is "the line of flight" along which the human manages to escape Oedipal triangulation and identification. Again, it must not be imagined that the subject has literally to *be* like an animal. It is possible, for example, to step into the stream of animal-becoming through an act as couth and as civilized as writing. Hence Deleuze and Guattari insist that " 'Mimicry' is a very bad concept, since it relies on binary logic to describe phenomena of an entirely different nature."[6] This is contrasted with writing where "there is no longer a tripartite division between a field of reality (the world) and a field of representation (the book) and a field of subjectivity (the author)."[7] Kafka's writings, especially his novels, present what are perhaps the best examples of this arrangement of radically heterogeneous elements. Not only do they depict the metamorphosing of the human into an animal, such as a beetle, they also produce the chimerical becoming-animal of the author (Kafka) himself. Indeed, "this is the essential object of the stories." Correcting any misconception that Deleuze and Guattari are advocating here something like a "return to nature," James Urpeth shows how the notion of becoming-animal is to be understood both as a critique of some of the basic assumptions and values prevalent in the philosophical and humanistic tradition, as well as a continuation of the Nietzschean project of affirming the priority of becoming over being. The two projects are linked owing to the fact that animal-becoming is precisely the manner in which the subject is able to free itself from a humanistic straightjacket without being posited as a subject behind the becoming in turn. Urpeth shows that two conclusions follow from this: first, the traditional hierarchical opposition of being and becoming is overcome, attested by Deleuze and Guattari's claim that "there is a reality of becoming-animal, even though one does not in reality become animal." And second, the subject becomes an animal that is itself changed in the process. In Deleuze and Guattari's words: "Becoming is always double, that which one becomes becomes no less than the one that becomes." Urpeth finishes by demonstrating how Deleuze and Guattari are successful in their identification of the theme of animal-becoming with art, such as Olivier Messiaen's famous *Catalogue d'oiseaux*.

Among the philosophers under discussion in this volume, Jacques Derrida (1930–) stands out as one who has perhaps gone the farthest in thinking through the *place* of animals within the Western philosophical tradition. Although Derrida hinted at the importance of the question of the animal for his work as early as the 1960s and 1970s, it was not until the mid-1980s that it came to occupy center stage in his writings. In the "*Geschlecht* II: Heidegger's Hand" (1985), *Of Spirit* (1987), "'Eating Well'" (1991), and *Aporias* (1992), Derrida presented highly sophisticated deconstructive analyses of the human/animal distinction as it operates in both Heidegger's work and the broader philosophical tradition. He went on in 1997 to publish "The Animal That Therefore I Am," his most extended set of reflections on the animal question to date. In this essay, Derrida moves beyond the project of deconstructing the human/animal binary and seeks to develop a positive thought of being-with animals that has its origins in the uncanny experience of being watched by the other animal – in this instance, a cat. Derrida goes on to present two hypotheses concerning the radical finitude and multiplicity of other animals. The first hypothesis is that there has been an unprecedented transformation in our relationship with animals over the past two centuries to the point where their subjugation and suffering has been accelerating and intensifying at an incalculable rate and level. The second hypothesis is that we ought to refrain from speaking of animals in the general singular ("The Animal") and speak instead of "the plural of animals heard in the singular." Derrida coins the term *animot* in order to speak about animals in a way that is intended to respect their radical multiplicity and singularity with regard to each other and those beings called "human." In his wide-ranging response to Derrida's essay, David Wood affirms several aspects of Derrida's analysis and acknowledges its importance for a post-metaphysical thought of animals, while also contesting other aspects of Derrida's thinking, especially his staunch rejection of continuist approaches to the human/animal distinction. If the merit of Derrida's essay lies in its calling attention to the conceptual, philosophical, and ideological forces that have stifled thinking through the question of the animal, the importance of Wood's response is to be found in its insistence on dealing with the material conditions (e.g., the human population problem) that create much of the suffering that animals encounter. Finally, Wood's essay also demonstrates the importance of uniting the question of the animal with broader issues in environmental philosophy, a move that is consistent with Derrida's thinking, but one that Derrida himself has so far failed to make with any real conviction.

The neo-humanist Luc Ferry's (1951–) essay "Neither Man or Stone" is taken from his enormously popular *The New Ecological Order*, which won the Prix Medicis de l'Essai in France in 1992. Ferry's main argument in his book is that contemporary forms of radical environmentalism, including animal liberation, deep ecology, and ecofeminism, are the ideological outgrowths of an anti-humanist strain of Continental philosophy that has failed to engage sufficiently with those aspects of the humanist heritage promoting progressive views about the natural world and its inhabitants. Ferry largely concurs with such critics as Nietzsche and Heidegger that Cartesian forms of humanism have led to the destruction and technological domination of the earth. But – and this is Ferry's chief point – the anti-humanist argument that we ought to reject Cartesian humanism does not entail the rejection of humanism *tout court*. On the contrary, Ferry argues that the humanism of Rousseau and Kant that stresses the diversity of the various orders of reality (in contrast to the Cartesian dualism) offers us an alternative ethic of human/animal interaction, one that respects the radical freedom of human beings and the enigmatic nature of animals. It is not rights for animals that follow from this version of humanism, according to Ferry, but rather a "circumscribed respect" that acknowledges their sentience and avoids reducing them to "mere things." Although Ferry's essay is rhetorically persuasive, Verena Conley points out that a number of problems remain for this kind of neo-humanist approach to animal philosophy. First, an ethic of animal welfare is perhaps not as effective as one might wish against animal abuses at the institutional level, a point that has been made forcefully in the recent work of Gary Francione.[8] Further, Ferry's recourse to a Kantian philosophy of the freedom of "man" fails to address the decentering of the human that has occurred in science and technology and which has de facto rendered human beings post-human. Conley argues that the "manly" values espoused by Ferry will not suffice to transform our relations to animals. What is needed, she argues, is a new metaphysics that thoroughly rethinks the relations between human beings, animals, and the natural world, one "that goes *through* technologies" and leads to "other ways of being and of sharing the world between humans and animals."

Hélène Cixous's (1937–) reflections on the troika "birds, women, and writing" contrast sharply with Ferry's emphasis on "man," humanism, and subjectivity. Whereas Ferry seeks to recover a Promethean humanism whereby human beings attain their unique essence in being separated from animals and the rest of nature, Cixous aims to explore the space of abandonment into which those beings traditionally denied full human status have been cast. The words "birds, women, and writing" might seem a random association, but Cixous maintains they share the common feature of being regarded as *immonde* by the dominant religious and metaphysical tradition. *Immonde* literally means unworldly, but also carries the sense of being unclean or improper. In order to develop this thought, Cixous investigates a passage from novelist Clarice Lispector's *The Passion according to G. H.* in which the main character, G. H., has a face-to-face encounter with a cockroach, which she almost kills by crushing it. With the cockroach half-dead and white paste oozing out of its body, G. H. stops to consider her relation to the paste and how the male religious tradition – which G. H. calls "those He-Bible" – declares such things to be "abominations." Following Lispector, Cixous suggests that the task is to rethink one's relation to all forms of being that are considered abominable, not only because of their marginalized existence, but also because the "elsewhere" of abomination is a site of profound joy. Cixous does not deny that the state of exile common to birds, women, writing, and other others is an "uncomfortable situation," but she insists that it is simultaneously "a magical situation." Thus, her aim is not to make light of the experience of exile, but to learn to "endure it differently," to learn to understand the *immonde* otherwise. Stephen David Ross finds just such a recasting of the association of birds, women, and writing in Remedios Varo's painting *Creation of the Birds* (1957), which depicts a bird-woman sitting at a desk in the process of writing-painting, surrounded by birds and other forms of animal and non-animal life. Ross threads his reading of Cixous's essay into a series of reflections on Varo's painting in which the association of birds, women, and writing is figured in terms of a mutually transforming process of *poiēsis*, becoming, *mimēsis*, and touching. Varo's painting thus opens the viewer-reader onto the un-worldly existence and becoming of all those beings, which, according to Ross "*crack the edges of our world.*" Ross is not concerned to compare this proto-linguistic touch and *mimēsis* with the rational discourse that Descartes and others attribute to "man." He wants instead to underscore the ways in which animals and other forms of life "*speak another language, or practice a language they do not speak, or know a reason we can never know because it knows nothing of our language.*" Ross finds in these languages and practices the joy that Cixous tells us is to be found in the space of exile. He writes: "*In the face, the eyes, the paws, fangs, and claws, the fur and skin, in the touch of animals is joy. The cacophony and* mimēsis *of the world is strange and impure joy.*"

Luce Irigaray (1930–) begins her essay with the question of the difficulty of understanding animal life from within: "How can we talk about them? How can we talk to them? These familiars of our existence inhabit another world, a world that I do not know. Sometimes I can observe something in it, but I do not inhabit it from the inside – it remains foreign to me." The alterity of animal worlds is not a source of distress for Irigaray, however, but corresponds to a certain joy, not unlike the joy Cixous associates with the elsewhere of birds, women, and writing. The greatest joys of her childhood, she recounts, were

bound up with her encounters with other an
But the most remarkable animal encounter
life. During times of acute anxiety and illnes
animals of various sorts which brought her
ionship. In particular, it was the visitatic
Irigaray. She calls birds our "friends," "guid
she uses elsewhere to refer to beings that
woman, and serve as "mediators of that wh
still going to happen, of what is on the hori
birds and other angel-animals thus appears
human becoming. For Irigaray, the accom
"learning to meet the other and to welco
reborn thus in a fidelity to ourselves and to
have been unable to accomplish this calli
inability to learn from animal compassion
partake in the "sharing of speech, of love,

We hope that you find this volume as st
it was for us to prepare. But more than t
toward breaking the thick silence that h
question in Continental philosophy, as tho
hour had not come, his morning, his day w
great noon!" (Nietzsche).

bound up with her encounters with other animals such as butterflies and rabbits. But the most remarkable animal encounters were those that occurred in adult life. During times of acute anxiety and illness, Irigaray was recurrently visited by animals of various sorts which brought her comfort, compassion, and companionship. In particular, it was the visitations from birds that most affected Irigaray. She calls birds our "friends," "guides," "scouts" – even "angels," a term she uses elsewhere to refer to beings that circulate between God, man, and woman, and serve as "mediators of that which has not yet happened, of what is still going to happen, of what is on the horizon."[9] The compassion shown us by birds and other angel-animals thus appears to announce another possibility for human becoming. For Irigaray, the accomplishment of our humanity lies in "learning to meet the other and to welcome them in their difference, to be reborn thus in a fidelity to ourselves and to this other." The extent to which we have been unable to accomplish this calling is directly proportionate to our inability to learn from animal compassion, that is to say, our unwillingness to partake in the "sharing of speech, of love, of desire" that other animals offer.

We hope that you find this volume as stimulating and provocative to read as it was for us to prepare. But more than that, we hope that it goes some way toward breaking the thick silence that has too often surrounded the animal question in Continental philosophy, as though Zarathustra had not ripened, his hour had not come, his morning, his day were not breaking: *"rise now, rise, thou, great noon!"* (Nietzsche).

CHAPTER ONE: NIETZSCHE

O MY ANIMALS

Friedrich Nietzsche

"O my animals," replied Zarathustra, "chatter on like this and let me listen. It is so refreshing for me to hear you chattering: where there is chattering, there the world lies before me like a garden. How lovely it is that there are words and sounds! Are not words and sounds rainbows and illusive bridges between things which are eternally apart?

"Speaking is a beautiful folly: with that man dances over all things. How lovely is all talking, and all the deception of sounds! With sounds our love dances on many-hued rainbows."[1]

* * *

To the plants all things are usually in repose, eternal, every thing identical with itself. It is from the period of the lower organisms that man has inherited the belief that there are *identical things* (only knowledge educated in the highest scientificality contradicts this proposition). It may even be that the original belief of everything organic was from the very beginning that all the rest of the world is one and unmoving.[2]

* * *

Animals and morality. – The practices demanded in polite society: careful avoidance of the ridiculous, the offensive, the presumptuous, the suppression of one's virtues as well as of one's strongest inclinations, self-adaptation, self-deprecation, submission to orders of rank – all this is to be found as social morality in a crude form everywhere, even in the depths of the animal world – and only at this depth do we see the purpose of all these amiable precautions: one wishes to elude one's pursuers and be favored in the pursuit of one's prey. For this reason the animals learn to master themselves and alter their form, so that many, for example, adapt their coloring to the coloring of their surroundings (by virtue of the so-called "chromatic function"), pretend to be dead or assume the forms and colors of another animal or of sand, leaves, lichen, fungus (what English researchers designate "mimicry"). Thus the individual hides himself in the general concept "man," or in society, or adapts himself to princes, classes, parties, opinions of his time and place: and all the subtle ways we have of appearing fortunate, grateful, powerful, enamored have their easily discoverable parallels in the animal world. Even the sense for truth, which is really the sense for security, man has in common with the animals: one does not want to let oneself be deceived, does not want to mislead oneself, one hearkens mistrustfully to the promptings of one's own passions, one constrains oneself and lies in wait for oneself; the animal understands all this just as man does, with it too self-control springs from the sense for what is real (from prudence). It likewise assesses the effect it produces upon the perceptions of other animals and from this learns to look back upon itself, to take itself "objectively," it too has its degree of self-knowledge. The animal assesses the movements of its friends and foes, it learns their peculiarities by heart, it prepares itself for them: it renounces war once and for all against individuals of a certain species, and can likewise divine from the way they approach that certain kinds of animals have peaceful and conciliatory intentions. The beginnings of justice, as of prudence, moderation, bravery – in short, of all we designate as the *Socratic virtues*, are *animal*: a consequence of that drive which teaches us to seek food and elude enemies. Now if we consider that even the highest human being has only become more elevated and subtle in the nature of his good and in his conception of what is inimical to him, it is not improper to describe the entire phenomenon of morality as animal.[3]

*　　*　　*

A few theses. – Insofar as the individual is seeking happiness, one ought not to render him any prescriptions as to the path to happiness: for individual happiness springs from one's own unknown laws, and prescriptions from without can only obstruct and hinder it. . . .

It is not true that the *unconscious goal* in the evolution of every conscious being (animal, man, mankind, etc.) is its "highest happiness"; the case, on the contrary, is that every stage of evolution possesses a special and incomparable happiness neither higher nor lower but simply its own. Evolution does not have happiness in view, but evolution and nothing else. . . .[4]

*　　*　　*

The situation that faced sea animals when they were compelled to become land animals or perish was the same as that which faced these semi-animals, well adapted to wilderness, to war, to prowling, to adventure: suddenly all their instincts were disvalued and "suspended." From now on they had to walk on their feet and "bear themselves" whereas hitherto they had been borne by the water; a dreadful heaviness lay upon them. They felt unable to cope with the simplest undertakings; in this new world they no longer possessed their former guides, their regulating, unconscious and infallible drives: they were reduced to thinking, inferring, reckoning, coordinating cause and effect, these unfortunate creatures; they were reduced to their "consciousness," their weakest and most fallible organ![5]

*　　*　　*

Against the slanderers of nature. – I find those people disagreeable in whom every natural inclination immediately becomes a sickness, something that disfigures them or is downright infamous: it is *they* that have seduced us to hold that man's inclinations and instincts are evil. *They* are the cause of our great injustice against our nature, against all nature. There are enough people who *might well* entrust themselves to their instincts with grace and without care; but they do not, from fear of this imaged "evil character" of nature. That is why we find so little nobility among men; for it will always be the mark of nobility that one feels no fear of oneself, expects nothing infamous of oneself, flies without scruple where we feel like flying, we freeborn birds. Wherever we may come there will always be freedom and sunlight around us.[6]

* * *

What changes the general taste? The fact that some individuals who are powerful and influential announce without any shame, *hoc est ridiculum, hoc est absurdum,* in short, the judgment of their taste and nausea. ... The reason why these individuals have different feelings and tastes is usually to be found in some oddity of their lifestyle, nutrition, or digestion, perhaps a deficit or excess of inorganic salts in their blood and brain; in brief, in their *physis.* They have the courage to side with their *physis* and to heed its demands down to the subtlest nuances.[7]

* * *

What makes a person "noble"? ... It involves the use of a rare and singular standard and almost a madness: the feeling of heat in things that feel cold to everybody else; the discovery of values for which no scales have been invented yet; offering sacrifices on altars that are dedicated to an unknown god; a courage without any desire for honors; a self-sufficiency that overflows and gives to men and things.[8]

* * *

The most comprehensive soul, which can run and stray and roam farthest within itself; the most necessary soul, which out of sheer joy plunges itself into chance; the soul which, having being, dives into becoming; the soul which *has,* but *wants* to want and will; the soul which flees itself and catches up with itself in the widest circle; the wisest soul, which folly exhorts most sweetly; the soul which loves itself most, in which all things have their sweep and countersweep and ebb and flood – oh, how should the highest soul not have the worst parasites?[9]

* * *

A kind of atavism. – I prefer to understand the rare human beings of an age as suddenly emerging late ghosts of past cultures and their powers – as atavisms of a people and its *mores.* ... Now they seem strange, rare, extraordinary; and whoever feels these powers in himself must nurse, defend, honor, and cultivate them against another world that resists them, until he becomes either a great human being or a mad and eccentric one – or perishes early.

Formerly, these same qualities were common and therefore considered *common* – not distinguished. Perhaps they were demanded or presupposed; in any case, it was impossible to become great through them, if only because they involved no danger of madness or solitude.

It is preeminently in the generations and castes that *conserve* a people that we encounter such recrudescences of old instincts. . . .[10]

*   *   *

Brave is he who knows fear but *conquers* fear, who sees the abyss, but with *pride*.

Who sees the abyss but with the eyes of an eagle; who grasps the abyss with the talons of an eagle – that man has courage.[11]

*   *   *

But courage and adventure and pleasure in the uncertain, the undared – *courage* seems to me man's whole prehistory. He envied the wildest, most courageous animals and robbed all their virtues; only thus did he become man.[12]

*   *   *

Then he looked into the air, questioning, for overhead he heard the sharp call of a bird. And behold! An eagle soared through the sky in wide circles, and on him there hung a serpent, not like prey but like a friend: for she kept herself wound around his neck.

"These are my animals," said Zarathustra and was happy in his heart. "The proudest animal under the sun and the wisest animal under the sun – they have gone out on a search. They want to determine whether Zarathustra is still alive. Verily, do I still live? . . . May my animals lead me!"

When Zarathustra had said this he recalled the words of the saint in the forest, sighed, and spoke thus to his heart: "That I might be wiser! That I might be wise through and through like my serpent! But there I ask the impossible: so I ask my pride that it always go along with my wisdom. And when my wisdom leaves me one day – alas, it loves to fly away – let my pride then fly with my folly."[13]

*   *   *

"O Zarathustra," the animals said, "to those who think as we do, all things themselves are dancing: they come and offer their hands and laugh and flee – and come back. Everything goes, everything comes back; eternally rolls the wheel of being. Everything dies, everything blossoms again; eternally runs the year of being. Everything breaks, everything is joined anew; eternally the same house of being is built. Everything parts, everything greets every other thing again; eternally the ring of being remains faithful to itself. In every Now, being begins; round every Here rolls the sphere There. The center is everywhere. Bent is the path of eternity."[14]

NIETZSCHE AND ANIMALS

Alphonso Lingis

EVOLUTION AND ATAVISM

Like every other species, our species evolved in a complex natural ecosystem. We are coming to realize that with each species that goes extinct, our planet loses something of the ecosystem that was able to sustain the evolution of our species. Soon 50, then 60 percent of humanity will be living in megacities, in high-rise buildings where the materials, the furnishings, the very air will be man-made. Long before us, Nature included the termites of the African savannah who never leave the high-rise constructions within which they raise their food, circulate the air. Biotechnology is reconstructing our nature: in vitro fertilization, surrogate maternity, cloning, brain cell splicing, genetic manipulation are bringing on the ability to reproduce the physical, physiological, and psychological traits we choose in our offspring. "Man is something that shall be overcome," Zarathustra affirmed. "What have you done to overcome him?" Such is our answer.

In the work of Friedrich Nietzsche we can find a strikingly distinctive assessment of the long association of our species with other species. It leaves us troubled about the future of the ever greater percentage of humanity for which this association is no more.

NATURALIZATION OF VALUES

Philosophers since Anaximander divided thoughts into true and false, but Hume divided them first into strong and weak. Nietzsche divides thoughts into healthy and sick. There are thoughts that arise out of a healthy body and are invigorating and empowering, and there are thoughts that arise out of a sick body, and that sicken the body. Nietzsche likewise divides values, sciences, religions, institutions, artworks, music according to this physiological criterion.

An ancient and dominant conception in Western culture conceives the body as a material conglomerate which is porous, leaks, and also respires and excretes wastes. Lacks and wants arise which open the organism to perceive and reach for substances in its environment. Life would be the force of this negativity. For Nietzsche the organism is a plenum which generates more energy than it needs to satisfy its needs and wants. The upsurge of excess energies is felt inwardly as exhilaration. Joy is natural; it is not in self-conscious consciousness only but everywhere in Nature and in our nature, inasmuch as we are natural. Joy is expansive and active. It is because the organism must discharge these excess energies that it acts, and in acting develops hungers and thirsts. These are not the primary phenomena; it is because the organism is a positive force that it develops these negativities. The feelings turned back upon unsatisfied lacks and wants are reactive. Resentment is turned back upon the organism itself, feeling its hurts, its mortification. It is vengeful. Nietzsche elaborates a genealogy of thoughts, values, sciences, religions, institutions, artworks, music according to the active, joyous or reactive, resentful and vindictive feelings from which they issue and which they intensify.

For Nietzsche the human species is a transitional species in the course of evolution; the question what man is entails the question what he can become. Nietzsche categorizes observed traits in view of evaluating them and evaluating the values with which they are evaluated. This evaluation does not proceed by a comparison of observed traits and a ranking of them according to natural criteria ("survival of the species," "survival of the fittest") or cultural criteria ("social utility," "benevolence," "virtue," "rationality"). Instead, Nietzsche affirms positively what life itself affirms positively and he identifies as negative movements by which life turns against itself. Health, the production of excess energies radiates upon itself, feels itself, is intrinsically joyous. This feeling intensifies the upsurge of energies. It is affirmative and self-affirmative. The songs and words that issue in these states radiate them and intensify them further. "How happy I am!" "How good to be alive!" "How strong I am!" "How beautiful life is!" The value terms – good, strong, beautiful, real, true – get their meaning in these exclamations. They intensify and radiate inner feelings of exultation: the beautiful words beautify; the noble words ennoble; the strong words strengthen; the healthy words vitalize. A living organism is positive, a plenum which generates excess energies; the lacks and needs that arise in it are secondary, intermittent and superficial. The positive, affirmative and self-affirmative feelings, and the positive, affirmative and self-affirmative value terms, are primary.

Weakness, sickness, neediness, want, dependence, vulnerability are reactive; they are forces of life turned against themselves: "Woe says, 'Break, bleed, heart! Wander, leg! Wing, fly! Get on! Up! Pain!' ... *Woe implores, 'Go!'*"[1] These states give rise to resentment and to negative, resentful, value terms. These reactive value terms intensify the weakness from which they issue. The ugly words sully; the servile words debase those who speak them but also those to whom they are spoken; the weak words emasculate and debilitate; the sick words contaminate. To prevail in their weakness, the weak transform these negative terms into positive values by reacting against the affirmative and self-affirmative exclamations of the strong and joyous; denigrating the happiness of the strong as frivolity, their pride as vanity, their health as sensuality, the weak vaunt their anxiety as humility, their timidity as prudence, their dependence as obedience, their inoffensiveness as patience. Nietzsche does not devalue the states that the weak value; he exposes their intrinsically negative and reactive movement.

NOBLE AND SERVILE ANIMALS

Nietzsche divides thoughts, values, sciences, religions, institutions, artworks, music into noble and servile. "Noble" and "servile" are to be sure categories from the feudal politic-economic system but Nietzsche naturalizes them. He associates them with animal species: eagles, lions, and serpents are noble; sheep, cattle, and poultry are servile. This transference of the identifying characteristics of the noble animal upon the human animal that rises from the herd is far older than feudal class society; we see the falcon-man, lion-man, stallion-man, eagle-man, bull-man, cobra-man in the necropolises of Egypt, on the temple friezes of the Assyrians, the Hittites, and on the seals of Mohendo-daro and Harrappa on the Indus two thousand years older still.

There are solitary, independent animals and there are gregarious, dependent animals. Naturally dependent upon a herd leader, gregarious animals – sheep and goats, cattle, pigs, horses, camels – accept a human leader; they can be domesticated.

Among humans there are gregarious individuals and there are individuals as solitary as beasts of prey. In fact there are independent, solitary impulses in individuals along with gregarious impulses. It is then not that there are healthy specimens and sick specimens in the human species, noble specimens and gregarious specimens; each major historical epoch has its own form of great health and its own form of nobility, its own form of sickness and its own form of gregariousness. And within each major historical epoch there are many kinds of health and of sickness, many kinds of nobility and of gregariousness. Even each life is destined to go through many kinds of health and many kinds of sickness, to cultivate many kinds of nobility and many kinds of gregariousness.

Humans in whom gregarious impulses dominate have made humans a self-domesticated species. For it is not the independent, solitary individuals who have imposed a herd leader on them; their own deepest instinct is to subject themselves to one another. The leaders of the human herds – priests and despots – understand these instincts because they share them; they need the dependence of others on them; they depend on the dependent.

ETHOLOGY AND ANTHROPOMORPHISM

Like other animal species in Nature humans nourish themselves, rest, take shelter, defend themselves from wounding by inert things and hostile animals, indulge in sexual contacts for pleasure as well as for reproduction, dance and perform display rituals. Like them humans feel the exhilaration of upsurging excess energies, know affection, pride, parental care, serenity, anger, trust and distrust. Like other gregarious species humans know feelings of dependency, wariness, timidity, and rancor.

For its modern founders, ethology's destiny as a science required the resolute repudiation of anthropomorphism. Not only were the "higher" activities of thought, aesthetic appreciation, and learning to be denied animal species other than human, but even for perceptions and feelings distinctive technical terminology and descriptions had to be devised for nonhuman species. Eagles could not be said to be "proud" nor serpents "wise." Nietzsche's procedure is the reverse of anthropomorphism; he naturalizes the human species, attributing to humans the perceptions, feelings, and behaviors of other natural species.

> The beginnings of justice, as of prudence, moderation, bravery – in short, of all we designate as the *Socratic virtues*, are *animal*: a consequence of that drive which teaches us to seek food and elude enemies. Now if we consider that even the highest human being has only become more elevated and subtle in the nature of his good and in his conception of what is inimical to him, it is not improper to describe the entire phenomenon of morality as animal.[2]

It has been argued, however, that Nietzsche's work does not depart from classical anthropocentrism in that humans are taken to be the most advanced animal species, although destined to evolve into a still higher species. Yet Nietzsche denies that the fittest is produced by evolution; what human evolution is realizing is the last man, weakest and sickest species which can only will nothingness, and for which Nature contemplates no sort of cure.[3] The species to come, the overman, will not evolve progressively out of the last man, but, in a pathos of distance from all continuity, by a new birth.

It has been argued that there is a classical anthropocentrism in the way Nietzsche describes the other species. Other species are identified with one characteristic trait: camels are responsible, lions sovereign, eagles are proud, serpents wise; they figure as allegories of human characters.

It is true that not only are distinctive forms of behavior characteristic of different animal species, but distinctive forms of sensibility and intelligence. Hibernating and migrating species have distinctive forms of perception and adaptive intelligence, as have diurnal and nocturnal species. The ability to foresee where a prey animal now unseen will turn up, the ability to identify the mere traces a prey animal has left on the ground is part of predator intelligence. Biologists argue that it is meaningless to compare the intelligence of one species with another: every species that survives over time develops the extent and kind of intelligence required for its environment. It is also true that every animal is moved by individual perceptions, memories, and feelings.

Part of the program for scientific ethology was to exclude the practice of seeing animals exemplifying virtues and vices; specialists argue that predators are not cruel, even to those they prey on. In the African savannah predators and hoofed herbivores evolved together, the antelopes becoming swifter and more wary as the great felines culled out the weak and diseased among them. Ethologists elaborate environmental explanations for infanticide among lions and birds. Yet if cruelty in humans is wanton destruction which yields at most only psychological satisfaction in the perpetrator, one cannot fail to observe the same kind of wanton destruction in other species. During the idle season bees will engage in veritable wars to extermination on other bee colonies and self-extermination. If a flock of birds pecking to death a weak individual can be said to serve unwittingly for the reproduction of the genetically strongest in the species, could not the same be said for the cruelty with which human children and adults pick on weaklings?

Though Nietzsche designates animal species by distinctive or dominant traits, he does not really take animal species as allegories of human virtues and vices, morally praiseworthy or reprehensible. Beneath or rather beyond the right, objectively observable and judgeable, and the good, subjectively appraised morally, the *virtù* of those humans Nietzsche evaluates positively (and who first evaluate themselves positively) is a matter of sound instincts, instincts that surge out of health, independence, and excessive and exultant energies. It is not Zarathustra's pride and wisdom that Nietzsche attributes to the eagle and the serpent, but the eagle's pride and the serpent's wisdom he attributes to Zarathustra.

SYMBIOSIS

And as so many species live in symbiosis, algae with sea anemones, egrets with water buffalos, hornbills with elands, in their association aristocrats and warriors take on the feelings and behavioral traits of tigers and eagles, as sedentary populations took on the feelings and behavioral traits of gregarious animals. (As well as their diseases; the principal infectious diseases such as smallpox, tuberculosis, influenza, measles, and syphilis have passed to humans as mutations of diseases that subsist among gregarious animals.)[4] Sedentary populations even took on the perspective and perceptions of plants, for which all things are usually in repose, eternal, every thing identical with itself. The thought governed by the belief in identical things, governed by principles of identity, non-contradiction, and excluded middle, Nietzsche says, would have been picked up from plants.

The earliest gods of humanity were not the abstract forces of Nature, but the lordly beasts and birds – tigers, lions, jaguars, eagles, condors, cobras. The earliest hominids lived in fear and awe of the beasts of prey that prowled their camps by night. Sacrifice is the fundamental religious act, and Barbara Ehrenreich[5] speculates that it originated in the practice of exposing deformed infants and the sick and dying to those beasts of prey. And the oldest religions taught humans to become half-lion, half-bull, half-stag, half-fox, half-ibis.

European aristocrats, Assyrian lords, Japanese samurai, the kshatriyas of Rajasthan, Maasai and Papuan warriors decorated themselves with lion pelts and eagle plumes, and took on the silent, stealthy movements of lions and the upright stance of eagles. They acquired the splendor of quetzal and birds of paradise plumes as well as the stately bearing and courtly dances of black-necked cranes and tragopans. The sharing of traits with other species is the most ancient ethics. What humans looked up to, what they admired and sought for, was the sensibility of eagles and wolves, the strength and endurance of elands and bears, the sacrificial loyalty of small birds defending their offspring. It is in interaction with these species that humans acquire their traits: the courage of the torero rises in his confrontation with that of the black bull; in hunting them or with them, humans acquire the single-mindedness, sensibility, and intelligence of predators. In long association only with eagles and serpents in the high mountains, Zarathustra acquires pride and wisdom. Sedentary and gregarious humans came to acquire the restricted and monotonous diet of their domesticated herds and flocks, became dependent on one another and on herd leaders, came to prize security, regularity, predictability, conformity, came to value wariness, prudence, nonaggression.

Modern ethics concedes that Nature is thoroughly amoral and sees morality as distinctively human. What morality calls virtues, established by conscious choice and for which a self-conscious ego is responsible, would be specifically "human," dependent on thinking, inferring, reckoning, coordinating cause and effect. The traits that Nietzsche identifies in the noble, their *virtù* – truthfulness, courage, pride, the presence in the present that disconnects the regrets and remorse of the past and the goals of the future – are the traits of noble animal species other than human and acquired by association with those species. The noble have strong healthy instincts, have an instinct for health, for beauty, for vitality, for joy, and live by instincts. They do not understand the others; their riches are squandered; they are victimized by the calculating; they are not very intelligent. The first trait Nietzsche recognizes in the noble is truthfulness; they are real, they truly are, and they are as good as their word. By instinct they declare what they see to be the case. It is the weak and the servile that have developed wariness, dissimulation, and cleverness.

BREEDING

Nietzsche envisions then the cultures in which values are given, cultures where deeds and results are evaluated, as cultures of selective conservation of things, selective transformation of production, and education of people. But he envisions the evolution or devolution of the evaluators from the point of view of nature and breeding.

The word of honor distinctive of the noble, which Nietzsche characterizes as the right to make promises (because one has the power to keep them), he does not see as something that developed out of its perceived general utility, as thus something dependent on reckoning and coordinating cause and effect. Instead he explains its emergence as a result of breeding: "To breed an animal *with the right to make promises* – is not this the paradoxical task that nature has set itself in the case of man? is it not the real problem regarding man?"[6] The selective breeding of this new species was accomplished by making memory cloying and painful (reflection necessitating a suspension of immediate gratification) and resolutely punishing and eventually liquidating those who do not keep their word. Nietzsche says it has taken virtually the greater part of the existence of the human race.

Breeding means that animal specimens that are healthy can be cultivated. The characteristic thoughts, instincts, and volitions of noble humans then are seated in their physiological natures. They are physically strong and healthy. But that health is not simply determined negatively: the absence of deformity, incapacity, or disease. It is the "great health" that is multiple, a health for many different kinds of activities and ways of life. It does not exclude suffering, for suffering anneals us and evinces the breakup of old structures and the emergence of new ones. It does not even exclude deformity and disease: Nietzsche's own physical afflictions are well known, yet he boasted he was the healthiest man in Europe, for able to take upon himself all the ailments of his century and overcome them.

THE ANIMAL IS POOR IN WORLD

Martin Heidegger

Man is not merely a *part of the world* but is also master and servant of the world in the sense of "*having*" world. Man has world. But then what about the other beings which, like man, are also part of the world: the animals and plants, the material things like the stone, for example? Are they merely parts of the world, as distinct from man who in addition *has* world? Or does the animal too have world, and if so, in what way? In the same way as man, or in some other way? And how would we grasp this otherness? And what about the stone? However crudely, certain distinctions immediately manifest themselves here. We can formulate these distinctions in the following three theses: [1.] the stone (material object) is *worldless*; [2.] the animal is *poor in world*; [3.] man is *world-forming*. ...

The lizard basking in the sun on its warm stone does not merely crop up in the world. It has sought out this stone and is accustomed to doing so. If we now remove the lizard from its stone, it does not simply lie wherever we have put it but starts looking for its stone again, irrespective of whether or not it actually finds it. The lizard basks in the sun. At least this is how we describe what it is doing, although it is doubtful whether it really comports itself in the same way as we do when we lie out in the sun, i.e., whether the sun is accessible to it *as* sun, whether the lizard is capable of experiencing the rock *as* rock. Yet the lizard's relation to the sun and to warmth is different from that of the warm stone simply lying present at hand in the sun. ... It is true that the rock on which the lizard lies is not given for the lizard *as* rock, in such a way that it could inquire into its mineralogical constitution for example. It is true that the sun in which it is basking is not given for the lizard *as* sun, in such a way that it could ask questions of astrophysics about it and expect to find the answers. But it is not true to say that the lizard merely crops up as present at hand *beside* the rock, *among* other things such as the sun for example, in the same way as the stone lying nearby is simply present at hand among other things. On the contrary, the lizard has its *own relation* to the rock, to the sun, and to a host of other things. ... The animal's *way of being*, which we call "*life*," is *not without access* to what is around it and about it, to that among which it appears as a living being.[1]

HEIDEGGER'S ZOONTOLOGY

Matthew Calarco

1. INTRODUCTION

Readers familiar with Heidegger's writings will be aware that the question of the relation between human *Dasein* and non-human animals is one that haunts nearly all of his work. Although he rarely elaborates this question at length, a careful reading of Heidegger's texts leaves no doubt that he is highly interested in rethinking the distinction between human beings and animals in a way that challenges traditional metaphysical characterizations. Yet, at first glance, this project of critically rethinking the human/animal distinction seems to offer little more than a new determination of what is essential to *human* existence, thereby leaving the question of *animal* life unexamined; indeed, it is precisely this focus on the human that has led some critics to argue that Heidegger's thought represents simply another instance (albeit a highly sophisticated one) of the dogmatic anthropocentrism that has characterized much of the Western philosophical tradition.[1] There is certainly considerable textual evidence to support this kind of critical reading. Not only are the overwhelming majority of Heidegger's remarks on non-human animals intended to highlight the comparative uniqueness of the human, but they also tend to portray animals in purely negative and oppositional terms in relation to human *Dasein*. The following passages might be taken as representative examples of such anthropocentric tendencies:

The leap from living animals to humans that speak is as large if not larger than that from the lifeless stone to the living being.[2]

Mortals are they who can experience death as death. Animals cannot do so. But animals cannot speak either. The essential relation between death and language flashes up before us, but remains still unthought.[3]

Because captivation belongs to the essence of the animal, the animal cannot die in the sense in which dying is ascribed to human beings but can only come to an end.[4]

Ek-sistence can be said only of the essence of the human being, that is, only of the human way "to be." For as far as our experience shows, only the human being is admitted to the destiny of ek-sistence. Therefore ek-sistence can also never be thought of as a specific kind of living creature among others. ... Thus even what we attribute to the human being as *animalitas* on the basis of the comparison with "beasts" is itself grounded in the essence of ek-sistence. The human body is something essentially other than an animal organism.[5]

Of all the beings that are, presumably the most difficult to think about are living creatures, because on the one hand they are in a certain way most closely akin to us, and on the other they are at the same time separated from our ek-sistent essence by an abyss.[6]

The [human] hand is a peculiar thing. In the common view, the hand is part of our bodily organism. But the hand's essence can never be determined, or explained, by its being an organ which can grasp. Apes, too, have organs that can grasp, but they do not have hands. The hand is infinitely different from all grasping organs – paws, claws, or fangs – different by an abyss of essence.[7]

For Rilke, human "consciousness," reason, *logos*, is precisely the limitation that makes man less potent than the animal. Are we then supposed to turn into "animals"?[8]

Of course, in order to be able to give these remarks a charitable reading they would have to be reinserted into their original context, and then given careful consideration in relation to the text itself as well as to the larger question of the place of animals and "life" within Heidegger's work. I do not have the space to undertake such a massive task here.[9] I have cited these passages simply to give the reader a sense of the tenor of Heidegger's treatment of animal life, and also to give some idea as to why his work has sometimes been charged with being dogmatically and naïvely anthropocentric. I will offer my own brief assessment of whether Heidegger's thinking remains anthropocentric in the closing section of the chapter.

So, rather than developing an interpretation of the passages cited above, I propose in this chapter to examine the issue that is perhaps most recurrent for Heidegger with regard to the human/animal distinction: trying to determine the difference between the human relation to world and the animal relation to world. Heidegger addressed this particular question on several occasions, in both his early and late writings. In one of the most widely read essays from his later period, "Letter on 'Humanism'" (1946), Heidegger offers the following oft-cited statement concerning the animal's relation to world in the context of a reflection on language and the animal's environment:

Because plants and animals are lodged in their respective environments but are never placed freely into the clearing of being which alone is "world," they lack language. But in being denied language, they are not thereby suspended worldlessly in their environment. Still, in this word "environment" converges all that is puzzling about living creatures.[10]

Eleven years prior, in a series of lectures at Freiburg (which were eventually published under the title *An Introduction to Metaphysics*), Heidegger offers a somewhat different account of the animal world in a discussion of the phenomenon of the darkening of the world and the emasculation of spirit (which Heidegger associates with the flight of the gods, the destruction of the earth, the standardization of human beings, and the preeminence of mediocrity). Heidegger asks:

> What do we mean by world when we speak of a darkening of the world? World is always world of the spirit. The animal has no world nor any environment.[11]

And in his well-known essay from the same year, "The Origin of the Work of Art," Heidegger makes a similarly ambiguous statement about the animal's lack of world in contrast to the world-relation of the peasant woman.

> A stone is worldless. Plant and animal likewise have no world; but they belong to the covert throng of a surrounding into which they are linked. The peasant woman, on the other hand, has a world because she dwells in the overtness of beings, of the things that are.[12]

In order to gain some insight into the significance of the status of animality in these passages, and to see why Heidegger's seemingly contradictory statements may not be contradictory once properly understood, it will be helpful to turn to the 1929–30 Freiburg lecture course *The Fundamental Concepts of Metaphysics*.[13] This lecture course is Heidegger's most sustained attempt by far to come to grips with both the question of the animal's relation to world in particular, and with determining the ontology of animal life in general. What we will discover in our reading of this lecture course is that Heidegger's statement concerning the world-poverty of animals is meant to indicate a simultaneous having and not-having of world, something which appears to be a blatant contradiction from the perspective of formal logic and common sense. By penetrating into and disclosing the ambiguous world-relation of animals, we will also track Heidegger's efforts to establish the foundations for a new ontology of animal life that contests the continuism of Darwinism as well as classically mechanistic and vitalistic interpretations of animal life.

Before examining the lecture course in more detail, it is important to bear in mind that the tacit orientation of Heidegger's entire analysis of animality lies in the direction of understanding what he takes to be the uniquely *human* relation to world. (We will have occasion to call this orientation into question below.) Heidegger states that he addresses the issue of the animal's relation to world only in order to highlight, by way of contrast and comparison, what is essential to the human capacity for world-formation. At the same time, however, Heidegger does make a genuine effort to understand the animal's relation to world on the animal's own terms. It is this latter aspect of the text that at least partially justifies reading this portion of the lecture course in isolation from the rest of Heidegger's argument.

2. ESSENTIAL POVERTY

Heidegger's examination of the theme of "world" in *The Fundamental Concepts of Metaphysics* emerges in an attempt to answer one of the three questions deriving from the discussion of boredom that occupies the first half of the lecture course (1–167). Of the three questions – What is world? What is finitude? What is individuation? – Heidegger begins with the first: What is world? Prior to this text, he had allotted considerable space to discussions of the concept of "world," both in *Being and Time* and in his essay "On the Essence of Ground" (1929).[14] In contrast with these previous attempts to determine the meaning of "world," Heidegger here seeks to uncover the specifically human relation to world by way of a *comparative* examination with the world relations of the animal and stone. Heidegger begins with the assumption that human beings are not simply a part of the world but also, in some sense which is to be further clarified, *have* world. But what about the animal and stone? Do they have world in a way that parallels the human being's having? Or are they denied access to world a priori? Concerning these questions, Heidegger suggests that certain distinctions, however crude they might at first appear, immediately manifest themselves in the form of three theses: "[1.] the stone (material object) is *worldless* [weltlos]; [2.] the animal is *poor in world* [weltarm]; [3.] man is *world-forming* [weltbildend]" (177).

These theses clearly have an ambivalent status for Heidegger. He does indeed intend to show that they are fundamentally correct in a certain respect, but they trouble him insofar as they presuppose essential distinctions between entities that are difficult to establish with any clarity. Heidegger himself admits that the distinction between human and animal "is difficult to determine" (179). This difficulty raises the need for a more exacting determination of the essence of animality so that human and animal (as well as animal, *qua* living being, and stone, *qua* non-living material object) can be clearly distinguished. The question that immediately arises for the skeptical reader is: How can the essence of animality be determined if one doesn't already have essential knowledge of what constitutes inclusion in the category "animal"? This skeptical question has little purchase for Heidegger, however, as the kind of metaphysical questioning he is undertaking proceeds and moves about in a pre-logical space, unfettered by the charge of circular reasoning that would force common sense and logic to seek a different approach.

Of greater importance to Heidegger than answering the skeptical question concerning circularity is to ensure that his thesis – "the animal is poor in world" – not be understood in terms of a hierarchical value judgment. He insists repeatedly throughout the lecture course that the thesis "the animal is poor in world" does not mean to say that the animal is "poor" in comparison with, and by the measure of, man who is "rich" in having world. Such a difference of degree, which implies a continuist and hierarchical scale of evaluation, is firmly rejected by Heidegger (194) in the name of a different understanding of poverty. According to Heidegger, the animal is poor in world *on its own terms*, poor in the sense of being deprived: "[B]eing poor means *being deprived* [Entbehren]" (195). Hence, what poverty and deprivation ultimately mean here can only be understood "by taking a look at animality itself" (195), rather than evaluating the animal using the measure of the human.[15]

In order to explain the animal's deprivation of world, Heidegger begins by comparing the animal's world-relation with that of the stone. He suggests that the animal's being deprived of world is quite different from the stone's lack of world, for the stone is "essentially *without access* [Zugangslosigkeit]" (197) to those things that surround it; consequently, the stone does not even have the possibility, as the animal does, of being deprived of world. Unlike stones, animals are not merely present-at-hand (*vorhanden*) material objects. A lizard (Heidegger's primary example of a living being in the opening pages of his discussion) that is warming itself in the sun by basking on a warm stone does not merely "crop up [*kommt . . . vor*]" in the world like the stone does; rather, it actively seeks out the stone upon which it lies. And if the lizard is removed from the stone and placed in another, cooler area, it will not stay put as the stone does, but will in all likelihood try once again to seek out a warm stone or another place to bask in the sun. This strongly suggests that the lizard is a being that has a responsive and interactive relation with the environment that surrounds it. Heidegger can thus maintain that, unlike the stone, the lizard has world inasmuch as it has some form of access to other beings. The real question for Heidegger, though, is whether the behavior exhibited by the lizard is comparable to "same" act when it is carried out by a human being. When a human being basks in the sun, is it any different than the lizard lying on the warm stone? Is the human being's mode of access to other beings in such acts substantially different from the lizard's?

According to Heidegger, these two acts, and the modes of access that they presuppose, are in fact radically different. The lizard, it seems, is incapable of relating to the stone and the sun in the same way that we do. That is to say, Heidegger doubts "whether [the lizard] really comports itself in the same way as we [presumably the "we" here denotes only human *Daseins*] do when we lie out in the sun" (197). When we lie out in the sun, Heidegger goes on to argue, the sun is accessible to us *as* sun, and rocks are accessible to us *as* rocks in a way that is simply not possible for the animal. Thus, even though an animal might have access to the beings that surround it inasmuch as it has "a specific set of relationships to its sources of nourishment, its prey, its enemies, its sexual mates, and so on" (198), Heidegger believes that animals can never gain access to the other entities it encounters in its environment *as* entities. The animal[16] is incapable of grasping the ontological difference – which is to say, it has access to other beings, but not to other beings *as such* (*als solche*).

The conclusion Heidegger has arrived at in his initial analysis of the animal's relation to world, then, is as follows: if by "world" is meant accessibility to other beings, we can say that the animal has world; but if "world" is in some way related to having access to the being of beings, to beings *as such*, then the animal does not have world.

3. LIFE HELD CAPTIVE

This ambiguous and seemingly contradictory conclusion – the animal has and does not have world – suggests that the concepts of "world" and "world-poverty" have not yet been properly clarified. In order to move past this limitation, and to keep to his original goal of understanding the animal's relation to world on its own terms, Heidegger considers the possibility of transposing himself into the animal's world in order to describe it from within. Heidegger does not ultimately pursue this option, however, because animals have a radically different mode of being-in-the-world than do human beings. Heidegger suggests that a more promising means of achieving insight into the animal's world-poverty would be to determine first what the essence of the animal is, and then deduce the animal's specific world-relation beginning from this determination.

With this task in mind Heidegger launches into a rather lengthy and dense discussion of what he takes to be the essentially "organismic" character of life, with a specific emphasis on animal life. In addition to preparing the ground for the analysis of the animal's world relation, these sections (§§51–61) are used to develop an understanding of life's essence in such a manner that the twin pitfalls of mechanism and vitalism are avoided. A living being *qua* organism on Heidegger's account is not a mere machine any more than it is an entity guided by an underlying, subject-based vital process or entelechy; rather it consists of a group of organs that function in order to further and maintain the life processes of the organism. Organs, though, are not to be understood as mere instruments or tools (e.g., the eye as an instrument for sight); they should be seen as secondary to, and in the service of, potentialities inherent to specific animals. As Heidegger explains, it is "the *potentiality for seeing* which first makes the possession of eyes possible, makes the possession of eyes necessary in a specific way" (218). This rather peculiar account of the function of organs helps to explain in part Heidegger's constant references to the human body and its parts (e.g., the hand) as being something "essentially other" than an animal organism. The animal potentialities that give rise to such organs as paws, claws, or fangs are seen as essentially different from the human potentialities that give rise to human hands. Although such organs may appear physiologically similar (and in some cases indistinguishable), for Heidegger, they have their conditions of possibility in two wholly different modes of potentiality, and thus their being is likewise essentially different.

Consideration of the living being's capacity for governing its own reproduction, nourishment, and other such processes might lead us to believe that there is an underlying agent that controls these vital processes. As I just mentioned, Heidegger firmly rejects any form of vitalism that would attribute conscious subjectivity to animal life. He argues that the self-governing activities of animals happen purely at an instinctual level, and that there is no gap between an animal's activities and itself. Thus, even though the animal is thrust toward the world and deals with its external environment in a responsive and interactive way, it brings itself along so closely and so immediately in the process that no gap for reflection or self-awareness can arise. In the animal's instinctual behavior toward itself and the world, its specific capacity for being thus "becomes and remains *proper to itself* – and does so *without* any so-called *self-consciousness* or any *reflection* at all, without any relating back to itself" (233). Not surprisingly, in this context Heidegger reserves the terms "self" and "selfhood" for human beings, and defines the animal's self-relation as simply "proper being": "The way and manner in which the animal is proper to itself is not that of personality, not reflection or consciousness, but simply its *proper being* [Eigentum]" (233).

But this denial of full subjectivity to the animal should not be taken to imply that Heidegger maintains an uncritically Cartesian stance on animal life. Although he is clearly anxious about any attempt to attribute language, consciousness, or selfhood to animals (as was Descartes), Heidegger does not want to suggest that an animal's reactions to stimuli are ontologically indistinguishable from, say, the inner mechanistic workings of a clock (as Descartes seems to).[17] He is willing to grant the animal a certain amount of responsivity to external stimuli, but wants to limit such responsivity to the level of instinct. Animals on this account would be open to other beings, but their openness would be conditioned, and made possible, by species-specific instincts. The image that Heidegger uses to convey this double relation is an instinctual "ring." This ring both (1) *encircles* the animal, and thereby strictly limits its access to specific types of other beings, and, at the same time, (2) *disinhibits* and opens the animal up beyond itself to the surrounding environment. In this sense, we can say that animal life literally holds itself captive: captive to its own instincts, but also captive to other beings in such a way that no gap is able to be inserted between the animal and its other. Phrased differently, living beings open themselves to other beings, but in such a way that the other is not recognized *as* an other being, that is, *as such*.

4. THE BODY WITHOUT ORGANS

We have arrived at the moment of the "example" in Heidegger's text (241), the moment in which the ontological and metaphysical analysis of animality is supplemented with empirical examples meant to illustrate, clarify, and bolster the thesis that the animal lacks access to other beings as such. Here Heidegger offers an interpretation of experiments done with bees and other insects (the results of which were presented in the works of Emanuel Radl and Jakob von Uexküll) that helps to clarify the difference between the animal's instinctual, driven behavior (*Benehmen*) and human comportment (*Verhaltung*).

Heidegger's initial example concerns the bee's act of collecting nourishment. What is revealed in carefully analyzing this act is that the worker bee is not indifferent to the scent or color of the flower with which it is engaged. Such distinctions are important to the bee if it is to complete its task. Its task, of course, is to collect honey, and, when it sucks up all of the honey, it flies away. Now, if we ask *why* the bee flies away, the simplest answer is: because the honey is gone, it is no longer present. While this might seem to explain clearly why the bee flies away, it does not answer the question that most interests Heidegger: Does the bee fly away because it recognizes the honey *as* no longer present? Is there any evidence that would conclusively prove that the bee recognizes the presence or absence of the honey *as such*? "Not at all," answers Heidegger, "especially if we can and indeed must interpret" the comings and goings of the bee in terms of a "driven performing and as drivenness, as behavior – as behavior rather than comportment" (241).

Now the skeptical reader might raise some questions about Heidegger's interpretation of this example or not be fully convinced of the bee's inability to recognize the presence or absence of the honey as such. In support of his own interpretation, Heidegger has recourse to an experiment with bees that is quite convincing but, at the same time, quite disturbing. In this experiment:

> A bee was placed before a little bowl filled with so much honey that the bee was unable to suck up the honey all at once. It begins to suck and then after a while breaks off this driven activity of sucking [*dieses Treiben des Saugens*] and flies off, leaving the rest of the honey still present in the bowl. If we wanted to explain this activity, we would have to say that the bee recognizes [*stellt fest*] that it cannot cope with all the honey present [*vorhandenen*]. It breaks off its driven activity because it recognizes the presence of too much honey for it. Yet, it has been observed that if its abdomen is carefully cut away while it is sucking, a bee will simply carry on regardless even while the honey runs out of the bee from behind. This shows conclusively that the bee by no means recognizes the presence of too much honey. It recognizes neither this nor even – though this would be expected to touch it more closely – the absence of its abdomen. There is no question of it recognizing any of this ... [because] the bee is simply taken by its food. This *being taken* is only possible where there is an *instinctual* "toward . . . ." Yet such a driven being taken also excludes the possibility of any recognition of presence. It is precisely being taken by its food that prevents the animal from taking up a position over and against this food. (242)

After reading Heidegger's analysis of the experiment, most readers would probably be convinced of the bee's inability to recognize the presence or absence of food as such. Perhaps bees as such, or at least this particular bee, are unable to recognize the presence of too much honey and only depart from the bowl based on a kind of driven behavior.[18] Heidegger uses two further examples – (1) an experiment designed to demonstrate that the bee's flight to and from the hive is based not on cognition but on instinct, and (2) instances where moths, in their instinctual search for light, often fly directly into a flame and kill themselves in the process – to drive home the point that "the animal" lacks access to other beings in their being, to beings *as such*. With these theses established to his satisfaction, and with a provisional ontology of the essence of animal life (as the capacity for captivated, driven behavior) established, Heidegger is then able to return to his original question of what being "poor in world" means from the animal's own perspective.

But before examining Heidegger's closing remarks on the animal's world poverty, I want to pause for a moment and raise some questions about the analysis of animality given thus far.

First, it is highly revealing in the context that Heidegger has nothing to say about the domination of life in these experiments, particularly the experiment where a bee's abdomen is cut away, and this despite his railings against the techno-scientific domination of nature which is prevalent throughout several of his texts. One perhaps wonders why the double sacrifice of this bee – sacrificed once (literally) in the name of scientific knowledge and a second time (symbolically) in the name of the ontological difference – even if it does not touch the bee at a cognitive level, does not "touch" *thought* more closely.

Second, Heidegger makes two rather hasty and questionable generalizations concerning the essence of animal life. The first generalization we might want to question concerns the particular behaviors (gathering honey, the movement toward light, etc.) from which Heidegger draws his generalization about the animal's captivation. It should be said that simply because a particular behavior on the part of an animal or insect demonstrates an inability to access beings as such does not mean that careful examination of other behaviors might not produce different results. It also seems reasonable to be suspicious of the claim that the capacities for *Dasein* and world are strictly coextensive with the human species. For his part, Heidegger insists repeatedly that there is "no indication that the animal does or ever could comport itself toward beings as such" (253); but such a claim cannot be confirmed or disconfirmed unless we are given a list of certain signs (e.g., culture, history, advanced linguistic capacities, tool use, a relation to finitude, etc.) that *would* indicate the capacity for comportment. One gets the sense, however, that any animal act that might indicate such a capacity would be quickly thrust aside by Heidegger and labeled as "essentially different" from similar human acts, much as the ape's "grasping organ" is deemed to be essentially different from the human hand. The second generalization raises an even more difficult question. Heidegger's analysis of animal life tends to move quickly, and with very little justification, from generalizations about one species of animal to broader claims about the essence of animality. While such gestures are perhaps inevitable in the construction of any "productive logic" of animal life, the choice of examples from which the generalizations are drawn is nevertheless suspect. Not only are Heidegger's primary examples drawn solely from the realm of insects, but he deliberately avoids examining the behavior of what he calls "higher animals" inasmuch as their behavior seems to "correspond so closely to our own comportment" (241). What kinds of conclusions about the essence of animal life might have been drawn if his analysis had sought to account for behaviors from, say, chimpanzees or elephants?

Third, Heidegger's entire text is strongly anti-Darwinian in its refusal of any form of human/animal continuism, but the reasons for this opposition, and the alternative offered in its place, are far from unproblematic. As I suggested above, Heidegger opposes all mechanist and vitalist accounts of life; yet Darwinism, which seems to offer a promising means of overcoming the limits of these two theories, also receives a summary dismissal from Heidegger. Toward the end of the sections on the essence of the organism, he argues that the Darwinian interpretation of the animal's relation to its environment is

> based upon the fundamentally misconceived idea that the animal is present at hand, that it then subsequently adapts itself to a world that is present at hand, that it then comports itself accordingly and that the fittest individual gets selected. Yet the task is not simply to identify the specific conditions

of life materially speaking, but rather to acquire insight into the *relational structure between the animal and its environment.* (263)

Heidegger then goes on to show how this supposed misunderstanding of the animal's relationality allows for a mistaken conflation of the different manners in which human beings and animals encounter other beings.

> We ... think that the particular animals and species of animal adapt themselves in different ways to these beings that are intrinsically present at hand, present in exactly the same way for all beings and thus for all human beings. (277)

What interests me in these passages is less Heidegger's specific reading of Darwin (which in itself is inadequate inasmuch as it fails to take into account the complex interplay of genetic, environmental, and hereditary factors that determine an animal's or a human being's relation to its environmental niche), and more his underlying reasons for rejecting the continuist implications of Darwinian evolutionary theory. Beyond the rejection of the idea that beings are fundamentally present at hand for us, Heidegger primarily wants to avoid flattening out differences in relational structures among various life forms. If, as Heidegger seems to imply, Darwinian evolutionary theory resulted in a homogenization of the various world relations among human and animal life (and it is not at all clear that it does), then one could perhaps go along with this critique. But what Heidegger offers in place of a continuist thought of relation – the reduction of all forms of world relation among living beings to three distinct and essential kinds (plant, animal, and human) – presents its own difficulties. If, as Aristotle reminds us, "life is said in many ways [*pleonachōs de tou zēn legomenou*]" (*De Anima* 413a 23), then perhaps the world relations characteristic of life are themselves to be said in many ways. And perhaps the project of elaborating a productive logic of these world relations has to begin with a resolute refusal to diminish the radical multiplicity and singularity of relations characteristic of life, whether in its so-called "plant," "animal," or "human" form.

5. DEAD END

Let us leave these questions aside and return to Heidegger's text in order to examine his final remarks on the thesis with which we began: "the animal is poor in world." The seeming contradiction concerning the animal's relation to world (the animal has and does not have world) that led us into the discussion of the essence of animal life can now be resolved. If the essence of animal life can be said to reside in being captivated, then, strictly speaking, the animal's specific mode of relationality cannot be assimilated to a having of world. Inasmuch as the animal is open to, and has access to other beings, it has "world" in a way that the stone does not. But this way of speaking about world is misleading. The concept of "world," while not identical with the "as such" relation to the being of beings, is nevertheless inextricably intertwined with it such that any being which is deprived access to other beings *as such* is deprived of world altogether.

In comparison with the human, then, the animal is not poor in world but is completely deprived of world:

> in distinction from what we said earlier we must now say that it is precisely because the animal in its captivation has a relation to everything encountered within its disinhibiting ring that it precisely does *not* stand alongside man and precisely has *no* world. (269)

What the animal *has*, positively, is a certain openness toward beings; what it *lacks*, negatively, is the capacity to encounter beings in their manifestness, in their being, a capacity that is, for Heidegger at least, unique to human *Dasein*.

We seem, however, to have gotten off track somewhere. Wasn't Heidegger's express intention to understand the animal's mode of relationality on the animal's own terms? How can we say *from the perspective of animal life itself* that the animal's being is characterized by being deprived of world? If it knows nothing of world, how could it be deprived of world? Heidegger recognizes the importance of this objection when he notes that it is "only from the human perspective that the animal is poor with respect to world, yet animal being in itself is not a deprivation of world" (270–1). Heidegger also acknowledges that the entire discussion of the essence of animal life in terms of captivation is not only incomplete (265), but is, like the analysis of world, shot through with anthropocentric comparative analyses, where the human functions as the measure of animal life. When Heidegger speaks of captivation, he is concerned not only with disclosing the essence of animal life, but also with trying to distinguish human comportment from animal behavior. Thus, any thesis about the animal's relation to world that is grounded in the animal's captivation is also questionable inasmuch as the notion of captivation only takes on meaning by way of comparative considerations with human *Dasein*'s comportment toward beings as such. In the final analysis, Heidegger is forced to reduce radically the scope and significance of his original thesis:

> Captivation as the essence of animality is the condition of the possibility of a merely comparative definition of animality in terms of poverty in world, insofar as the animal is viewed from the perspective of man to whom world-formation belongs. Our thesis that the animal is poor in world is accordingly far from being a, let alone *the*, fundamental metaphysical principle of the essence of animality. At best it is a proposition that follows from the essential determinations of animality, and moreover one which follows only if the animal is regarded in comparison with humanity. (271)

For all intents and purposes, then, the discussion of animality in *The Fundamental Concepts of Metaphysics*, despite its extreme prudence, patience, and sophistication, results in a dead end – at least with respect to a non-anthropocentric understanding of the animal's mode of being and relationality. The upshot of the analysis of animal world, though, is that it sheds light on human *Dasein* and the specifically human mode of world-formation. As I noted at the outset of our reading of this portion of Heidegger's lecture course, the tacit orientation of the discussion of animality is directed toward uncovering the essence of the human and its relation to world. To cite Heidegger on this point, in the analysis of the animal's relation to world, "we ourselves have also been in view all the time" (272).

This kind of narrow orientation toward human *Dasein* is the source of much of the criticism that has been directed at Heidegger's lecture course. The critical position is summed up nicely by Michel Haar's complaint that "the phenomenology of animality teaches us more about man than about animals!"[19] But as William McNeill points out, isolating the analysis of animality from the larger project of *The Fundamental Concepts of Metaphysics* tends to make the reader overlook the fact that what is primarily at stake for Heidegger is an attempt to recover another thought of human relationality, not for the sake of the human alone, but in the name of recalling us to our radical finitude and proto-ethical responsivity toward all others: human, animal, and other others.[20] While one can only agree with the basic thrust of this rejoinder, it seems to miss the larger point of the kinds of criticisms Heidegger has received from figures such as Jacques Derrida, Jean-Luc Nancy, and Giorgio Agamben.[21] The problem with Heidegger's discussions of animality, both in *The Fundamental Concepts of Metaphysics* and elsewhere, it seems to me, does not lie with the task of rethinking a specifically human finitude in terms of ek-sistence, relation, and responsivity, but rather with the fact that this project is inseparable from Heidegger's insistence on *essential and oppositional determinations* of the difference between human beings and animals. From this perspective, what Heidegger's reflections on the human/animal distinction present is an effective challenge to metaphysical *humanism* on the one hand (where the human is defined in terms of animality plus "X," where X is figured as *logos, ratio,* freedom, selfhood, etc.), but an extremely problematic reinforcement of metaphysical *anthropocentrism* on the other. By "anthropocentrism" I mean simply the dominant tendency within the Western metaphysical tradition to determine the essence of animal life by the measure of, and in opposition to, the human. Heidegger, as we know, contests the classically Christian anthropocentric view that human beings are the center of all creation,[22] but generally he has little problem reinforcing the idea that the animal's being can be explained in negative and oppositional terms in comparison with the human, an idea that forms one of the central dogmas of philosophical anthropocentrism from Aristotle to Descartes to Kant.[23]

I do not mean to suggest, however, that Heidegger's discussions of animality are anthropocentric in any simple sense, and ought therefore to be dismissed.[24] On the contrary, it is precisely the tension between Heidegger's non-anthropocentric commitment to approach the animal's relationality on its own terms and his inability ultimately to carry through on this project that makes his text so rich and interesting. Perhaps the most fruitful way to read Heidegger's remarks on animal life is to see them as a resource for working through the two dominant approaches to animal issues within the Continental tradition. On the one hand, Heidegger's work prefigures the writings of a number of philosophers who seek, after the "death of God" and the closure of metaphysical humanism, to recover a definition and meaning for "the human" in opposition to its animal other. On the other hand, his work resonates with and creates the conditions for other figures who are trying to think through relation, ethics, politics, and ontology in radically non-anthropocentric and trans- or post-humanist terms. Which of these two approaches will prevail remains to be seen, but it is clear that any effort to work through the question of the animal from a Continental philosophical perspective must begin with, and will benefit greatly from, a *thinking* confrontation with Heidegger's analysis of animal life.[25]

CHAPTER THREE: BATAILLE

ANIMALITY

Georges Bataille

IMMANENCE OF THE EATER AND THE EATEN

I consider animality from a narrow viewpoint that seems questionable to me, but its value will become clear in the course of the exposition. From this viewpoint, animality is immediacy or immanence.

The immanence of the animal with respect to its milieu is given in a precise situation, the importance of which is fundamental. I will not speak of it continually, but will not be able to lose sight of it; the very conclusion of my statement will return to this starting point: *the situation is given when one animal eats another.*

What is given when one animal eats another is always the fellow creature of the one that eats. It is in this sense that I speak of immanence.

I do not mean a *fellow* creature perceived as such, but there is no transcendence between the eater and the eaten; there is a difference, of course, but this animal that eats the other cannot confront it in an affirmation of that difference.

Animals of a given species do not eat one other. . . . Perhaps, but this does not matter if the goshawk eating the hen does not distinguish it clearly from itself, in the same way that we distinguish an object from ourselves. The distinction requires a positing of the object as such. There does not exist any *discernible* difference if the object has not been posited. The animal that another animal eats is not yet given as an object. Between the animal that is eaten and the one that eats, there is no relation of *subordination* like that connecting an object, a thing, to man, who refuses to be viewed as a thing. For the animal, nothing is given through time. It is insofar as we are human that the object exists in time where its duration is perceptible. But the animal eaten by another exists this side of duration; it is consumed, destroyed, and this is only a disappearance in a world where nothing is posited beyond the present.

There is nothing in animal life that introduces the relation of the master to the one he commands, nothing that might establish autonomy on one side and dependence on the other. Animals, since they eat one another, are of unequal strength, but there is never anything between them except that quantitative difference. The lion is not the king of the beasts: in the movement of the waters he is only a higher wave overturning the other, weaker ones.

That one animal eats another scarcely alters a fundamental situation: every animal is *in the world like water in water*. The animal situation does contain a component of the human situation; if need be, the animal can be regarded as a subject for which the rest of the world is an object, but it is never given the possibility of regarding itself in this way. Elements of this situation can be grasped by human intelligence, but the animal cannot *realize* them.

DEPENDENCE AND INDEPENDENCE OF THE ANIMAL

It is true that the animal, like the plant, has no autonomy in relation to the rest of the world. An atom of nitrogen, of gold, or a molecule of water exist without needing anything from what surrounds them; they remain in a state of perfect immanence: there is never a necessity, and more generally nothing ever matters in the immanent relation of one atom to another or to others. The immanence of a living organism in the world is very different: an organism seeks elements around it (or outside it) which are immanent to it and with which it must establish (relatively stabilize) relations of immanence. Already it is no longer like water in water. Or if it is, this is only provided it manages to *nourish* itself. If it does not, it suffers and dies: the flow (the immanence) from outside to inside, from inside to outside, which is organic life, only lasts under certain conditions.

An organism, moreover, is separated from processes that are similar to it; each organism is detached from other organisms: in this sense organic life, at the same time that it accentuates the relation with the world, withdraws from the world, isolates the plant or the animal which can theoretically be regarded as autonomous worlds, so long as the fundamental relation of nutrition is left aside.

THE POETIC FALLACY OF ANIMALITY

Nothing, as a matter of fact, is more closed to us than this animal life from which we are descended. Nothing is more foreign to our way of thinking than the earth in the middle of the silent universe and having neither the meaning that man gives things, not the meaninglessness of things as soon as we try to imagine them without a consciousness that reflects them. In reality, we can never imagine things without consciousness except arbitrarily, since *we* and *imagine* imply consciousness, our consciousness, adhering indelibly to their presence. We can doubtless tell ourselves that this adhesion is fragile, in that we will cease to *be there*, one day even for good. But the appearance of a thing is never conceivable except in a consciousness taking the place of my consciousness, if mine has disappeared. This is a simple truth, but animal life, halfway distant from *our* consciousness, presents us with a more disconcerting enigma. In picturing the universe without a man, a universe in which only the animal's gaze would be opened to things, the animal being neither a thing nor a man, we can only call up a vision in which we see nothing, since the object of this vision is a movement that glides from things that have no meaning by themselves to the world full of meaning implied by man giving each thing his own. This is why we cannot describe such an object in a precise way. Or rather, the correct way to speak of it can *overtly* only be poetic, in that poetry describes nothing that does not slip toward the unknowable. Just as we can speak fictively of the past as if it were a present, we speak finally of prehistoric animals, as well as plants, rocks, and bodies of water, *as if* they were things, but to describe a landscape tied to these conditions is only nonsense, or a poetic leap. There was no landscape in a world where the eyes that open did not apprehend what they looked at, where indeed, in our terms, the eyes did not see. And if, now, in my mind's confusion, *stupidly* contemplating that absence of vision, I begin to say: "There was no vision, there was nothing – nothing but an empty intoxication limited by terror, suffering, and death, which gave it a kind of thickness ... " I am only abusing a poetic capacity, substituting a vague fulguration for the nothing of ignorance. I know: the mind cannot dispense with a fulguration of words that makes a fascinating halo for it: that is its richness, its glory, and a sign of sovereignty. But this poetry is only a way by which a man goes from a world full of meaning to the final dislocation of meanings, all of meaning, which soon proves to be unavoidable. There is only one difference between the absurdity of things envisaged without man's gaze and that of things among which the animal is present; it is that the former absurdity immediately suggests to us the apparent reduction of the exact sciences, whereas the latter hands us over to the sticky temptation of poetry, for, not being simply a thing, the animal is not closed and inscrutable to us. The animal opens before me a depth that attracts me and is familiar to me. In a sense, I know this depth: it is my own. It is also that which is farthest removed from me, that which deserves the name depth, which mean precisely *that which is unfathomable to me.* But this too is poetry. ... Insofar as I can also see the animal as a thing (if I eat it – in my own way, which is not that of another animal – or if I enslave it or treat it as an object of science), its absurdity is just as direct (if one prefers, just as near) as that of stones or air, but it is not always, and never entirely, reducible to that kind of inferior reality which we attribute to things. Something tender, secret, and painful draws out the intimacy which keeps vigil in us, extending its glimmer into that animal darkness. In the end, all that I can maintain is such a view, which plunges me into the night and dazzles me, brings me close to the moment when – I will no longer doubt this – the distinct clarity of consciousness will move me farthest away, finally from the unknowable truth which, from myself to the world, appears to me only to slip away.

THE ANIMAL IS IN THE WORLD LIKE WATER IN WATER

I will speak of the unknowable later. For the moment, I need to set apart from the dazzle of poetry that which, from the standpoint of experience, appears distinctly and clearly.

I am able to say that the animal world is that of immanence and immediacy, for that world, which is closed to us, is so to the extent that we cannot discern in it an ability to transcend itself. Such a truth is negative, and we will not be able to establish it absolutely. We can at least imagine an embryo of that ability in animals, but we cannot discern it clearly enough. While a study of those embryonic aptitudes can be done, such a study will not yield any perspectives that invalidate our view of immanent animality, which will remain unavoidable *for us.* It is only within the limits of the human that the transcendence of things in relation to consciousness (or of consciousness in relation to things) is manifested. Indeed transcendence is nothing if it is not embryonic, if it is not constituted as solids are, which is to say, immutably, under certain given conditions. In reality, we are incapable of basing ourselves on unstable coagulations and we must confine ourselves to regarding animality, from the outside, in the light of an absence of transcendence. Unavoidably, in our eyes, the animal is in the world like water in water.

The animal has diverse behaviors according to diverse situations. The behaviors are the starting points for possible distinctions, but distinguishing would demand the transcendence of the object having become distinct. The diversity of animal behaviors does not establish any conscious distinction among the diverse situations. The animals which do not eat a fellow creature of the same species still do not have the ability to recognize it as such, so that a new situation, in which the normal behavior is not triggered, may suffice to remove an obstacle without there being an awareness of its having been removed. We cannot say concerning a wolf which eats another wolf that it violates the law decreeing that ordinarily *wolves do not eat one another.* It does not violate this law; it has simply found itself in circumstances where the law no longer applies. In spite of this, there is, for the wolf, a continuity between itself and the world. Attractive or distressing phenomena arise before it; other phenomena do correspond either to individuals of the same species, to food, or to anything attractive or repellant, so that what appears has no meaning, or is a sign or something else. Nothing breaks a continuity in which fear itself does not announce anything that might be distinguished before being dead. Even the fighting between rivals is another convulsion where insubstantial shadows emerge from the inevitable responses to stimuli. If the animal that has brought down its rival does not apprehend the other's death as does a man behaving triumphantly, this is because its rival had not broken a continuity that the rival's death does not reestablish. This continuity was not called into question, but rather the identity of desires of two beings set one against the other in mortal combat. The apathy that the gaze of the animal expresses after the combat is the sign of an existence that is essentially on a level with the world in which it moves like water in water.

BATAILLE AND THE POETIC FALLACY OF ANIMALITY

Jill Marsden

According to the French philosopher Georges Bataille "nothing is more closed to us than this animal life from which we are descended."[1] Closed – but nothing is more terrifyingly close. In a series of writings, most notably his *Theory of Religion, Eroticism* and *The Accursed Share*, Bataille returns obsessively to a central paradox: human nature is fundamentally animal yet it is in negation of our animality that our self-definition is achieved. Death, cruelty, horror, sexual union, and its concomitant dissolution mark the borders of the "human" for Bataille. His abiding engagement with the erotic and violent extremes of human experience is in no sense a valorization of the "animal" or the "animalistic." His transgression of disciplinary boundaries – philosophical, anthropological, aesthetic, economic, psychoanalytic, and theological – is entirely consonant with his enduring consideration of the limits of that paradoxical creature – the "human animal."

To be fully "continuous" with our animality would be to abandon the cultivated discontinuity of both knowledge and human being. Asserting that "man differs from animal in that he is able to experience certain sensations that wound and melt him to the core,"[2] Bataille suggests that our suffering is qualitatively distinct from the wounding of an animal by another animal. Obscenity, incest, madness, disgust, betrayal are uniquely available to civilized discontinuous beings. Consciousness of death, restricted sexual activity, and the work imperative are all regarded by Bataille as expressions of a cultural logic of prohibition and limit that reduces "nature" to an "order of things" – the vast reaches of intimate continuity being obscured in the process. In *Theory of Religion*, written in the 1940s, and published in 1973, Bataille argues that religion is a search for this lost intimacy. A basic problem addressed by the text is "how to get out of the human situation" (*ME*, 13). Bataille speculates that human longing for the sacred world can be attributed to a primitive fascination for animal continuity (*ME*, 43). Accordingly, his discourse on animality involves an excursion of the intellect outside its privileged domain (which he characterizes as solid, stable, and discontinuous) to engage with a trajectory of dissolution and collapse.

Bataille's starting point in *Theory of Religion* is to define animality as "immediacy" or "immanence." Immanence, in Bataille's vocabulary, is an economic rather than an epistemological term, designating an unknowable inherence or "continuity" that resists categorization. Its meaning emerges in its interplay with the term "transcendence," which Bataille uses in his writings on the sacred to signify a state of separation or isolation. It is important to recognize that when Bataille alludes to the immanence of the animal with respect to its milieu, he speaks from the necessary perspective of "theoretical" detachment. From this vantage point, the human observer struggles to demarcate determinate differences between animals, their environments, and each other. He suggests that the animal that eats another does not distinguish what it eats in the same way that a human being distinguishes an object. There is no "opposition" between the animals in question. On the contrary, this act confirms the similarity between the eater and the eaten.

One might insist that the recognition of a similarity presupposes a minimal recognition of a difference between the creature that consumes and the one that is consumed, but this apparent identity is not *perceived* by the participants. It would be utterly anthropomorphic to say that the former confronts the other "in an affirmation of that difference" (*ME*, 18). This claim relies for its force on a certain understanding of Hegel's account of self-consciousness that Bataille encountered through the seminars of Alexandre Kojève. With apparent approval, Bataille cites as an epigraph to his discussion of animality Kojève's claim that it is desire that transforms being. Kojève asserts that animal desire is a necessary but not sufficient condition of self-consciousness. Human desire takes the form of the revelation of an "object" to a "subject" that is different from the object, and opposed to it. In *The Phenomenology of Spirit*, Hegel had argued that self-consciousness experiences itself primarily in relation to its encounter with otherness. The existence of the other mediates the existence of the subject but the former is also understood by the subject in terms of its availability for appropriation. At the most basic level, this has to do with whether something can be consumed. While desire for self-preservation is achieved through the consumption of food, this is no more than mere self-awareness conditioned by an object. What is essential to self-consciousness can only be discovered by it when it comes into a relation with another self-conscious being. According to Hegel's account of the struggle for recognition, the positions of master and slave are determined when one subject, fearful of death, sacrifices freedom and submits to the other as victor. In this instance, one loses one's autonomy and becomes thing-like. However, in Kojève's version of the master/slave dialectic, the slave eventually regains autonomy through work. Indeed, the dialectical passage from "animal hunger" to self-conscious desire is achieved through work that is the "foundation for knowledge and reason"[3] above all else. Although relations of domination and subordination may be discerned in terms of unequal strength, Bataille asserts that "there is never anything between animals except this quantitative difference" (*TR*, 18). Tempting though it may be to regard the lion as the "king" of the beasts, its actions are the mere expression of a superior force – a "higher wave" overturning the weaker ones. One might add, too, that a humanist interpretation of "nature" in terms of hierarchical notions such as "the food chain" tends to neglect the plethora of micro bacteria and parasites that feed on the great beasts of prey.

In submitting to the master, the slave posits a world beyond the present. The temporal horizon against which the relations between subjects and objects unfold does not form the necessary framework against which animal interaction takes place. From the perspective of the human being at least, animal being is sheer immediacy. Although the coordinates of time and space may be regarded as an a priori "grammar" of sentience, the observer may not assume that they are species-universal forms of intuition. To say that, for the animal, nothing is given in time is not to deduce that animals lack a temporal sense, but simply to say that *serial* time is a distinctly human invention, trimmed to the requirements of the industrial calendar. While it is possible, if not inevitable, that the inquirer will introduce the conceptual grammar of subject and object into speculation about the animal condition, this model is nothing that the animal could be said to "realize." From the human perspective, the animal is in the world "like water in water" (*TR*, 19).

Bataille's maxim alludes to an indistinct flow of being into being or unlimited immanence. Inscrutable and illegible *for us*, the domain of immanence is resistant to transcendent description. For this reason, there is a tendency to regard it in terms of the inertia of "being-in-itself." However, Bataille insists that a living organism, unlike molecules and atoms, has a relation of dependence to its environment inasmuch as it is required to seek its nourishment. Indeed, insofar as the organism is defined by boundary conditions it is possible to acknowledge relations between that which is "inner" and that which is "outer." It is worth noting that these boundaries only last "under certain conditions," that is, they are provisional rather than constitutive. (For example, a protozoan such as the amoeba constantly remakes its boundaries as its pseudopodia surround and incorporate food.) Immanence is presented as a space without transcendent limit, yet within which there is a difference between "perfect immanence" – the immanence of the molecule – and the immanent relation of the animal to its environment. The key point is that there is no absolute (transcendent) measure of this difference. It is a *differentiation that remains immanent* to its terms.

The animal appears to be "like water in water" but is not the *same* as water in water. On the basis of Bataille's notion of immanent differentiation, there is reason to regard immanence as a generative materiality rather than as an indifferent being-in-itself. Indeed, his work may be regarded as a challenge to the dogma that something which makes no difference at the level of the concept makes no difference whatsoever. Since "knowing" has historically been approached in terms of the question of how a subject relates to an object, epistemology – whether idealist, realist, or skeptical in its orientation – has required a prior distinction between "subject" and "object." What gets elided in pre-critical epistemology is the question of how both subject and object are generated. Bataille suggests that through the manufacture and distribution of "tools," both nature and the human become subjugated. When nature becomes "our" property, we cease to be immanent to it. In subjugating nature, we become subjugated in turn. To regard nature as a passive resource or "object" for cultural speculation is to persist with this belief. Consequently, Bataille makes it clear that from the perspective of the "subject," the world of the animal is unfathomable.

Like water in water, animality constantly evades conceptual determination. The animal only becomes a "thing" when classified as a zoological entity or when it is consumed as meat yet is never entirely reducible to that utile "inferior reality" (*TR*, 22). It is only an epistemological prejudice that the "formless" is perceived as something which is in want of shape.

This theme of unknowability is continued in Bataille's intriguing account of the "poetic fallacy of animality" (*TR*, 20). The attempt to imagine the world prior to its apprehension by human consciousness is presented as both an impossibility and a naïveté. Despite the phenomenological appeal of bracketing out predetermined meanings, it is a fantasy *for us* to imagine phenomena "without a consciousness that reflects them" (*TR*, 20). This is because the condition of consciousness is presupposed in the act of imagining it away. Bataille does not imply that the world is dependent on my perception of it. We can imagine that one day we will cease to "be there" but this thought can only be articulated this side of consciousness. However, since animal being has the status neither of human being nor of a thing, the world of the animal is neither meaningful nor meaningless. Animal life is "halfway distant from *our* consciousness" (*TR*, 21) – a phrase which suggests that the distance between meaning and meaninglessness is straddled by animality. Yet this is not to imply that animality offers an openness to being. Although there is a temptation to express the animal "gaze" poetically (Rilke's Eighth "Duino Elegy" comes to mind), Bataille insists that to see the world as the animal would see it is to see *nothing*. We do not see a landscape through the eyes of a tiger: we imagine what it would be like for us to do so which is to content ourselves with fictions. While many non-human animals appear to have sight, "vision" is a value-laden concept that implies a specific framework of perception (seeing is always "seeing-as"). Since animality cannot be known, our representations of it must of necessity be "false." However, Bataille suggests that the object of this imagined vision is a "movement that glides" (*TR*, 21) from meaning to meaninglessness. Accordingly, to employ poetic formulations to describe it may be appropriate given that poetry is itself a flight-vector towards the unknowable. It is a sign of "sovereignty" that the human being employs rich "fulgurations" for this drift of meaning. The idea that a world unconditioned by human knowing can be posited has a scientific appeal, but is logically "absurd" because a relation of knowledge implies prior conditioning, whereas imagining the world through the presence of the animal has an intractable allure because the gulf dividing human and animal *is* knowable.

Interestingly, Bataille describes the difference in terms of depth rather than distance. There is no measurable relation between two "states" of being, understood on a horizontal axis (e.g., a chain of being or evolutionary scale). Rather, there is an unfathomable depth – one that can be experienced otherwise – as non-knowledge. One might call this a tacit knowledge "something tender, secret, and painful" (*TR*, 23), which is glimpsed only at the moment of self-loss. Poetic language "intimates" that which resists conceptuality – the "draw of intimacy" that subtends the snare of calculative thought. What is communicated in the encounter with animality is the defeat of knowledge, a realization of the estrangement of the human from the animal, *and* an estrangement from this realization. This double negation has the character of "truth" but one which must also slip away in a trajectory of loss.

One cannot help but notice that the formulation "the animal is in the world like water in water" is a poetic one. Is it significant that having resisted analogical reasoning in his reflection on the differences between humans and animals, Bataille should have recourse to metaphor when considering the impossibility of analogy? Perhaps this is a question of whether poetry is to be regarded as representation of "reality" (an approximation to measure) or as the mark of an encounter with the limits of language.

In this regard, it is worth noting that Bataille does not seek to differentiate animals from humans by means of measurable difference. Discernible traits have to be identified in order to establish species-membership. While a diversity of animal behaviors are easily noticed, to *distinguish* behaviors "would demand the transcendence of the object having become distinct" (*TR*, 24). In any case, what could ever be said to unite a lobster, an ant colony, a condor, an elephant? Bataille claims that the diversity of animal behaviors does not establish any "conscious distinction" (*TR*, 24) among diverse situations. There might be change – such as the removal of an obstacle – without there being reflective awareness of the change as such. This does not mean that there is no difference. The failure of the dialectic is the failure of conceptual difference, not the failure of difference as such. At the extreme limit of knowing, one encounters the reaches of the unknown that is "distinct from Nothingness by nothing which discourse can enunciate."[4]

If epistemology collapses in the abyss of brute existence, this is because the categories of knowing are ill suited to negotiate the unstable trajectory of immanence. The closure of the world of the animal to human consciousness is a "negative truth," but one that is perhaps different from the negative determination of "world-poverty" proposed by Heidegger. Indeed, despite his recourse to the Kojèvian notion that the organism is propelled by hunger, animality is never presented by Bataille as lacking. It can only be thought so from the point of consciousness. From the perspective of immanence, there is no "essential" difference between humanity and animality. The relation is one between discontinuity and continuity. Rather than consolidating identity through otherness, the encounter with the unknowability of the animal reflects the extent to which we are strangers to ourselves. It is the unknowability of our immanent immensity that is touched.

This is a thinking based on participation rather than knowledge. For Bataille, poetry is sacred in that it is consumed immediately and is unthinkable in terms of the recuperative and profane logic of exchange. It is by way of participation that the human engages with its erotic animality (as immediacy or immanence), but it is also here that its difference from animality (defined in relation to the human) is most distinct (the animal is wholly driven by instinct but erotic pleasure is ineluctably lucid). This animality, of which we are a part yet from which we strive to distinguish ourselves, hovers at the edge of consciousness, extending its glimmer into the night of unknowing. The simultaneity of the lunge toward transcendence and the mute imperative of continuity signals a distinction between that which distinguishes itself (the human) and that from which it is distinguished (immanence) – an asymmetrical movement that is illegible within the paradigm of reciprocal determination. The human animal remains fused at all costs, despite itself, to the base matter of dissolvant flow while striving at all costs to expend itself in its violent craving to be human. This is a "heterogeneity" that the profane or "homogenous" logic of transcendent thinking tends to conceal. For example, Bataille may seem to perpetuate the profane logic of the reduction of difference to quantifiable identities of market capitalism in his insistence on the mere quantitative difference between animals, whereby animals would be instrumental (as a kind of "resource") to the cultivation of modern subjectivity, but it is through continuity rather than discontinuity that Bataille understands heterogeneity. The dissolution of boundaries in poetic and erotic activity is not a reduction of difference to sameness, which would be to understand difference conceptually, but a dissolution of the strictures that shore up recalcitrant identities.

This notwithstanding, it may remain unclear as to how the desire for sacred intimacy differs from a desire to "return to nature" or to a prior animalistic state. Bataille appears to follow Kojève in proposing a fundamental difference between the immediacy of animal craving and the mediated nature of human desire. It would seem that the animal – conceived as immediacy – is unburdened by work, prohibition, and the fear of death, and yet by the same token is condemned to apathetic immersion in the natural world. If the "goal" of religious intimacy is this bovine stupor, Bataille's preoccupation with the torments of self-consciousness is hard to understand (as is his obsession with violation of boundaries in general). At this juncture, it is worth noting that whatever narrative one favors regarding the transition from animal to human, it is only from the perspective of the latter that the former is "produced" as a "primary" state. It is in this spirit that Bataille's considerable exploration of transgression and taboo, particularly the ritualized breaking of prohibitions specific to totemic societies, is best appreciated. Bataille's contention that the horror of incest is a humanizing power, one that distinguishes humans from the "natural and unformulated life of the animals,"[5] is a story that can only be told after the institution of taboo, for it is the latter that "gives" the originary terms. Although laws against sexual relations between particular members of a clan and taboo on killing totem animals may be upheld as evidence of the fundamental principles of social organization, there is no violation of law when an animal consumes another, even if animals of a given species tend to refrain from killing one another. The tendency of a wolf to refrain from killing another wolf is not explicable according to a logic of recognition. Fear before death explains a human terror and fascination that cannot be extended to animal life. The conflict between human rivals involves a threat to discrete identity that is at once attractive and repellent, with the return of continuity promised by the death of the rival. However, in the case of animals there is no conflict of desire, and the rupture of continuity is never called into question.

This is not to deny that Bataille does speak of a "nostalgia" and a longing for lost continuity that the human being feels in its discontinuous state, even going so far as to express regret at not existing in the world "like a wave lost amongst waves."[6] Despite these lapses into sentimentality, Bataille expresses total dread for those who would seek to dismiss sexual taboos and advocate a return "to the good old days of animalism" (*ME*, 138). To see the overcoming of taboos as a goal or in any way desirable is to miss the point – both historically and philo-sophically – of the claim that human nature is an ingenious aberration of nature. The state of nature to which civilized man might "return" is not a state that he ever left. Rather, it is an idea produced in and by the civilized order it is deemed to precede.

With these caveats, the sacred desire for "intimacy" may be linked to the desire to "become-animal." This is best thought of as openness to exteriority rather than as identification with any given form. Since one cannot think from the perspective of the animal, direction is to be sought among the poetic and erotic dimensions of life. Although Bataille offers little in the way of analysis as to how humans might treat animals, this is largely because the question is itself "profane," implying as it does that animals are available for our appropriation. It is taken as given that "an animal exists for itself and in order to be a thing it must be dead or domesticated" (*TR*, 39). To make a horse draw a plough is to render it thing-like, but the farmer is likewise rendered servile and foreign to the "immanent immensity, where there are neither separations nor limits" (*TR*, 42).

One might object that Bataille is precipitate in insisting on the uniquely human nature of work. Many empirical examples could be cited of beasts using "tools," including the use of other beasts as tools. However, such objections have limited validity owing to Bataille's understanding of immanence. He does not make the error of allowing an empirical example bear the weight of a universal point. One might add that "animality" is addressed transcendentally in his work as an immanent condition for thinking the human. No claim is made as to what specific animals "do." Bataille's failure to reflect on the playfulness or "non-productive expenditure" of animals is likewise unsurprising when considered in this light. It must not be assumed, given Bataille's (often impassioned) critique of utility, that the value he accords to human labor is minimal or that escape from the "human situation" is the "goal" of his meditation. Bataille may share Nietzsche's view that the breeding of the human animal has been an exercise in self-cruelty (particularly in the production of modesty and shame), but also like Nietzsche would also confirm that it is through the cultivation of "slavish values" that the human animal has become interesting. Bataille makes it clear in *Theory of Religion* that it is the human being's resistance to immanence that regulates its resurgence. Indeed, to surrender unreservedly to immanence would result in a loss of sacred tension – a return to the "unconscious intimacy" and "slumber" of animals (*TR*, 53).

Bataille's frequent references to the dumb passivity of the animal might be regarded as evidence of the most blatant speciesism. However, his insistence on the failure of reciprocity between human and animal is born of a refusal to commute his meditation on animality to humanist paradigms of thought. It is also important to note that the failure of recognition between human and animal is not commensurate with a failure of communication. In default of a bilateral or dialectical communication between separate entities, there is a "base" or immanent connection – the legacy of the paradox of life turned against itself. It is this animality that is touched in the poetic – not as a "symbol" but as the eruption of vital force – a revitalization of our animal sense. This is not a knowledge that can be grasped any more than the animal can be recognized or known. Rather, it is submission to the forces that resist the "order of things": movement, fluidity, flow, the hemorrhaging of identity into the yawning depths. Such contact with animality, however poetic, is not a return to the bosom of a benevolent nature; it is the re-intensification of anguish, dread, and utter loss. What the human may see in the eye of the animal is not the answer to the question of being, but rather a blind and steadily dilating abyss staring back into the heart of the human.

CHAPTER FOUR: LEVINAS

THE NAME OF A DOG,* OR
NATURAL RIGHTS

Emmanuel Levinas

You shall be men consecrated to me; therefore you shall not eat any flesh
that is torn by beasts in the field; you shall cast it to the dogs. (Exodus 22:31)

Is the biblical verse guilty, as one will later accuse it, of attaching too much
importance to what "goes into man's mouth" and not enough to what comes
out? Unless the sight of flesh torn by beasts in the field seems meat too strong
for the digestion of the honest man who, even if he is carnivore, still feels he is
watched over by God. This flesh torn by beasts in the field, and the remains of
bloody struggles between wild animals that half-devour one another, from the
strong species to the weak, will be sublimated by intelligence into hunting
games. This spectacle suggesting the horrors of war, this devouring within
species, will provide men with the artistic emotions of the *Kriegspiel.* Such ideas
make one lose one's appetite! In fact, they can also come to you at the family
table, as you plunge your fork into your roast. There is enough, there, to make
you a vegetarian again. If we are to believe Genesis, Adam, the father of us all,
was one! There is, at least, enough there to make us want to limit, through
various interdictions, the butchery that every day claims our "consecrated"
mouths! But enough of this theology! It is the dog mentioned at the end of the
verse that I am especially interested in. I am thinking of Bobby.

So who is this dog at the end of the verse? Someone who disrupts society's
games (or Society itself) and is consequently given a cold reception [*que l'on
reçoit comme un chien dans un jeu de quilles*]? Someone whom we accuse of being
rabid when we are trying to drown him? Someone who is given the dirtiest work
– a dog's life – and whom we leave outside in all weathers, when it is raining cats
and dogs, even during those awful periods when you would not put a dog out
in it? But all these, in spite of their misery, reject the affront of a repulsive prey.

---

* Emmanuel Levinas, *Difficult Freedom*, trans. Seán Hand (Baltimore: Johns Hopkins University
Press, 1990), pp. 151–3. Translator's note: *nom d'un chien* [name of a dog] is also in French a
mild expletive (crikey!), and recognizably a polite version of *nom de Dieu* [in the name of
God/bloody hell!].

So does it concern the beast that has lost the last noble vestiges of its wild nature, the crouching, servile, contemptible dog? Or, in the twilight [*entre chien et loup*] (and what light in the world is not, already this dusk?), does it concern the one who is a wolf [*loup*] under his dogged faithfulness, and thirsts after blood, be it coagulated or fresh?

But enough of allegories! We have read too many fables and we are still taking the name of a dog in the figurative sense. So, in the terms of a venerable hermeneutics, more ancient than La Fontaine, orally transmitted from early antiquity – the hermeneutics of the talmudic Doctors – this biblical text, troubled by parables, here challenges the metaphor in Exodus 22:31, the dog is a dog. Literally a dog! Beyond all scruples, by virtue of its happy nature and direct thoughts, the dog transforms all this flesh cast to it in the field into good flesh. This feast is its right.

High hermeneutics, however, which is so caught up here in a word-for-word approach, allows itself to explain the paradox of a pure nature leading to rights.

It therefore unearths some forgotten dogs lying in a subordinate proposition in another verse from Exodus. In Chapter 11, verse 7, strange dogs are struck by a light in the middle of the night. They will not growl! But around them a world is emerging. For this is the fatal night of the "death of the first-born" of Egypt. Israel is about to be released from the house of bondage. Slaves who served the slaves of the State will henceforth follow the most high Voice, the most free path. It is a figure of humanity! Man's freedom is that of an emancipated man remembering his servitude and feeling solidarity for all enslaved people. A rabble of slaves will celebrate this high mystery of man, and "not a dog shall growl." At the supreme hour of his institution, with neither ethics nor *logos*, the dog will attest to the dignity of its person. This is what the friend of man means. There is a transcendence in the animal! And the clear verse with which we began is given a new meaning. It reminds us of the debt that is always open.

But perhaps the subtle exegesis we are quoting gets lost in rhetoric? Indeed?

There were seventy of us in a forestry commando unit for Jewish prisoners of war in Nazi Germany. An extraordinary coincidence was the fact that the camp bore the number 1492, the year of the expulsion of the Jews from Spain under the Catholic Ferdinand V. The French uniform still protected us from Hitlerian violence. But the other men, called free, who had dealings with us or gave us work or orders or even a smile – and the children and women who passed by and sometimes raised their eyes – stripped us of our human skin. We were subhuman, a gang of apes. A small inner murmur, the strength and wretchedness of persecuted people, reminded us of our essence as thinking creatures, but we were no longer part of the world. Our comings and goings, our sorrow and laughter, illnesses and distractions, the work of our hands and the anguish of our eyes, the letters we received from France and those accepted for our families – all that passed in parenthesis. We were beings entrapped in their species; despite all their vocabulary, beings without language. Racism is not a biological concept; anti-Semitism is the archetype of all internment. Social aggression, itself, merely imitates this model. It shuts people away in a class, deprives them of expression and condemns them to being "signifiers without a signified" and from there to violence and fighting. How can we deliver a message about our humanity which, from behind the bars of quotation marks, will come across as anything other than monkey talk?

And then, about halfway through our long captivity, for a few short weeks, before the sentinels chased him away, a wandering dog entered our lives. One day he came to meet this rabble as we returned under guard from work. He survived in some wild patch in the region of the camp. But we called him Bobby, an exotic name, as one does with a cherished dog. He would appear at morning assembly and was waiting for us as we returned, jumping up and down and barking in delight. For him, there was no doubt that we were men.

Perhaps the dog that recognized Ulysses beneath his disguise on his return from the Odyssey was a forebear of our own. But no, no! There, they were in Ithaca and the Fatherland. Here, we were nowhere. This dog was the last Kantian in Nazi Germany, without the brain needed to universalize maxims and drives. He was a descendant of the dogs of Egypt. And his friendly growling, his animal faith, was born from the silence of his forefathers on the banks of the Nile.

*   *   *

INTERVIEW

But is there something distinctive about the human face which, for example, sets it apart from that of an animal?

One cannot entirely refuse the face of an animal. It is via the face that one understands, for example, a dog. Yet the priority here is not found in the animal, but in the human face. We understand the animal, the face of an animal, in accordance with *Dasein*. The phenomenon of the face is not in its purest form in the dog. In the dog, in the animal, there are other phenomena. For example, the force of nature is pure vitality. It is more this which characterizes the dog. But it also has a face.[1]

According to your analysis, the commandment "Thou shalt not kill" is revealed by the human face; but is the commandment not also expressed in the face of an animal? Can an animal be considered as the other that must be welcomed? Or is it necessary to possess the possibility of speech to be a "face" in the ethical sense?

I cannot say at what moment you have the right to be called "face." The human face is completely different and only afterwards do we discover the face of an animal. I don't know if a snake has a face. I can't answer that question. A more specific analysis is needed.

But there is something in our attraction to an animal. . . . In the dog, what we like is perhaps his childlike character. As if he were strong, cheerful, powerful, full of life. On the other hand, there is also, even with regard to an animal, a pity. A dog is like a wolf that doesn't bite. There is a trace of the wolf in the dog. In any case, there is here the possibility of a specific phenomenological analysis. . . . Children are often loved for their animality. The child is not suspicious of anything. He jumps, he walks, he runs, he bites. It's delightful.

If animals do not have a face in an ethical sense, do we have obligations toward them? And if so, where do they come from?

It is clear that, without considering animals as human beings, the ethical extends to all living beings. We do not want to make an animal suffer needlessly and so on. But the prototype of this is human ethics. Vegetarianism, for example, arises from the transference to animals of the idea of suffering. The animal suffers. It is because we, as human, know what suffering is that we can have this obligation.

The widespread thesis that the ethical is biological amounts to saying that, ultimately, the human is only the last stage of the evolution of the animal. I would say, on the contrary, that in relation to the animal, the human is a new phenomenon. And that leads me to your question. You ask at what moment one becomes a face. I do not know at what moment the human appears, but what I want to emphasize is that the human breaks with pure being, which is always a persistence in being. This is my principal thesis. A being is something that is attached to being, to its own being. That is Darwin's idea. The being of animals is a struggle for life. A struggle of life without ethics. It is a question of might. Heidegger says at the beginning of *Being and Time* that *Dasein* is a being concerned for this being itself. That's Darwin's idea: the living being struggles for life. The aim of being is being itself. However, with the appearance of the human – and this is my entire philosophy – there is something more important than my life, and that is the life of the other. That is unreasonable. Man is an unreasonable animal. . . .[2]

ETHICAL CYNICISM

Peter Atterton

Plato having defined man to be a two-legged animal without feathers, Diogenes the Cynic plucked a cock and brought it into the Academy, and said, "This is Plato's man." On which account this addition was made to the definition, – "With broad nails." (Diogenes Laërtius)

INTRODUCTION

Levinas seldom addresses the animal question in his philosophy. There are, however, two notable exceptions: an essay called "The Name of a Dog, or Natural Rights,"[1] written in 1975, and an interview that took place in 1986.[2] "The Name of a Dog" is without question one of the most bizarre things Levinas ever published, but also one of the most interesting. It originally appeared in a collection of essays dedicated to the Dutch expressionist painter Bram Van Velde, and was reprinted in the second edition of Levinas's book *Difficult Freedom* the following year. A hybrid mixture of biblical criticism, whimsy, autobiography, and philosophy, written with humor and pathos, it leaves the reader amused and bemused, ultimately unsure how to interpret it in the context of Levinas's work as a whole. By contrast, Levinas's remarks on animality during the course of an interview conducted a decade later present a rather more sober reflection, though they are no less difficult to assimilate to the main body of his work. The question why Levinas was clearly uncomfortable talking about the animal question, and why on the few occasions that he did he relegated it to the margins of his philosophy, is one that philosophers are still asking themselves.[3] It may be conjectured that had he given the discussion a more prominent place in his magnum opus *Totality and Infinity* (1961),[4] for example, it would have posed a threat to the preeminence of the human face as described there. When he did not ignore the animal question completely, Levinas gave it a secondary status no doubt so as not to displace "the humanism of the other man" that has become a catchword for his ethics.[5]

In both "The Name of a Dog" and the 1986 interview, Levinas appears to grant something like a human status to the nonhuman animal, and, in a non-parallel way, to attribute animality to humans, two gestures that serve at one and the same time to redraw and blur the traditional humanist line between humans and animals. In the following two-part discussion, I want to pinpoint several places in the essay and interview where this occurs, while leaving it to the reader to decide for him- or herself what the implications are for Levinas's ethical philosophy. For even if Levinas's general tendency to disregard the animal question provides evidence that he himself did not consider ethics to extend very far beyond the human sphere, the question can still be asked whether a Levinasian ethics *ought* nevertheless to include the other animal, and, if so, to what extent and on what basis. As we will see, such questions are not easy to answer, if only because almost every consideration in the two texts we are considering that leads in one direction is counterbalanced by a decision leading in the opposite direction.

I shall begin with "The Name of a Dog" and the story of Bobby, the stray dog that befriended Levinas and his companions for a few short weeks during their long internment (1940–5) in a camp for Jewish prisoners of war in Nazi Germany.

1. "THE NAME OF A DOG, OR NATURAL RIGHTS"

Bobby would seem to be different from other animals – almost human in fact. We first encounter him in the penultimate paragraph of Levinas's essay:

> And then, about halfway through our long captivity, for a few short weeks, before the sentinels chased him away, a wandering dog [*chien errant*] entered our lives. One day he came to meet this rabble as we returned under guard from work. He survived in some wild patch in the vicinity of the camp. But we called him Bobby, an exotic name, as befits a cherished dog. He would appear at morning assembly and was waiting for us as we returned, jumping up and down and barking in delight. For him – it was incontestable – we were men. (*DF*, 153)

The first thing I wish to draw attention to is that Bobby was an *actual* dog, not a fictive dog, not a dog from literature, from *Odyssey* to Exodus, from Spencer's *Beth Gelert* to London's *The Call of the Wild*, but a dog of flesh and blood.[6] Homer's story of the dog that recognized his master, Ulysses, after an absence of 20 years has about as much veracity as that of Circe's transforming Ulysses' men into swine. In contrast, Levinas's story of Bobby and the welcome he showed Levinas and the other prisoners is no fable. Bobby really did recognize them. Nor is this a mere anecdote. Levinas seems to want to give the impression that Bobby's welcome had an ethical dimension. He seems to want to say that Bobby's response really was ethics, which in *Totality and Infinity* is described as "attention to speech or welcome of the face" (*TI*, 299). Levinas could not be more emphatic: "For him – it was incontestable – we were men."

But Bobby is different from Ulysses' dog in yet another way:

> Perhaps the dog that recognized Ulysses beneath his disguise on his return from the Odyssey was a forebear of our own. But no, no! There, they were in Ithaca and the Fatherland. Here, we were nowhere. This dog was the last

Kantian in Nazi Germany, without the brain needed to universalize maxims and drives. (*DF*, 153)

I must confess that I have never quite known what to make of the ascription of Kantian ethics to Bobby. I have never known whether Levinas meant his comment to be taken literally or whether he was merely speaking figuratively, perhaps anthropomorphizing Bobby to show how it is possible for an animal to rise above human beings when they treat each other as animals. I say this because earlier in the essay Levinas had written:

The other men, called free, who had dealings with us or gave us work or orders or even a smile – and the children and women who passed by and sometimes raised their eyes – stripped us of our human skin. We were merely a quasi-humanity [*une quasi-humanité*], a gang of apes. (*DF*, 153)

It is impossible not to see Levinas in the essay under discussion attributing to animals contradictory values: to be like animals ("apes") is to be without freedom and dignity. But the so-called free men who palpably failed to recognize the freedom and dignity of Levinas and his companions appeared to fall short of the humanity of an animal (Bobby). Without wishing to downplay the injurious impact of racial epithets intended to denote one's inferior status by resorting to a comparison with animals, we might wonder all the same whether Levinas does not too readily accept the *logic* of such a racist affront, namely, that to be anything other than fully human is ipso facto a degradation.

There was no doubt, of course, in the mind of Levinas and his fellow prisoners that they were men. Even before Bobby arrived to confirm it, even in their solitariness, they knew, as Descartes put it, that their essence was to think: "A small inner murmur, the strength and wretchedness of a persecuted people, reminded us of our rational essence. But we were no longer part of the world" (*DF*, 153). No longer in the "world," which had been taken from them by an evil regime, the prisoners were reminded of their "rational essence" by way of a mediation or interior monologue – a *logos*. Not that the prisoners, of course, were in a position to do much else with that *logos* apart from remind themselves that they were men. What Aristotle in Books II and X of the *Nicomachean Ethics* presented as the royal road to human flourishing (*eudaimonia*), namely, the skillful exercise of the logos in both the practical (moral) and theoretical (contemplative) sphere was well and truly blocked for them. As prisoners forced to do hard labor for the Nazis, their status was that of slaves. They were unable to make the transition beyond what Hegel described as subjective self-certainty ("an inner murmur"), having been deprived of recognition by their Nazi "masters." Levinas presents this refusal by the Nazis to recognize the distinctly *rational* (i.e., human) nature of the prisoners as a refusal to regard the *logos* of the prisoners as anything other than the chatter of an ape:

We were beings entrapped in their species; despite all their vocabulary, beings without language [*langage*]. Racism is not a biological concept; anti-Semitism is the archetype of all internment. Social oppression, itself, but imitates this model. It shuts people away in a class, deprives them of expression and condemns them to being "signifiers without a signified" and from there to violence and fighting. How can they deliver a message about their humanity which, behind the bars of quotation marks, will come across as anything other than monkey-like [*simiesque*]? (*DF*, 153)

For the language of the prisoners to "deliver a message about their humanity," for it to be regarded as more than a mere mimicking ("behind the bars of quotation marks") of speech, the words that are spoken must be reunited with men and women who say them. It must constitute "expression" as that word is used by Levinas in *Totality and Infinity* (see *TI*, 72–9).

Prima facie this would seem to make it impossible for an animal such as Bobby to be regarded as anything other than a representative of the type genus of the *Canidae*. For if Levinas and his companions found it impossible to escape the typology, characterization, and classification given to them by their Nazi oppressors, what chance has Bobby when he can only bark, jump up and down, and wag his tail? Because Bobby lacks the speech required for the ethical recognition to take place, he seems destined to be deprived of the possibility of transcendence. With no radical and unsubstitutable singularity to his name ("we called him Bobby, an exotic name, as befits [*convient à*] a cherished dog"), he remains forever "entrapped in [his] species." In "Language and Proximity" (1967), Levinas appears to cite with approval Descartes' argument as to why animals are mere *machinae animatae*:

In a well-known text of Part V of the *Discourse of Method* Descartes refutes the opinion of "some ancients that brutes talk, although we do not understand their language" by advancing that "since they have many organs which are allied to our own, they could communicate their thoughts to us just as easily as to those of their race." Descartes thus refuses to admit a language that would be imprisoned in the particularisms of a species. An animal is a machine not only because it does not know how to utilize its organs in polyvalent way, but *because it is imprisoned in its constitution.*[7] (italics added)

Levinas goes on to say that "our analyses have brought us to see fraternity with the neighbor as the essence of the original language; it finds universality ... starting with singularities."[8] The "singularities" Levinas has in mind, however, are *human* singularities – never animal.

Let me now mention some perplexities in "The Name of a Dog" that assail the attempt to draw an indivisible line between Bobby and the human prisoners. To begin with, we might note that while Levinas in the essay under discussion clearly wishes to guard against the racist aspersions that he and his fellows were anything other than fully human by recounting "the small inner murmur ... that reminded us of our rational essence," his philosophy in general displaces the Cartesian and Kantian definition of man as a rational being when the question of ethics is posed. It is not reason that makes humans human, according to Levinas, but the relationship with the Other. "Reason speaking in the first person is not addressed to the other, [and] conducts a monologue" (*TI*, 72). Indeed, it would be difficult to ignore the implicit challenge that "The Name of a Dog" presents to traditional humanism, first, by inviting an obvious comparison between the "wandering Jew" and the "errant dog" named Bobby; and secondly, by appearing to ascribe some kind of singular moral status to Bobby despite his inability to reason and "universalize his maxims." It is worth examining both of these points in more detail.

Both Bobby and the prisoners have no "Fatherland;" they live "nowhere." To be sure, Levinas makes a point of saying that he and the other prisoners were protected by the "French uniform" against the worst of Hitler's excesses. But this point, however, can be overstated. As already mentioned, Levinas and his companions were nothing short of slaves. Living in a "forestry commando unit for Jewish prisoners" (*DF*, 152), they were denied the "natural rights" guaranteed to citizens living under common laws or a *politei*. They were prisoners who were forcibly deprived of freedom and equality secured by the social contract itself. In a certain sense, their situation was even worse than that of an animal – one of Aristotle's many "natural slaves" (*Politics* 1256 b) – since Bobby was at least free to rove where he pleased "for a few short weeks before the sentinels chased him away." In the *Social Contract*, Rousseau argues that injustice in society is capable of making the situation for human beings even more disagreeable than it would otherwise be in a purely instinctual state of nature:

> This passage from the state of nature to the civil state produces quite a remarkable change in man, for it substitutes justice for instinct in his behavior and gives his actions a moral quality they previously lacked. ... Although, in this state he deprives himself of several of the advantages belonging to him in the state of nature, he regains such great ones. ... [I]f the abuse of this new condition did not often lower his status to beneath the level he left, he ought constantly to bless the happy moment that pulled him from away from it forever and which transformed him from a stupid, limited animal into an intelligent being and a man [*d'un animal stupide et borné, fit un être intelligent et un homme*].[9]

Notice that this passage contains a paradox: man ought constantly to celebrate his transition from animal to man in society, were it not for the fact that the injustice of men *in society* did "often lower his status beneath the level he left." In *The Kreutzer Sonata*, Tolstoy writes: "When a man does not live as a man, he is beneath the animal."[10] Heidegger too writes in *The Fundamental Concepts of Metaphysics* that "man can sink lower than any animal. No animal can become depraved in the same way as man."[11] Levinas seems to be making a similar claim in "The Name of a Dog," not admittedly in reference to the condition of the prisoners themselves, but in reference to the guards and "the other men, called free," whose injustice makes them morally inferior to a dog. To be sure any positive value Levinas attaches to the notion of animality in the essay is continually vitiated. Insofar as Bobby's entrance into the society of men amounts to his recognizing the humanity of the prisoners ("For him – it was incontestable – we were men"), he would seem to transcend the guards and the villagers who are morally inferior by comparison. However, inasmuch as their moral inferiority consists in treating the prisoners as animals ("a gang of apes"), then the implication is that animals have a moral status that is a priori inferior to that of humans.

For the most part, however, Levinas is reluctant in his philosophy to exalt the animal to the moral rank of the human (as he understands these terms), or, conversely, to disparage human beings by considering them little more than animals. This is not to say, of course, that Levinas is not prepared to criticize man's inhumanity to man. He frequently does; but he is also careful not to conflate such inhumanity with the behavior of what he presumably would regard as *mere* animality. In *Totality and Infinity*, his caution is expressed thus: "there exists a tyranny of the universal and of the impersonal, an order that is inhuman though distinct from the brutish [*brutal*]" (*TI*, 242). The internment of the Jewish prisoners was indeed "inhuman" – a crime against humanity – but it was not animal. There is transcendence it would seem even in totalitarianism.

Unlike men who are racists, however, Bobby himself doesn't discriminate. Or rather, Bobby discriminates without discriminating. He receives the message concerning the humanity of Levinas and the prisoners loudly and clearly. Again: "For him – it was incontestable – we were men." But does Levinas really mean what he says? For Bobby to be able to recognize the humanity of Levinas and his companions, he would have to have the power of the famous Heideggerian "as such" (*als solche*). He would have to be rich in understanding well beyond what Heidegger called "poverty in world" (*Weltarmut*).[12] This would require him to have something like *logos*. But Bobby is traditionally *zoōn alogon*; he cannot speak and reason, and is altogether incapable, says Levinas, of universalizing his maxims. How, then, is it possible for him to be a Kantian – indeed "the last Kantian in Nazi Germany"? His Kantianism would have to consist in the fact he was somehow able to follow the second formula of the Moral Law and recognize the "humanity in his own person or in the person of any other." His welcoming gestures ("jumping up and down and barking in delight") would have to be caused by the idea in him of "personality" (*Persönlichkeit*) as opposed to being simply a Pavlovian response to the excitation of need. In other words, Bobby would have to be capable of *feeling* respect. ("The idea of personality awakens respect.")[13] Kant insists that this feeling pertains to all humans – and indeed only to humans:

> No man is entirely without moral feeling, for were he lacking in susceptibility to it, he would be morally dead; and if (to speak in medical terms) the moral vital force could no longer excite this feeling, then humanity would dissolve (by chemical laws, as it were) into mere *animality* and be mixed irretrievably with the mass of other natural beings.[14]

Animals are bereft of reason and respect, according to Kant, and thus cannot escape pathological determination by need.[15]

In *Totality and Infinity*, Levinas shows how much he is in agreement with Kant here. He wrote:

Animal need is liberated from vegetable dependence, but this liberation is itself dependence and uncertainty. The need of a wild animal [*fauve*] is inseparable from struggle and fear; the exterior world from which it is liberated remains a threat. *But need is also the time of labor: a relation with an other yielding its alterity.* (*TI*, 116)

Levinas acknowledges that humans, like animals, have certain biological needs. Unlike animals, however, they are able to anticipate those needs in advance through tool making and commerce. Before man is *animal rationale*, he is *Homo habilis* and *zoōn politikon*:

The animal fabricating tools frees itself for its animal condition when its momentum seems interrupted and broken, when instead of going itself to its goal as an inviolable will it fabricates tools and fixes the powers of its future action in transmissible and receivable things. Thus a political and technical existence ensures the will its truth, renders it objective. (*TI*, 241)

Where is Bobby in this story? Well Bobby is certainly *wild* and *needy* ("He survived in some wild patch in the region of the camp"), but he has no tools to fend off need and few friends to feed him. He is nevertheless able to anticipate the future, for Levinas explicitly says: "He would appear at morning assembly and was waiting for us [*nous attendons*] when we returned, jumping up and down and barking with delight." As we know, Bobby's happiness is abruptly brought to an end by his being "chased away" by the guards. Presumably it was no less risky for him to remain in the camp than it was for the prisoners to try to escape. In both cases the punishment would have been the same: death. In *Totality and Infinity*, Levinas writes:

the happiness of enjoyment is greater than every disquietude, but disquietude can trouble it; here lies the gap between the animal and the human. ... Before defining man as the animal that can commit suicide it is necessary to define him as capable of living for the Other and *being* on the basis of the Other who is exterior to him. (*TI*, 149)

Perhaps Bobby did not see his eventual expulsion from the camp coming, but it would still be a mistake to describe his delight in the company of men as an "animal complacency in oneself" (*TI*, 149). For Bobby's "friendly barking" is in response to the encounter with the Other who is Levinas himself in this instance.

Perhaps the diehard humanist who does not like the way the discussion is going at this point will insist that Bobby, not having the wherewithal to transcend the immediacy of need through the practical employment of reason and autonomy, remains incapable of anything like Kantian morality. But this only begs a new question: Even if animals are not moral agents, are they not owed certain obligations as moral patients? If animals live in constant fear and anxiety, do we not have obligations toward them as we do to the human Other whose *face* is the face of destitution and hunger (*TI*, 75)? Levinas's answer to that question is no less ambiguous than his answer to the question of whether an animal such as Bobby has the capacity to stand outside his type genus and rise to the level of humanity.

2. INTERVIEW 1986

Despite his rejection of the traditional subject (ego, person, substance, spirit, consciousness, etc.), there seems little room for doubt that Levinas retains traditional humanist elements in his thinking. This is never more evident than in the context of the interview he gave in 1986 to graduate students from the universities of Essex and Warwick. Asked whether there is something distinctive about the face of the human that sets it apart from the face of an animal, Levinas replied:

> One cannot entirely refuse the face of an animal. It is via the face that one understands, for example, a dog. Yet the priority here is not found in the animal, but in the human face. ... The phenomenon of the face is not in its purest form in the dog. ... But it also has a face. (*PL*, 169)

Perhaps with Bobby in mind, Levinas seems to want to attribute something like a face to an animal such as a dog, but he is evidently unwilling to extend to it the same moral consideration as extends to the human face. He says that "one cannot entirely refuse the face of an animal." I think what he means is that the face of the animal such as a dog has the power to address us ethically in such a way that makes it difficult to ignore. But we are still a long way from the "epiphany" of the human face described so rhapsodically in *Totality and Infinity.* "This [human] gaze that supplicates and demands, deprived of everything because entitled to everything" (*TI*, 75).[16] The noncommittal or ambiguous stance on Levinas's part regarding the question of animal obligation is conspicuous later in the interview when his questioners, perhaps because they suspected that Levinas was avoiding the question, asked: "Can an animal be considered as the other that must be welcomed? Or is it necessary to possess the possibility of speech to be a 'face' in the ethical sense?" Again, Levinas equivocated:

> I cannot say at what moment you have the right to be called "face." The human face is completely different and only afterwards do we discover the face of an animal. I don't know if a snake has a face. I can't answer that question. A more specific analysis is needed. (*PL*, 171–2)

Notice the way in which Levinas appears to want to leave open the possibility that an animal has a face in the ethical sense, while at the same time saying that only human beings have a face in the ethical sense ("The human face is completely different"). He claims not to know whether an animal such as a snake has a face because a "more specific analysis is needed," though it is almost impossible not to get the sense that Levinas himself did not undertake such an analysis during the 40 years he spent talking about the ethical significance of the human face because he already considered the result to be something of a forgone conclusion.

When his interviewers – who deserve credit for pushing the animal question so far that Levinas was forced to break new ground in his philosophy – pressed him on the question of whether we have obligations to animals regardless of whether or not they have a face, Levinas replied that we do, at least to some extent:

> It is clear that, without considering animals as human beings, the ethical extends to all living beings. We do not want to make an animal suffer needlessly and so on. But the prototype of this is human ethics. Vegetarianism, for example, arises from the transference to animals of the idea of suffering. The animal suffers. It is because we, as human, know what suffering is that we can have this obligation. (*PL*, 172)

Some readers might find in the claim that "the ethical extends to all living beings" the roots of a Levinasian ecological ethics.[17] I think, however, that it is fairly clear that Levinas himself means to say that the ethical extends to all *sentient* living beings, that is, only to animals with a relatively complex nervous system. That would explain why Levinas immediately shifts the focus to animal *suffering*, which reminds us of the type of utilitarian defense of the ethical treatment of animals advocated by Singer and Bentham.[18]

However, Levinas is no utilitarian. Inasmuch as he insists that "the prototype of [ethics] is human ethics," it might be thought instead that he is paying lip service to Kantianism, for which all prima facie duties to animals are really "indirect duties towards humanity."[19] But this is not true either. According to Kant, kindness toward animals is obligatory only insofar as it helps us cultivate and strengthen a good will that is a necessary and sufficient condition for our performance of duties to each other. Levinas, by contrast, appears to be arguing that we have a *direct* duty to animals not to make them suffer "needlessly" (whatever that means), even though we only become *cognizant* of that duty indirectly through some kind of transference of suffering from the human realm. Levinas does not tell us what transferential mechanism is at work here, so it is difficult to know how much philosophical weight to give to such a pronouncement. Levinas clearly cannot claim it is self-certifying and thus in no need of justification. Indeed, it would have been just as plausible to my mind had Levinas simply said "we know" what animal suffering is because we are animals ourselves, at least biologically speaking. Obviously the type of knowledge I am speaking of here is knowledge by acquaintance, which Russell defined as a type of experience of which we are "directly aware, without the intermediary of any process of inference or any knowledge of truths."[20] According to Russell, this type of knowledge is open to animals even though he, like Aristotle, Descartes, Rousseau, Kant, and Levinas, considered them unable to introspect (i.e., become aware that they are aware of pain). This inability would certainly make it impossible for a nonhuman animal to transfer the idea of pain onto another, but again it is not clear why the inability to intro-spect implies that animals have a secondary moral status and why the "prototype" of ethics is *human* ethics. For if the fact that the extension of the idea of suffering beyond sense-data would not be possible without acquaintance by *human* introspection is presented as an argument for giving ethical priority to human interests, I am at a loss to see how this does not commit the genetic fallacy.

One of the questions that the preceding account presents us with is: Where does Levinas draw the line between human and animal *biologically?* Again, Levinas has an answer that is far from ambiguous:

> The widespread thesis that the ethical is biological amounts to saying that, ultimately, the human is only the last stage of the evolution of the animal. I would say, on the contrary, that in relation to the animal, the human is a new phenomenon. And that leads me to your question. You ask at what moment one becomes a face. I do not know at what moment the human appears, but what I want to emphasize is that the human breaks with pure being, which is always a persistence in being. This is my principal thesis. A being is something that is attached to being, to its own being. That is Darwin's idea. The being of animals is a struggle for life. A struggle of life without ethics. ... However, with the appearance of the human – and this is my entire philosophy – there is something more important than my life, and that is the life of the other. That is unreasonable. Man is an unreasonable animal. (*PL*, 172)

Clearly Levinas does not deny the irrefutable evidence that man is biologically an animal. What he denies is that Darwinian thesis that man is *reducible* to an animal. This amounts to a repudiation of supervenient explanations of moral action and the sociobiological claim that ethics has evolved from the "selfish gene." But Levinas's rejection of Darwinism is anything but the traditional repudiation of instinct in favor of reason – a trait Darwin and his two greatest followers, Nietzsche and Freud, considered to be selected for in virtue of the advantage it confers upon the human species. For Levinas, on the contrary, it is man's capacity to break with reason by putting the needs of the Other first that constitutes his human essence.

Of course, it will be said that only a being that is capable of reasoning is also capable of being unreasonable. Levinas has not so much gone beyond the tradition of *animal rationale* as put a new spin on it. But before we inhale what appears to be the bouquet of old wine in new bottles, it is important to realize that Levinas's definition of man as *animal irrationale* allows for the very untraditional possibility that we have direct duties to nonhuman animals. For what could be more unreasonable or more unintelligible from a *sociobiological* perspective for members of one species to sacrifice themselves for the members of another? What greater asininity has he than he who gives up his life for "man's best friend" – a dog? Does this not directly meet the requirements of an ethics that Levinas is "against-nature, against the naturality of nature"?[21]

I am not preaching traditional animal sacrifice such as substituting a ram for Isaac – or vice versa. Indeed, should we not be more than a little suspicious of an ethics that vaunts the fact that it is *against* nature? Despite his attempt to move beyond the ontotheological tradition, does not Levinas show himself to be firmly rooted in the Judeo-Christian tradition of what Nietzsche calls in his

Twilight of the Idols "anti-natural morality,"[22] characterized by hostility toward instinctual life? By absolutely refusing to accept the theory of evolution ("I would say, on the contrary, that in relation to the animal, the human is a new phenomenon"), by insisting on privileging the human over everything that walks and crawls on the earth, by drawing an absolute and non-traversable ethical divide between man and every other species, by failing to extend to other animals equal consideration of moral interests for no other apparent reason than that they cannot speak or reason, what is Levinas's ethics if not traditional? For one to describe it *otherwise* is liable to appear a *bêtise* – a true vindication of the claim that "man is an unreasonable animal."

CONCLUSION

Let me sum up. Levinas himself did not make much of an effort when it came to thinking about extending ethical consideration to animals. Even though he did not completely refuse the face of an animal, and even presented Bobby, a dog, as something of a moral exemplar for humans, he persistently pulled on the reins of his discussion as soon as it appeared to him that the animal question was threatening to take priority away from the human. Or, to reverse the metaphor, whenever the animal question encroached too much on the terrain of ethics, Levinas would chase it away, just as the guards were to chase away Bobby after he had overstayed his welcome in the company of the men. It seems to me that the lesson Levinas ought to have learned from Bobby was *not* that humans are like animals or animals are like humans, which would be to lack the sophistication required for a discussion of ethics that seeks to respect the absolute otherness of the Other. The lesson he should perhaps have learned was that his ethical theory was perhaps the best equipped of all the theories – with the exception of utilitarianism – to accommodate the inclusion of the other animal, and thereby truly go beyond the very humanism – and human chauvinism – that has served as a philosophical justification for the mistreatment of animals for over two millennia. His failure to learn that lesson leaves to others the task of providing us with a Levinasian ethics that does not perpetuate in the name of ethics the same humanism, the same hatred of the other animal.

Levinas is fond of a line from Eugène Ionesco's *The Bald Soprano*: "In short, we still do not know if, when someone rings the doorbell, there is someone there or not ..." (cited *CPP*, 60). I wonder whether we are agnostic enough, whether our agnosticism extends as a far as the scratching at the bedroom door, late on a Sunday morning, when the blinds are still down ... Or is that being *cynical*?

CHAPTER FIVE: FOUCAULT

ANIMALITY AND INSANITY

Michel Foucault

MADNESS IN THE RENAISSANCE

The dawn of madness on the horizon of the Renaissance is first perceptible in the decay of Gothic symbolism; as if that world, whose network of spiritual meanings was so close-knit, had begun to unravel, showing faces whose meaning was no longer clear except in the forms of madness. The Gothic forms persist for a time, but little by little they grow silent, cease to speak, to remind, to teach anything but their own fantastic presence, transcending all possible language (though still familiar to the eye). Freed from wisdom and from the teaching that organized it, the image begins to gravitate about its own madness.

Paradoxically, this liberation derives from a proliferation of meaning, from a self-multiplication of significance, weaving relationships so numerous, so intertwined, so rich, that they can no longer be deciphered except in the esoterism of knowledge. Things themselves become so burdened with attributes, signs, allusions that they finally lose their own form. Meaning is no longer read in an immediate perception, the figure no longer speaks for itself; between the knowledge which animates it and the form into which it is transposed, a gap widens. It is free for the dream. One book bears witness to meaning's proliferation at the end of the Gothic world, the *Speculum humanae salvationis*, which, beyond all the correspondences established by the patristic tradition, elaborates, between the Old and the New Testament, a symbolism not on the order of Prophecy, but deriving from an equivalence of imagery. The Passion of Christ is not prefigured only by the sacrifice of Abraham; it is surrounded by all the glories of torture and its innumerable dreams; Tubal the blacksmith and Isaiah's wheel take their places around the Cross, forming beyond all the lessons of the sacrifice the fantastic tableau of savagery, of tormented bodies, and of suffering. Thus the image is burdened with supplementary meanings, and forced to express them. And dreams, madness, the unreasonable can also slip into this excess of meaning. The symbolic figures easily become nightmare silhouettes. Witness that old image of wisdom so often translated, in German engravings, by a long-necked bird whose thoughts, rising slowly from heart to head, have time to be weighed and reflected on; a symbol whose values are blunted by being overemphasized: the long path of reflection becomes in the image the alembic of a subtle learning, an instrument which distills quintessences. The neck of the *Gutemensch* is endlessly elongated, the better to illustrate, beyond wisdom, all the real mediations of knowledge; and the symbolic man becomes a fantastic bird whose disproportionate neck folds a thousand times upon itself – an insane being, halfway between animal and thing, closer to the charms of an image than to the rigor of a meaning. This symbolic wisdom is a prisoner of the madness of dreams.

A fundamental conversion of the world of images: the constraint of a multiplied meaning liberates that world from the control of form. So many diverse meanings are established beneath the surface of the image that it presents only an enigmatic face. And its power is no longer to teach but to fascinate. Characteristic is the evolution of the famous gryllos already familiar to the Middle Ages in the English psalters, and at Chartres and Bourges. It taught, then, how the soul of desiring man had become a prisoner of the beast; these grotesque faces set in the bellies of monsters belonged to the world of the great Platonic metaphor and denounced the spirit's corruption in the folly of sin. But in the fifteenth century the gryllos, image of human madness, becomes one of the preferred figures in the countless *Temptations*. What assails the hermit's tranquillity is not objects of desire, but these hermetic, demented forms which have risen from a dream, and remain silent and furtive on the surface of a world. In the Lisbon *Temptation,* facing Saint Anthony sits one of these figures born of madness, of its solitude, of its penitence, of its privations; a wan smile lights this bodiless face, the pure presence of anxiety in the form of an agile grimace. Now it is exactly this nightmare silhouette that is at once the subject and object of the temptation; it is this figure which fascinates the gaze of the ascetic – both are prisoners of a kind of mirror interrogation, which remains unanswered in a silence inhabited only by the monstrous swarm that surrounds them. The gryllos no longer recalls man, by its satiric form, to his spiritual vocation forgotten in the folly of desire. It is madness become Temptation; all it embodies of the impossible, the fantastic, the inhuman, all that suggests the unnatural, the writhing of an insane presence on the earth's surface – all this is precisely what gives the gryllos its strange power. The freedom, however frightening, of his dreams, the hallucinations of his madness, have more power of attraction for fifteenth-century man than the desirable reality of the flesh.

What then is this fascination which now operates through the images of madness?

First, man finds in these fantastic figures one of the secrets and one of the vocations of his nature. In the thought of the Middle Ages, the legions of animals, named once and for all by Adam, symbolically bear the values of humanity. But at the beginning of the Renaissance, the relations with animality are reversed; the beast is set free; it escapes the world of legend and moral illustration to acquire a fantastic nature of its own. And by an astonishing reversal, it is now the animal that will stalk man, capture him, and reveal him to his own truth. Impossible animals, issuing from a demented imagination, become the secret nature of man; and when on the Last Day sinful man appears in his hideous nakedness, we see that he has the monstrous shape of a delirious animal; these are the screech owls whose toad bodies combine, in Thierry Bouts's *Hell,* with the nakedness of the damned; these are Stephan Lochner's winged insects with cats' heads, sphinxes with beetles' wing cases, birds whose wings are as disturbing and as avid as hands; this is the great beast of prey with knotty fingers that figures in Matthias Grünewald's *Temptation*. Animality has escaped domestication by human symbols and values; and it is animality that reveals the dark rage, the sterile madness that lie in men's hearts.

At the opposite pole to this nature of shadows, madness fascinates because it is knowledge. It is knowledge, first, because all these absurd figures are in reality elements of a difficult, hermetic, esoteric learning. These strange forms are situated, from the first, in the space of the Great Secret, and the Saint Anthony who is tempted by them is not a victim of the violence of desire but of the much more insidious lure of curiosity; he is tempted by that distant and intimate knowledge which is offered, and at the same time evaded, by the smile of the gryllos; his backward movement is nothing but that step by which he keeps from crossing the forbidden limits of knowledge; he knows already – and that is his temptation – what Jerome Cardan will say later: "Wisdom, like other precious substances, must be torn from the bowels of the earth." This knowledge, so inaccessible, so formidable, the Fool, in his innocent idiocy, already possesses. While the man of reason and wisdom perceives only fragmentary and all the more unnerving images of it, the Fool bears it intact as an unbroken sphere: that crystal ball which for all others is empty is in *his* eyes filled with the density of an invisible knowledge. Brueghel mocks the sick man who tries to penetrate this crystal sphere, but it is this iridescent bubble of knowledge – an absurd but infinitely precious lantern – that sways at the end of the stick Dulle Griet bears on her shoulder. And it is this sphere which figures on the reverse of the Garden of Delights. Another symbol of knowledge, the tree (the forbidden tree, the tree of promised immortality and of sin), once planted in the heart of the earthly paradise, has been uprooted and now forms the mast of the Ship of Fools, as seen in the engraving that illustrates Josse Bade's *Stultiferae naviculae*; it is this tree, without a doubt, that sways over Bosch's *Ship of Fools*.

What does it presage, this wisdom of fools? Doubtless, since it is a forbidden wisdom, it presages both the reign of Satan and the end of the world; ultimate bliss and supreme punishment; omnipotence on earth and the infernal fall. The Ship of Fools sails through a landscape of delights, where all is offered to desire, a sort of renewed paradise, since here man no longer knows either suffering or need; and yet he has not recovered his innocence. This false happiness is the diabolical triumph of the Antichrist; it is the End, already at hand. Apocalyptic dreams are not new, it is true, in the fifteenth century; they are, however, very different in nature from what they had been earlier. The delicately fantastic iconography of the fourteenth century, where castles are toppled like dice, where the Beast is always the traditional dragon held at bay by the Virgin, in short where the order of God and its imminent victory are always apparent, gives way to a vision of the world where all wisdom is annihilated. This is the great witches' Sabbath of nature: mountains melt and become plains, the earth vomits up the dead and bones tumble out of tombs; the stars fall, the earth catches fire, all life withers and comes to death. The end has no value as passage and promise; it is the advent of a night in which the world's old reason is engulfed. It is

enough to look at Dürer's Horsemen of the Apocalypse, sent by God Himself:
these are no angels of triumph and reconciliation; these are no heralds of serene
justice, but the disheveled warriors of a mad vengeance. The world sinks into
universal Fury. Victory is neither God's nor the Devil's: it belongs to Madness.

On all sides, madness fascinates man. The fantastic images it generates are not
fleeting appearances that quickly disappear from the surface of things. By a
strange paradox, what is born from the strangest delirium was already hidden,
like a secret, like an inaccessible truth, in the bowels of the earth. When man
deploys the arbitrary nature of his madness, he confronts the dark necessity of
the world; the animal that haunts his nightmares and his nights of privation is
his own nature, which will lay bare hell's pitiless truth; the vain images of blind
idiocy – such are the world's *Magna Scientia*; and already, in this disorder, in this
mad universe, is prefigured what will be the cruelty of the finale. In such images
– and this is doubtless what gives them their weight, what imposes such great
coherence on their fantasy – the Renaissance has expressed what it apprehended
of the threats and secrets of the world. . . .

MADNESS IN THE CLASSICAL AGE

When practices reach this degree of violent intensity, it becomes clear that they
are no longer inspired by the desire to punish nor by the duty to correct. The
notion of a "resipiscence" is entirely foreign to this regime. But there was a
certain image of animality that haunted the hospitals of the period [the "classical
age" – Eds.]. Madness borrowed its face from the mask of the beast. Those
chained to the cell walls were no longer men whose minds had wandered, but
beasts preyed upon by a natural frenzy: as if madness, at its extreme point, freed
from that moral unreason in which its most attenuated forms are enclosed,
managed to rejoin, by a paroxysm of strength, the immediate violence of
animality. This model of animality prevailed in the asylums and gave them their
cage-like aspect, their look of the menagerie. Coguel describes La Salpêtrière at
the end of the eighteenth century:

> Madwomen seized with fits of violence are chained like dogs at their cell
> doors, and separated from keepers and visitors alike by a long corridor
> protected by an iron grille; through this grille is passed their food and the
> straw on which they sleep; by means of rakes, part of the filth that
> surrounds them is cleaned out.

At the hospital of Nantes, the menagerie appears to consist of individual cages
for wild beasts. Never had Esquirol seen

> such an extravagance of locks, of bolts, of iron bars to shut the doors of the
> cells. . . . Tiny openings pierced next to the doors were fitted with iron bars
> and shutters. Quite close to this opening hung a chain fastened to the wall
> and bearing at its end a cast-iron receptacle, somewhat resembling a
> wooden shoe, in which food was placed and passed through the bars of
> these openings.

When François-Emmanuel Fodéré arrived at the hospital of Strasbourg in 1814, he found a kind of human stable, constructed with great care and skill: "for troublesome madmen and those who dirtied themselves, a kind of cage, or wooden closet, which could at the most contain one man of middle height, had been devised at the ends of the great wards." These cages had gratings for floors, and did not rest on the ground but were raised about fifteen centimeters. Over these gratings was thrown a little straw "upon which the madman lay, naked or nearly so, took his meals, and deposited his excrement."

This, to be sure, is a whole security system against the violence of the insane and the explosion of their fury. Such outbursts are regarded chiefly as a social danger. But what is most important is that it is conceived in terms of an animal freedom. The negative fact that "the madman is not treated like a human being" has a very positive content: this inhuman indifference actually has an obsessional value: it is rooted in the old fears which since antiquity, and especially since the Middle Ages, have given the animal world its familiar strangeness, its menacing marvels, its entire weight of dumb anxiety. Yet this animal fear which accompanies, with all its imaginary landscape, the perception of madness, no longer has the same meaning it had two or three centuries earlier: animal metamorphosis is no longer the visible sign of infernal powers, nor the result of a diabolic alchemy of unreason. The animal in man no longer has any value as the sign of a Beyond; it has become his madness, without relation to anything but itself: his madness in the state of nature. The animality that rages in madness dispossesses man of what is specifically human in him; not in order to deliver him over to other powers, but simply to establish him at the zero degree of his own nature. For classicism, madness in its ultimate form is man in immediate relation to his animality, without other reference, without any recourse.

The day would come when from an evolutionary perspective this presence of animality in madness would be considered as the sign – indeed, as the very essence – of disease. In the classical period, on the contrary, it manifested the very fact that *the madman was not a sick man.* Animality, in fact, protected the lunatic from whatever might be fragile, precarious, or sickly in man. The animal solidity of madness, and that density it borrows from the blind world of beasts, inured the madman to hunger, heat, cold, pain. It was common knowledge until the end of the eighteenth century that the insane could support the miseries of existence indefinitely. There was no need to protect them; they had no need to be covered or warmed. When, in 1811, Samuel Tuke visited a workhouse in the Southern Counties, he saw cells where the daylight passed through little barred windows that had been cut in the doors. All the women were entirely naked. Now "the temperature was extremely rigorous, and the evening of the day before, the thermometer had indicated a cold of 18 degrees. One of these unfortunate women was lying on a little straw, without covering." This ability of the insane to endure, like animals, the worst inclemencies was still a medical dogma for Pinel; he would always admire

the constancy and the ease with which certain of the insane of both sexes bear the most rigorous and prolonged cold. In the month of Nivôse of the Year III, on certain days when the thermometer indicated 10, 11, and as many as 16 degrees below freezing, a madman in the hospital of Bicêtre could not endure his wool blanket, and remained sitting on the icy floor of his cell. In the morning, one no sooner opened his door than he ran in his shirt into the inner court, taking ice and snow by the fistful, applying it to his breast and letting it melt with a sort of delectation.

Madness, insofar as it partook of animal ferocity, preserved man from the dangers of disease; it afforded him an invulnerability, similar to that which nature, in its foresight, had provided for animals. Curiously, the disturbance of his reason restored the madman to the immediate kindness of nature by a return to animality.

This is why, at this extreme point, madness was less than ever linked to medicine; nor could it be linked to the domain of correction. Unchained animality could be mastered only by *discipline* and *brutalizing*. The theme of the animal-madman was effectively realized in the eighteenth century, in occasional attempts to impose a certain pedagogy on the insane. Pinel cites the case of a "very famous monastic establishment, in one of the southern regions of France," where a violent madman would be given "a precise order to change"; if he refused to go to bed or to eat, he "was warned that obstinacy in his deviations would be punished on the next day with ten strokes of the bullwhip." If, on the contrary, he was submissive and docile, he was allowed "to take his meals in the refectory, next to the disciplinarian," but at the least transgression, he was instantly admonished by a "heavy blow of a rod across his fingers." Thus, by the use of a curious dialectic whose movement explains all these "inhuman" practices of confinement, the free animality of madness was tamed only by such discipline whose meaning was not to raise the bestial to the human, but to restore man to what was purely animal within him. Madness discloses a secret of animality which is its own truth, and in which, in some way, it is reabsorbed. Toward the middle of the eighteenth century, a farmer in the north of Scotland had his hour of fame. He was said to possess the art of curing insanity. Pinel notes in passing that this Gregory had the physique of a Hercules:

His method consisted in forcing the insane to perform the most difficult tasks of farming, in using them as beasts of burden, as servants, in reducing them to an ultimate obedience with a barrage of blows at the least act of revolt.

In the reduction to animality, madness finds both its truth and its cure; when the madman has become a beast, this presence of the animal in man, a presence which constituted the scandal of madness, is eliminated: not that the animal is silenced, but man himself is abolished. In the human being who has become a beast of burden, the absence of reason follows wisdom and its order: madness is then cured, since it is alienated in something which is no less than its truth.

A moment would come when, from this animality of madness, would be deduced the idea of a mechanistic psychology, and the notion that the forms of madness can be referred to the great structures of animal life. But in the seventeenth and eighteenth centuries, the animality that lends its face to madness in no way stipulates a determinist nature for its phenomena. On the contrary, it locates madness in *an area of unforeseeable freedom* where frenzy is unchained; if determinism can have any effect on it, it is in the form of constraint, punishment, or discipline. Through animality, madness does not join the great laws of nature and of life, but rather the thousand forms of a bestiary. But unlike the one popular in the Middle Ages, which illustrated, in so many symbolic visages, the metamorphoses of evil, this was an abstract bestiary; here evil no longer assumed its fantastic body; here we apprehend only its most extreme form, the truth of the beast which is a truth without content. Evil is freed from all that its wealth of iconographic fauna could do, to preserve only a general power of intimidation: the secret danger of an animality that lies in wait and, all at once, undoes reason in violence and truth in the madman's frenzy. Despite the contemporary effort to constitute a positivist zoology, this obsession with an animality perceived as the natural locus of madness continued to people the hell of the classical age. It was this obsession that created the imagery responsible for all the practices of confinement and the strangest aspects of its savagery.

MADNESS AND ANIMALITY IN MICHEL FOUCAULT'S *MADNESS AND CIVILIZATION*

Clare Palmer

INTRODUCTION

Madness and Civilization is one of Michel Foucault's earliest but most well-known books, and contains his only extended discussion of animality. In this paper, I shall outline the basic arguments of the book, then move on to consider different understandings of animality suggested in it, both by Foucault himself and in the texts on which he draws. In the later part of the paper, I shall indicate some difficulties that I consider to underlie Foucault's treatment of animality.[1]

Before embarking on this, however, it is important to locate this paper with respect to two controversial issues surrounding the text of *Madness and Civilization*. The original version of *Madness and Civilization* was Foucault's doctoral thesis. It was published in 1961 and was over 500 pages long. In 1964, Foucault published an abridged edition, which was considerably shorter albeit with the inclusion of one extra chapter from the original 1961 text, a small amount of other new material and a new introduction. This text was translated into the English by Richard Howard and given the title *Madness and Civilization*, from which these extracts are taken.[2] However, in France, Foucault's original thesis *Histoire de la folie à l'age classique* was republished with only minor alterations, and at the original length, in 1964. No English translation of this longer version exists. This has led to a number of difficulties, and in particular raises the question of whether criticisms of Foucault's work based on the English text of *Madness and Civilization* also apply to the longer French version of *Histoire de la folie*. In discussing the extracts here, as well as the book more widely, I have used the English version of *Madness and Civilization* – since it was an abridgement created by Foucault himself – but have also referred to *Histoire de la folie*. Indeed, all of the text reproduced here appears in the same form in *Histoire de la folie*.

A second problem, which is relevant to these extracts but which runs throughout *Madness and Civilization*, concerns the historical basis for Foucault's arguments. Some critics maintain that the historical evidence and artistic interpretations Foucault presents in *Madness and Civilization* are in a variety of ways fundamentally flawed.[3] I am inclined to think that at least part of this criticism may be accurate. Fortunately, for the purposes of this paper, the accuracy of Foucault's research in specific historical contexts is not central, although the extracts here do raise some of these questions. But one related issue is important. Foucault suggests that madness was commonly compared with animality, or viewed as animality, and that the mad were intentionally treated as animals in some of the texts of the periods he considers. Since Foucault does use supporting texts to substantiate these claims, it seems possible that some individuals did hold such views. However, how widely these views were held is contested. Roy Porter, for instance, argues that another image of the mad – as people who reason wrongly – was current in the Enlightenment and that Foucault does not address this interpretation.[4] Further – perhaps in part because of Foucault's elaborate, labyrinthine writing style in *Madness and Civilization* – it is very difficult to disentangle Foucault's *own* views of relationships between madness and animality from his presentation of the views of the periods he examines.[5] It seems evident from his more general discussion that some of the views he presents (especially some Renaissance ones) are – in part at least – congenial to his own interpretation, and both this and the way in which he presents other views raise doubts about how far his text does give us access to views of earlier periods (although, of course, one may argue that this is never possible to more than a limited extent). All that I will attempt to do here is to focus on Foucault's text itself, that is, on the perspective he seems to be adopting, and, based on this, to consider some of the issues raised by his discussion of madness and animality.

Finally, it is also worth noting that in later interviews and writing Foucault expressed concerns about aspects of the project undertaken in *Histoire de la folie*.[6] Some of these seem to have been triggered by Derrida's critique of the book in his paper "Cogito and the History of Madness" (1963); others by developments in Foucault's own thinking. We do not know whether Foucault's changing thoughts would have affected his discussion of animality; it is not a discussion specifically addressed elsewhere in his work. For this reason alone, this can only be the most provisional sketch of Foucault's ideas about animality in *Madness and Civilization*.

THE ARGUMENTS OF *MADNESS AND CIVILIZATION*

In order to make some sense of these extracts, it is important to understand their location within the context of the book as a whole. In *Madness and Civilization*, Foucault offers a "history of madness, rather than psychiatry – a history of the significance of madness, of how madness was experienced, rather than a disciplinary history of how specially trained professionals dealt with it as a perennial problem."[7] In particular, Foucault makes a series of claims about changing ideas of madness in the West. It should be noted, first of all, that – typically – Foucault does not regard madness as a single human phenomenon that presents itself identically in different periods. Rather, he regards what is understood as "madness" to be a construction that varies between historical epochs. In the history of the West he maintains, albeit controversially, three distinct epochs can be identified in which the understanding of madness, and thus the idea of how it should be treated, were regarded differently: the Renaissance, the Classical period (which he dates from about 1650 to 1800), and the Modern period (from about 1800 onward).[8]

Foucault argues that in the Renaissance two contrasting views of madness existed. The first extract here forms part of this discussion. One view of madness, manifest in much Renaissance art, saw it as a dark, dreamlike, tragic threat. The other, often manifest in Renaissance writing, regarded madness as a kind of ironic jousting-partner for Reason. (Foucault uses the terms *tragique* and *critique* for these two views respectively; Gutting refers to them as "cosmic madness" and "critical madness").[9] By the end of the Renaissance, Foucault maintains, it was the latter view that predominated. But both views had something in common: madness was regarded as giving access to an *inner human truth* not available to Reason, and was also thought of as being in constant dialogue with Reason, questioning it and exposing it to scrutiny. Because of this, Foucault suggests, those who were regarded as mad in the Renaissance were generally not treated harshly; they often wandered on the margins of society, and were not systematically confined.[10] (It is here that Foucault includes his famous narrative on the *Narrenschiff* – "the ship of fools" – the historical existence of which is now hotly contested.)

Foucault contrasts these Renaissance views with those of the Classical period. In the seventeenth century, Foucault argues, "the Great Confinement" suddenly occurred – an expansion of workhouses, hospitals, institutions, and prisons across Europe.[11] A variety of different kinds of individuals was confined, including the very poor, the sick, beggars, the unemployed, and the mad. All these groups were regarded, Foucault argues, as having deviated from reason in some way, as representing *déraison*, most significantly in terms of their relationship to the "imperative of labor."[12] Idleness, the failure to work, was regarded as a manifestation of unreason and as a moral failing, worthy of punishment. The mad constituted one group among others, and, as with all those who represented *déraison*, were seen as requiring confinement and control. Furthermore, it was believed that the mad had *chosen* to take this immoral path. Given this moral culpability, the community, Foucault says "acquired an ethical power of segregation which permitted it to eject, as into another world, all forms of social uselessness."[13] No longer was madness thought of as giving access to either cosmic or critical truth, as it was in the Renaissance; rather, madness was now seen as humanity in an ultimate state of degradation.

Foucault argues that a further shift with respect to madness occurred in the Modern period. Madness now became seen as "mental illness." It was thought that the mad should be interred in hospitals and medically treated, whereby the growth of the asylums began. But Foucault famously rejects a Whiggish view that this understanding of "mental illness" represented a humanitarian advance in the treatment of those called mentally ill. In fact, he argues, although asylums presented their work as medical, they operated with the principles of bourgeois ethics, creating new ways of repressing and disciplining those regarded as mad in an attempt to normalize their behavior. He implies that this modern treatment of madness was, in its own way, as much an attempt to control, mould, and repress as the confinement of the seventeenth and eighteenth centuries.

Foucault's own view, as has been widely noted, seems sympathetic (many have thought conservatively and romantically so) to Renaissance ideas of "cosmic madness." It is in relation to this kind of madness, Foucault suggests, that the works of genius of Nietzsche, Artaud, and Van Gogh were formed, notwithstanding his claim that "where there is a work of art, there is no madness."[14] Interrupting the work of art, madness "opens a void, a moment of silence, a question without answer, provokes a breach without reconciliation where the world is forced to question itself."[15] Madness, he suggests, may challenge the world; may even call the world to justify itself.

Madness and Animality
In the course of much of *Madness and Civilization*, Foucault associates madness with animality. Sometimes this association seems to come from Foucault himself, sometimes from his sources. As he presents changes in concepts of madness, so he also suggests that the madness/animality relation changes. Having said this, however, the study of Foucault's text also suggests some persistent assumptions of his own about what might be constituted by animality. I shall move on to discuss these later.

A madness/animality association is made – albeit obliquely – as early as the famous first paragraph of *Madness and Civilization*. Here, Foucault presents a vivid image of gated cities and the edges of communities, places previously "haunted" by lepers who had been excluded from their communities, scraping a living on the margins of society. But leprosy had now disappeared; the wastelands thus await the arrival of the next group of the excluded, which, in *Madness and Civilization*, is the mad.[16] In the meantime, the wastelands are both uninhabitable, and yet not empty; they "belong to the non-human." Immediately, Foucault associates lepers, the nonhuman, and the mad – all of whom inhabit marginal land, all of whom are outside human communities. As Cousins and Hussain note, the leper is a figure of particular significance in Foucault's writing, symbolizing exclusion, internment, an object of fear from whom purification was required.[17] In the same desolate space, between the occupation of one group of the excluded (the lepers) and a later group of the excluded (the mad), Foucault places the nonhuman. The separation of the nonhuman from the human is emphasized. The only kinds of humans with whom the nonhuman are associated are those humans ejected from human communities. This introduces one key theme of *Madness and Civilization*: the link between madness, animality, and that which is wild. Animality and wildness are, throughout, importantly and inextricably linked. Wild animals may be confined for display (in menageries) or they may be free (in the wasteland); but Foucault is not interested in their portrayal as domesticates or as human associates.[18] Furthermore, although the wilderness belongs to them, this is a strangely barren kind of belonging. Despite the presence of nonhumans – presumably reproducing as wild animals do – the wasteland is described as "sterile." In *Madness and Civilization*, nonhuman reproduction cannot bring sterility to an end.

Madness/Animality in the Renaissance

The first extract here follows on some pages after this evocative introduction, forming part of Foucault's exposition of Renaissance experiences of madness, that is to say, the experience of madness by those who are "sane." Here, Foucault discusses the "cosmic" and the "critical" views of madness. And although the "menacing" or "cosmic" understanding of madness dies out before the end of the Renaissance, it is this in which Foucault is most interested – and which he links with animality. This cosmic madness supercedes the medieval obsession with death. Madness, Foucault says, is the *déjà-la* of death; it concerns the "nothingness of existence"; "the tide of madness, its secret invasion ... shows that the world is near its final catastrophe."[19] This threat of fearful, cosmic madness is displayed in the dreamlike images of Renaissance art: in particular in the portrayals of creatures that are part-animal part-human; the development of the art of the gryllos embodying the "fantastic, the inhuman, all that suggests the unnatural, the writhing of an insane presence on the earth's surface."[20] This madness, Foucault suggests, filled with fantastic, writhing figures, was fascinating and tempting to man because it portrayed "one of the secrets and one of the vocations of his nature." Whereas in the Middle Ages, humans were those who, in Adam, named the animals, which thus symbolically bore the values of humanity, in the Renaissance the relations with animality are reversed: the beast is set free [*se libre*]; it escapes the world of legend and moral illustration to acquire a fantastic nature of its own. And, by an astonishing reversal, it is now the animal that will stalk man, capture him, and reveal him to his own truth. Impossible animals, issuing from a demented imagination, become the secret nature of man.[21]

How does Foucault understand "the animals" and "animality" here?[22] Adam's naming of the animals in Genesis 2 has long been interpreted as the establishment of a human power relation over animals. Animals are captured or confined by human language and human terminology. (That this is regarded as a kind of capture seems to be implied in Foucault's idea of reversal where animality is "set free," which is perhaps more appropriately translated as "frees itself.")[23] In the medieval period, the naming of the animals, he argues, was coupled with the symbolic attribution to them, for instance, in moral bestiaries, of particular human values (nobility, courage, deceit, and so on), a further form of capture. But, Foucault argues, in Renaissance conceptions of cosmic madness, animality acquires a life of its own; no longer captured, it frees itself and is the active agent in stalking and capturing; it is powerful, threatening, out of control. Animality here is not just the desolate inhabitant of the marginal wasteland; it now stands snarling at reason and the foundations of civilization. Indeed, "animality has escaped domestication by human symbols and values; and it is animality that reveals the dark rage, the sterile madness that lie in men's hearts."

Although this animality is portrayed as offering a tempting kind of wild freedom, it arises *within* human imagination; it is of human origin. Like Frankenstein, it is created by humans, although it is not under their control. So, while this animality may have escaped domestication, it is a human product. It is also *fantastic*. This animality is never presented in terms of real animal species, but of bizarre combinations of human and animal, animal with animal, outrageous bestial chimeras (calling to mind the animal categorization from Borges that Foucault uses to such good effect at the beginning of *The Order of Things*). These animal chimeras are characterized by their *unnaturalness*. Their fantastic forms run counter to nature, rather than emerging from it. It is in part their unnaturalness that renders them so terrifying, and (perhaps) also so sterile. And this animality provides access to a kind of truth about human beings; it reveals what is in their hearts, revelations not available to Reason. This dark, demented animality is associated not only with Unreason, with the unavailability and loss of Reason, but also with the dawning of a dark revelation, which, beyond the bounds of Reason, is "like an inaccessible truth."

The movement away from this view of cosmic madness as wild, fantastic animality later in the Renaissance seems to be regarded by Foucault as a loss. The ironic, critical view of madness that superseded it "tamed the violence of the mad," according to Foucault, a development that prevented its dark revelation. This wild animal madness resurfaces centuries later only in the genius writers who struggled with madness, such as Nietzsche, in whose work at least the idea of wild animality plays an important part – one that I noted earlier may have influenced Foucault himself.[24]

Foucault juxtaposes this account of Renaissance animality and cosmic madness with a rather different construal of animality and madness in the Classical period.

Madness/Animality in the Classical Period

Foucault maintains that the change in attitudes toward the mad, which he identifies with the Classical period, also led to a change in ideas about the relationship of madness and animality. Although the mad were confined in the Classical period with other groups considered to belong to the category of *déraison*, Foucault maintains that they were marked out from these other groups because the mad, and only the mad, were regarded as animal. This understanding of animality differs from that in the Renaissance. No longer is animality the tragic, stalking, inner beast that inspires both terror and truth. Animality is now what is left when humanity has been stripped of reason. The mad may have retained the form of humanity, but their lack of what was regarded as its distinguishing characteristic – reason or thought – meant that they had become what was left, namely, animal. Animality was the inevitable result of this annihilation of their humanity.

What Foucault understands by reason here does not necessarily exclude the *form* of logical reasoning; madness can present itself to reason in logical structures. A mad person might indeed use the form of reason, saying: "The dead do not eat; I am dead; hence I do not eat."[25] What is unreasonable about the mad is their attachment to an *image* bound up in a particular discourse ("I am dead"; "I am made of glass"; "I am being tempted by demons," etc.) rather than to reality. In a sense, then, this understanding of madness is the opposite to the one Foucault attributes to the Renaissance. In the Classical era, madness is seen as attachment to an image, to that which is untrue. It does not, unlike in the Renaissance, provide for the possibility of revelation of truth, however esoteric or inaccessible. In another sense, though, this Classical concept of madness was regarded as revealing a different kind of truth, one stripped of reason: humans are animals. Rather than the fantastic unnaturalness of Renaissance animality, what is revealed is animality in the form of degraded humanity, madness "in the state of nature":

> The animality that rages in madness dispossesses man of what is specifically human in him; not in order to deliver him over to other powers, but simply to establish him at the zero degree of his own nature. For classicism, madness in its ultimate form is man in immediate relation to his animality, without any other reference, without any recourse.[26]

The animality of madness is, by this account, the lowest state to which it was possible to fall. Furthermore, this fall was not regarded as being outside human responsibility for, in the Classical period, madness was regarded as a moral flaw. The mad had chosen their madness; they were self-deceived and persisted in a state of constant error.[27] Madness took humans to the edge of humanity, where they were in a state of "moral rapport" with animals. Foucault comments in a footnote here in *Histoire de la folie* (not in the text of *Madness and Civilization*) that this "moral rapport" between man and animality is not "like the power of metamorphosis" (a figure more common to medieval portrayals of humans-as-animals), but rather as the "border of his [man's] nature." This, he claims, is best expressed in a 1623 text by Le Picard, which begins: "he is a wolf in rapacity, in subtlety, a lion; in fraud and trickery, a fox; in hypocrisy, a monkey" and so on.[28] The mad were here regarded as displaying all the *negative* values associated with various animals. Yet, even at this low point, where human moral rapport was at the level of the animals, divine salvation of the mad was possible. "The scandal of madness showed men how close to animality their Fall could bring them; and at the same time how far divine mercy could extend when it consented to save man."[29]

Given this understanding of madness, it is not surprising that no dialogue could take place between reason and madness. Foucault suggests that for those looking on from a position of reason, animality was something to which, unlike the animality of the Renaissance, no relationship of any kind was felt: "madness was shown, but on the other side of bars." It was separated from reason by a moral chasm, and also by its fearful violence. Although Foucault used the language of "raging animality" of the Renaissance as well as the Classical period, now the raging is understood differently, as a dumb, degraded violence. It was a violence that generated fear, not only because of the physical danger it presented, but also because the mad were regarded as threateningly alien in the same way as animals were. But both these elements contributed to the idea that the mad should be displayed. As with fearful animals in menageries, mad humans presented a spectacle to be watched. And, indeed, the mad were often chained or kept on leashes; their living spaces resembled cages and "had the look of the menagerie." But these displays, Foucault maintains, could be justified because the spectacle was a moral one. It served as a warning to those who might be tempted to cross the moral chasm and plunge into madness themselves.

While such displays of the mad were not entirely new in the Classical period, Foucault suggests that, during the Great Confinement, displays of the mad became an extremely popular public attraction. Even in the late eighteenth century, when fear grew about the potential of disease and contamination spreading from madhouses, Foucault tells us of the work of Desmonceaux, who wanted to build asylums that "offered unreason as a spectacle without threatening the spectators, where it would have all the powers of example and none of the risks of contagion." Desmonceaux argued that being taken to see the mad-animals was a prudent act on the part of any parent, to prevent their children from morally lapsing into the ways of the mad, and becoming animals to be watched themselves. These displays of the mad seem to have been modeled on animal displays and on menageries, including the training of the mad to perform dancing and acrobatics "with a few flicks of the whip." Of course, this similarity is not surprising; it was the animality of the mad that made their display possible. Furthermore, one did not have to take care over the physical well-being of the mad; they could be displayed naked and hungry. According to Foucault, it was believed that "the animal solidity of madness, and the density it borrows from the blind world of beasts, inured the madman from hunger, heat, cold and pain."[30] Since animals did not feel cold or hunger, nor did the mad. This "insensibility" was regarded as a "kindness of nature." And, as animals, the mad could also be disciplined, by training, whips, and beating. These practices did not have the aim of restoring the mad to reason, and thus to humanity. Rather, they meant that the mad could be *true to their nature as animals*; animals should be mastered by human discipline. This view led to the spectacle of the mad being used, for instance, as beasts of burden on a farm where they were beaten into submission. Once they were submissive and obedient, the scandal of madness – and their humanity – was abolished; they were *properly* animals.

FOUCAULT'S PORTRAYAL OF ANIMALITY

Analyzing this complex portrayal of the association between madness and animality requires, first of all, some consideration of how Foucault deploys "animality" in the text. Sometimes he uses it to capture what his historical sources seem to be saying; on other occasions, it seems to reflect his own thinking, a term with which he himself seems comfortable. Is it possible, though, to identify further what he means when he uses the term "animality" or speaks of "the animal"?

Clearly, for Foucault, animality, like madness, is a constructed category, understood differently in different periods. Indeed, Foucault suggests that animality is constructed in different ways directly in relation to the way madness is constructed. In the Renaissance, animality was a figurative or symbolic portrayal of a dark and threatening, yet revelatory, aspect of the cosmos. Such symbolic use, though, did not mean that the mad were actually called animals, or were treated as animals. In contrast, in the Classical age animality was the "zero point of human nature," humans at their most depraved, their humanity annihilated; they could be regarded as animals and treated as animals. So in these two periods, "animality" meant something different, while always being inextricably related to the understanding of madness.

Does this imply, though, that the meaning of animality is entirely free-floating, that there is nothing at all to bind together the different historical interpretations of animality that Foucault presents, as well as, perhaps, Foucault's own interpretation? Looking closely, there are elements that these uses of animality share. They regard animality as in some sense a state of *déraison* and turbulent emotion. In Renaissance animality, it is the dark beast within that jousts with reason; in Classical animality the human is precisely without reason. Being without reason while still being a fear-inducing living being is distinctively animal.[31] In both accounts, Foucault describes animality as "raging," a manifestation of emotional and physical strength, severed from the rational workings of the mind. Animality is fundamentally wild and eludes domestication. This is not surprising. If reason is about order, and animals are in the contrary state of *déraison*, then they *must* primarily be seen as wild and disordered. It seems that wildness, however, can be disciplined into submission, perhaps tamed (rather than domesticated) by the use of force. It is always on the edge, however, of breaking through. Indeed, wildness for Foucault seems to be a normative as well as a descriptive category. Wildness resists conventional mores; it threatens to break out and overwhelm. It is dangerous; but from such danger, and the struggle against it, can come brilliance, revelation, and the breaking in of "other powers."

In this sense, Foucault's study in madness and animality maintains a positive regard for some ways of understanding animality, ways that recognize the significance of the expression of unreason, the possibility of revelation from sources other than reason, the power of the raging passions, and the proposed role of animality in stimulating works of genius. But there is, I think, some difficulty with such a view. At the heart of this difficulty lies the relationship between animality, madness, and reason in the text. Foucault is clearly working with discourses – and, indeed, apparently adopting a version of them himself – in which, as Derrida suggests, "reason constitutes itself by excluding and objectifying the free subjectivity of madness."[32] If reason constitutes itself by the exclusion of madness then the very establishment of a discourse of reason renders madness and animality outside reason. But, as Foucault himself argued in his later work, discourses of this kind are not just descriptively neutral. They reflect, express, and develop particular kinds of power relations. And so one might ask: If one operates with a discourse in which animality and madness are excluded from reason, what power relations are thereby reflected, expressed, and encouraged particularly with respect to their manifestations in power practices?

Of course, *Madness and Civilization* is, to some extent at least, just such a study of practices relating to those understood to be mad, although Foucault does not here use the language of power relations that appears in his later works such as *Discipline and Punish*. In the Classical period, as we have seen, the mad were confined, chained, beaten, starved, exposed, and displayed; Foucault gives us to believe that this is because of the link between madness, animality, and unreason. Regarded as being stripped of reason, humans were animals, and could be treated like animals. A particular conception of madness, linked with a set of ideas about animality, is bound up with violent power-practices acted on the bodies of those classified as mad. Although Foucault does not explicitly condemn those practices – nor endorse the less physically violent but more psychologically disciplinary practices that he maintained replaced them – nonetheless his text is, at the very least, uncomfortable with these kinds of power relationships. As most commentators have maintained, he seems to want to reject both the classical and the more modern approaches to madness in favor of a view more like that of the Renaissance, where the mystery and revelatory potential of madness is emphasized, and those thought to be mad are surrounded by less intense physical constraints or psychological discipline. One might read this as Foucault challenging such practices of power by attempting to revalue positively the "madness" or "unreason" side of the madness/reason binary divide. Madness may be the "other" of reason, as it were, but unreason can have its own value.

If one remains within a discourse where reason constitutes itself against madness and against animality, then revaluing the "other" of reason must be the only way of moving to a different understanding of power relations between "the reasonable," "the mad," and "the animal." On this basis emerges the view I attributed to Foucault above, namely, that animality could be regarded more positively – revalued – on the grounds of its raging passions, its potential for revelation, its wildness. But another possibility, which Foucault does not propose here, at least not directly, is an alternative discourse where the relationship between reason and animality is one whose terms do not necessarily exclude the other, that is, a discourse where some aspects, at least, of "being animal" overlap with some aspects, at least, of reason.

I say that Foucault does not straightforwardly propose this, but in fact his work, especially in the earliest version of *Histoire de la folie*, does suggest a certain unease with the mutual exclusiveness of madness–animality and reason. One aspect of this unease seems to concern the effects of the disvalue of madness, where madness is bound into a network of power relations involving physical harm and troubling forms of psychological discipline. But even where the "madness" side of the divide is revalued, at some level Foucault is still pushing at its boundaries. In the first preface to the 1961 edition of *Histoire de la folie* (later excised), Foucault indicated an interest in finding where

the man of madness and the man of reason, separating themselves, are not yet separate, and in a language that is very primal, very crude, far earlier than that of science, begin the dialogue of their rupture, which testifies in a fleeting way that they still speak to one another.[33]

The idea of some sort of dialogue between madness and reason also emerges in his portrayal of Renaissance madness. But this understanding of madness/reason, the idea that the mad and the reasonable may speak to one another, or that the reasonable may speak about madness itself, is precisely what cannot be done in the context (as Derrida maintains). If madness is constituted as unreason, then madness cannot use language, since language requires reason. A dialogue with madness and a history of madness are both either impossible or involve betraying madness. Any attempt to write a history of madness traps it in reason, whereby the "man of madness" cannot be spoken with as such. A similar line of thought seems to follow with respect to animality. If animality *just is* unreason, then – among other things – there is no possibility of communicating with the animals who embody animality. If the madness–animality/reason binary is fundamental, then dialogue, however "primal" or "crude," cannot take place. Yet Foucault did, at some stage at least, seem to want to affirm the possibility of such a dialogue. Even on Foucault's own terms, then, there might be grounds for rethinking the binary nature of this discourse.

What kind of alternative discourse, then, might be possible in relation to animality and reason? One alternative seems to exist within some of the current work on animal behavior in scientific disciplines, in particular within new work in cognitive ethology. Rather than starting from the view that animals are "without reason," careful study of the mental capacities of different animals and different species of animals has been undertaken. Animal abilities to communicate, to navigate, to play, and to deceive have been explored. What, in particular, emerges within scientific discourses of this kind (among others) is that both "reason" and "animality" are themselves deeply problematic as categorical terms. This is not just on the grounds that their meanings change in the kinds of ways Foucault identifies. Hauser comments that questions about whether animals "think" or are "conscious" are unhelpful because the concepts of thought and consciousness are too vague and general. It is better to ask about particular mental phenomena concerning issues such as problem-solving using symbols or understanding another's beliefs.[34] From this perspective, reason or rationality can similarly be viewed as a vague, general concept, to which a wide variety of very different abilities and capacities may contribute.[35] Further, different species display varying mental capacities and abilities that have emerged in the context of their particular evolutionary circumstances. It is not clear what characteristic, or cluster of features, all these kinds of beings have in common that justifies placing them under the umbrella term "animality."

This suggests, then, that very different kinds of discourse about animality and reason are possible. On the one hand, in *Madness and Civilization,* Foucault works with discourses in which reason and animality are mutually dependent but exclusive concepts. On the other hand, there are current scientific discourses where the mental capacities of different animals are explored without there being any binary division between reason and animality, and where, indeed, the usefulness of these categories is questioned. Foucault's discourse of animality is thus largely symbolic and imaginative, and has little or no contact with animals understood as living biological organisms.

CONCLUSION

Accepting that different, even competing discourses exist does not, of course, imply that one should be preferred to another. But, as I suggested earlier, even within Foucault's own thinking the reason/madness–animality divide emerges as problematic. I want to conclude by suggesting that there are grounds for contesting discourses with a reason/animality divide, at least when thinking about animals as *living biological organisms*, rather than as creatures of the literary and philosophical imagination.

At the root of this concern are the natures of the discourses in question: the symbolic, binary reason/animality discourse, and the modern biological discourse of animal mental capacities. I do not want to take the problematic step of claiming that the scientific discourse is more "foundational" than the other. (After all, questionable scientific discourses about the mad are just what Foucault goes on to discuss later in *Madness and Civilization*.) But Foucault's text does raise questions about the nature of some of the claims embedded in particular manifestations of the reason/madness–animality divide. For instance, in the Classical age, he tells us, it was "common knowledge" that the mad were animals, and that since animals did not feel cold or hunger, nor did the mad. Presumably, we are not supposed to think it the case – and, presumably, Foucault himself did not think it the case – that the mad, or animals, in the Classical age or at any other time, really did not feel cold or hunger; that they were in these ways "invulnerable."[36] If indeed this was "common knowledge," it was mistaken. But it was "knowledge" bound up with a series of power practices on the bodies of the mad (e.g., leaving them unclothed, exposing them, not feeding them) and presumably a series of practices on the bodies of animals too.

This is one example of precisely the kind of problem that arises from the whole discourse of reason/animality I have been discussing. While the discourse may have a particular symbolic role, it does not exist separated from power relations and effects. Animality is constructed in it as wild, emotional, and without reason. Even in this more abstract, symbolic sense, and even as Foucault appears to try to revalue more positively those "animal" qualities, such a discourse creates an understanding of "the animal" that homogenizes animals, and separates animals from "reasonable" humans.[37] And this idea of "the animal" and "animality" is united with particular kinds of practices and actions on the bodies of real animals. But the beliefs manifest in the discourse – like the beliefs that the mad do not get hungry or feel cold – can be contested. For instance, one may argue that animals – or at least some of them – are not "wild," emotional, and raging in Foucault's sense, and that many do have a variety of mental capacities and abilities that, using a more nuanced understanding, can be regarded as expressions of some forms of rationality.

Contesting the reason/animality discourse, as I have indicated, means turning to another discourse, for instance, a biological discourse of animal mental capacities. I am not suggesting, by making this move, that such an alternative discourse gives unmediated access to the "real" nature of animals. It is itself embedded in power relations in which animals are the objects of observation or experimentation, are kept in confinement, and are used as ends to achieve particular kinds of human knowledge. Indeed, Foucault's own later work on the repressive and creative effects of power on bodies offers a range of tools for thinking through just these kinds of human/animal relations.[38] Nonetheless, in terms of thinking about how different animals live in the world, both in wild ecosystems and in domestic or laboratory contexts, careful studies of animal behavior manifest, at least, an *attentiveness* to animal ways of being, to the differences between individual animals and species of animals, and to their varying mental abilities. The intricate details of the lives of individual animals, their interaction with members of their own and other species, their ways of acting and reacting to the world around them are here a focus of thoughtful reflection. This kind of attention does seem to be grounds for privileging such a discourse over discourses such as Foucault's, at least when thinking about animals as living biological organisms enmeshed in a network of power relations with humans.

In conclusion, then: Foucault's discussion of animality in *Madness and Civilization* tells us a lot not only about how animality was conceived in the past, but also about how Foucault understood it much more recently. I have argued that the reason/animality split, fundamental to Foucault's discourse, is problematic both on his own terms and in terms of the discourse of animals as living biological organisms. Indeed, inasmuch as Foucault's own discursive constructions of animality can be regarded as emerging from human–animal power relations, a fruitful future project might be to utilize Foucault's critical tools to uncover a genealogy of "animality," a task I have barely been able to pursue here.

CHAPTER SIX: DELEUZE AND GUATTARI

BECOMING-ANIMAL

Gilles Deleuze and Félix Guattari

MEMORIES OF A BERGSONIAN

We believe in the existence of very special becomings-animal traversing human beings and sweeping them away, affecting the animal no less than the human. . . . Structuralism clearly does not account for these becomings, since it is designed precisely to deny or at least denigrate their existence: a correspondence of relations does not add up to a becoming. When structuralism encounters becomings of this kind pervading a society, it sees them only as phenomena of degradation representing a deviation from the true order and pertaining to the adventures of diachrony. . . . It is always possible to try to explain these *blocks of becoming* by a correspondence between two relations, but to do so most certainly impoverishes the phenomenon under study. . . .

A becoming is not a correspondence between relations. But neither is it a resemblance, an imitation, or, at the limit, an identification. The whole structuralist critique of the series seems irrefutable. To become is not to progress or regress along a series. Above all, becoming does not occur in the imagination, even when the imagination reaches the highest cosmic or dynamic level, as in Jung or Bachelard. Becomings-animal are neither dreams nor phantasies. They are perfectly real. But which reality is at issue here? For if becoming animal does not consist in playing animal or imitating an animal, it is clear that the human being does not "really" become an animal any more than the animal "really" becomes something else. Becoming produces nothing other than itself. We fall into a false alternative if we say that you either imitate or you are. What is real is the becoming itself, the block of becoming, not the supposedly fixed terms through which that which becomes passes. Becoming can and should be qualified as becoming-animal even in the absence of a term that would be the animal become. The becoming-animal of the human being is real, even if the animal the human being becomes is not; and the becoming-other of the animal is real, even if that something other it becomes is not. This is the point to clarify: that a becoming lacks a subject distinct from itself; but also that it has no term, since its term in turn exists only as taken up in another becoming of which it is the subject, and which coexists, forms a block, with the first. This is the principle according to which there is a reality specific to becoming (the Bergsonian idea of a coexistence of very different "durations," superior or inferior to "ours," all of them in communication).

Finally, becoming is not an evolution, at least not an evolution by descent and filiation. Becoming produces nothing by filiation; all filiation is imaginary. Becoming is always of a different order than filiation. It concerns alliance. If evolution includes any veritable becomings, it is in the domain of *symbioses* that bring into play beings of totally different scales and kingdoms, with no possible filiation. There is a block of becoming that snaps up the wasp and the orchid, but from which no wasp-orchid can ever descend. There is a block of becoming that takes hold of the cat and baboon, the alliance between which is effected by a C virus. There is a block of becoming between young roots and certain microorganisms, the alliance between which is effected by the materials synthesized in the leaves (rhizosphere). If there is originality in neoevolutionism, it is attributable in part to phenomena of this kind in which evolution does not go from something less differentiated to something more differentiated, in which it ceases to be a hereditary filiative evolution, becoming communicative or contagious. Accordingly, the term we would prefer for this form of evolution between heterogeneous terms is "involution," on the condition that involution is in no way confused with regression. Becoming is involutionary, involution is creative. To regress is to move in the direction of something less differentiated. But to involve is to form a block that runs its own line "between" the terms in play and beneath assignable relations.

Neoevolutionism seems important for two reasons: the animal is defined not by characteristics (specific, generic, etc.) but by populations that vary from milieu to milieu or within the same milieu; movement occurs not only, or not primarily, by filiative productions but also by transversal communications between heterogeneous populations. Becoming is a rhizome, not a classificatory or genealogical tree. Becoming is certainly not imitating, or identifying with something; neither is it regressing-progressing; neither is it corresponding, establishing corresponding relations; neither is it producing, producing a filiation or producing through filiation. Becoming is a verb with a consistency all its own; it does not reduce to, or lead back to, "appearing," "being," "equaling," or "producing."

MEMORIES OF A SORCERER, I

A becoming-animal always involves a pack, a band, a population, a peopling, in short, a multiplicity. We sorcerers have always known that. It may very well be that other agencies, moreover very different from one another, have a different appraisal of the animal. One may retain or extract from the animal certain characteristics: species and genera, forms and functions, etc. Society and the State need animal characteristics to use for classifying people; natural history and science need characteristics in order to classify the animals themselves. Serialism and structuralism either graduate characteristics according to their resemblances, or order them according to their differences. Animal characteristics can be mythic or scientific. But we are not interested in characteristics; what interests us are modes of expansion, propagation, occupation, contagion, peopling. I am legion. The Wolf-Man fascinated by several wolves watching him. What would a lone wolf be? Or a whale, a louse, a rat, a fly? Beelzebub is the Devil, but the Devil as lord of the flies. The wolf is not fundamentally a characteristic or a certain number of characteristics; it is a wolfing. The louse is a lousing, and so on. What is a cry independent of the population it appeals to or takes as its witness? Virginia Woolf experiences herself not as a monkey or a fish but as a troop of monkeys, a school of fish, according to her variable relations of becoming with the people she approaches. We do not wish to say that certain animals live in packs. We want nothing to do with ridiculous evolutionary classifications à la Lorenz, according to which there are inferior packs and superior societies. What we are saying is that every animal is fundamentally a band, a pack. That it has pack modes, rather than characteristics, even if further distinctions within these modes are called for. It is at this point that the human being encounters the animal. We do not become animal without a fascination for the pack, for multiplicity. A fascination for the outside? Or is the multiplicity that fascinates us already related to a multiplicity dwelling within us? In one of his masterpieces, H. P. Lovecraft recounts the story of Randolph Carter, who feels his "self" reel and who experiences a fear worse than that of annihilation: "Carters of forms both human and non-human, vertebrate and invertebrate, conscious and mindless, animal and vegetable. And more, there were Carters having nothing in common with earthly life, but moving outrageously amidst backgrounds of other planets and systems and galaxies and cosmic continua. . . . Merging with nothingness is peaceful oblivion; but to be aware of existence and yet to know that one is no longer a definite being distinguished from other beings," nor from all of the becomings running through us, "that is the nameless summit of agony and dread."[1] Hofmannsthal, or rather Lord Chandos, becomes fascinated with a "people" of dying rats, and it is in him, through him, in the interstices of his disrupted self that the "soul of the animal bares its teeth at monstrous fate":[2] not pity, but *unnatural participation.* Then a strange imperative wells up in him: either stop writing, or write like a rat . . . If the writer is a sorcerer, it is because writing is a becoming, writing is traversed by strange becomings that are not becomings-writer, but becomings-rat, becomings-insect, becomings-wolf, etc. We will have to explain why. Many suicides by writers are explained by these unnatural participations, these unnatural nuptials. Writers are sorcerers because they experience the animal as the only population before which they are responsible in principle. The German preromantic Karl Philipp Moritz feels responsible not for the calves that die but before the calves that die and give him the incredible feeling of an unknown Nature – *affect.*[3] For the affect is not a personal feeling, nor is it a characteristic; it is the effectuation of a power of the pack that throws the self into upheaval and makes it reel. Who has not known the violence of these animal sequences, which uproot one from humanity, if only for an instant, making one scrape at one's bread like a rodent or giving one the yellow eyes of a feline? A fearsome involution calling us toward unheard-of becomings. These are not regressions, although fragments of regression, sequences of regression may enter in.

We must distinguish three kinds of animals. First, individuated animals, family pets, sentimental, Oedipal animals each with its own petty history, "my" cat, "my" dog. These animals invite us to regress, draw us into a narcissistic contemplation, and they are the only kind of animal psychoanalysis understands, the better to discover a daddy, a mommy, a little brother behind them (when psychoanalysis talks about animals, animals learn to laugh): *anyone who likes cats or dogs is a fool.* And then there is a second kind: animals with characteristics or attributes; genus, classification, or State animals; animals as they are treated in the great divine myths, in such a way as to extract from them series or structures, archetypes or models (Jung is in any event profounder than Freud). Finally, there are more demonic animals, pack or affect animals that form a multiplicity, a becoming, a population, a tale ... Or once again, cannot any animal be treated in all three ways? There is always the possibility that a given animal, a louse, a cheetah or an elephant, will be treated as a pet, my little beast. And at the other extreme, it is also possible for any animal to be treated in the mode of the pack or swarm; that is our way, fellow sorcerers. Even the cat, even the dog. ...

But what exactly does that mean, the animal as band or pack? Does a band not imply a filiation, bringing us back to the reproduction of given characteristics? How can we conceive of a peopling, a propagation, a becoming that is without filiation or hereditary production? A multiplicity without the unity of an ancestor? It is quite simple; everybody knows it, but it is discussed only in secret. We oppose epidemic to filiation, contagion to heredity, peopling by contagion to sexual reproduction, sexual production. Bands, human or animal, proliferate by contagion, epidemics, battlefields, and catastrophes. Like hybrids, which are in themselves sterile, born of a sexual union that will not reproduce itself, but which begins over again every time, gaining that much more ground. Unnatural participations or nuptials are the true Nature spanning the kingdoms of nature. Propagation by epidemic, by contagion, has nothing to do with filiation by heredity, even if the two themes intermingle and require each other. The vampire does not filiate, it infects. The difference is that contagion, epidemic, involves terms that are entirely heterogeneous: for example, a human being, an animal, and a bacterium, a virus, a molecule, a microorganism. Or in the case of the truffle, a tree, a fly, and a pig. These combinations are neither genetic nor structural; they are interkingdoms, unnatural participations. That is the only way Nature operates – against itself. This is a far cry from filiative production or hereditary reproduction, in which the only differences retained are a simple duality between sexes within the same species, and small modifications across generations. For us, on the other hand, there are as many sexes as there are terms in symbiosis, as many differences as elements contributing to a process of contagion. We know that many beings pass between a man and a woman; they come from different worlds, are borne on the wind, form rhizomes around roots; they cannot be understood in terms of production, only in terms of becoming. The Universe does not function by filiation. All we are saying is that animals are packs, and that packs form, develop, and are transformed by contagion.

These multiplicities with heterogeneous terms, cofunctioning by contagion, enter certain *assemblages*; it is there that human beings effect their becomings-animal. But we should not confuse these dark assemblages, which stir what is deepest within us, with organizations such as the institution of the family and the State apparatus. We could cite hunting societies, war societies, secret societies, crime societies, etc. Becomings-animal are proper to them. We will not expect to find filiative regimes of the family type or modes of classification and attribution of the State or pre-State type or even serial organizations of the religious type. Despite appearances and possible confusions, this is not the site of origin or point of application for myths. These are tales, or narratives and statements of becoming. It is therefore absurd to establish a hierarchy even of animal collectivities from the standpoint of a whimsical evolutionism according to which packs are lower on the scale and are superseded by State or familial societies. On the contrary, there is a difference in nature. The origin of packs is entirely different from that of families and States; they continually work them from within and trouble them from without, with other forms of content, other forms of expression. The pack is simultaneously an animal reality, and the reality of the becoming-animal of the human being; contagion is simultaneously an animal peopling, and the propagation of the animal peopling of the human being. The hunting machine, the war machine, the crime machine entail all kinds of becomings-animal that are not articulated in myth, *still less in totemism.* Dumézil showed that becomings of this kind pertain essentially to the man of war, but only insofar as he is external to families and States, insofar as he upsets filiations and classifications. The war machine is always exterior to the State, even when the State uses it, appropriates it. The man of war has an entire becoming that implies multiplicity, celerity, ubiquity, metamorphosis and treason, the power of affect. Wolf-men, bear-men, wildcat-men, men of every animality, secret brotherhoods, animate the battlefields. But so do the animal packs used by men in battle, or which trail the battles and take advantage of them. And together they spread contagion.[4] There is a complex aggregate: the becoming-animal of men, packs of animals, elephants and rats, winds and tempests, bacteria sowing contagion. A single *Furor.* War contained zoological sequences before it became bacteriological. It is in war, famine, and epidemic that werewolves and vampires proliferate. Any animal can be swept up in these packs and the corresponding becomings; cats have been seen on the battlefield, and even in armies. That is why the distinction we must make is less between kinds of animals than between the different states according to which they are integrated into family institutions, State apparatuses, war machines, etc. (and what is the relation of the writing machine and the musical machine to becomings-animal?). . . .

MEMORIES OF A SPINOZIST, II

There is another aspect to Spinoza. To every relation of movement and rest, speed and slowness grouping together an infinity of parts, there corresponds a degree of power. To the relations composing, decomposing, or modifying an individual there correspond intensities that affect it, augmenting or diminishing its power to act; these intensities come from external parts or from the individual's own parts. Affects are becomings. Spinoza asks: What can a body do? We call the *latitude* of a body the affects of which it is capable at a given degree of power, or rather within the limits of that degree. *Latitude is made up of intensive parts falling under a capacity, and longitude of extensive parts falling under a relation.* In the same way that we avoided defining a body by its organs and functions, we will avoid defining it by Species or Genus characteristics; instead we will seek to count its affects. This kind of study is called ethology, and this is the sense in which Spinoza wrote a true Ethics. A racehorse is more different from a workhorse than a workhorse is from an ox. Von Uexküll, in defining animal worlds, looks for the active and passive affects of which the animal is capable in the individuated assemblage of which it is a part. For example, the tick, attracted by the light, hoists itself up to the tip of a branch; it is sensitive to the smell of mammals, and lets itself fall when one passes beneath the branch; it digs into its skin, at the least hairy place it can find. Just three affects; the rest of the time the tick sleeps, sometimes for years on end, indifferent to all that goes on in the immense forest. Its degree of power is indeed bounded by two limits: the optimal limit of the feast after which it dies, and the pessimal limit of the fast as it waits. It will be said that the tick's three affects assume generic and specific characteristics, organs and functions, legs and snout. This is true from the stand-point of physiology, but not from the standpoint of Ethics. Quite the contrary, in Ethics the organic characteristics derive from longitude and its relations, from latitude and its degrees. We know nothing about a body until we know what it can do, in other words, what its affects are, how they can or cannot enter into composition with other affects, with the affects of another body, either to destroy that body or to be destroyed by it, either to exchange actions and passions with it or to join with it in composing a more powerful body.

Once again, we turn to children. Note how they talk about animals, and are moved by them. They make a list of affects. Little Hans's horse is not represen-tative but affective. It is not a member of a species but an element or individual in a machinic assemblage: draft horse-omnibus-street. It is defined by a list of active and passive affects in the context of the individuated assemblage it is part of: having eyes blocked by blinders, having a bit and a bridle, being proud, having a big peepee-maker, pulling heavy loads, being whipped, falling, making a din with its legs, biting, etc. These affects circulate and are transformed within the assemblage: what a horse "can do." They indeed have an optimal limit at the summit of horsepower, but also a pessimal threshold: a horse falls down in the street! It can't get back on its feet with that heavy load on its back, and the excessive whipping; a horse is going to die! – this was an ordinary sight in those days (Nietzsche, Dostoyevsky, Nijinsky lamented it). So just what is the becoming-horse of Little Hans? Hans is also taken up in an assemblage: his mother's bed, the paternal element, the house, the cafe across the street, the nearby warehouse, the street, the right to go out onto the street, the winning of this right, the pride of winning it, but also the dangers of winning it, the fall, shame ... These are not phantasies or subjective reveries: it is not a question of imitating a horse, "playing" horse, identifying with one, or even experiencing feelings of pity or sympathy. Neither does it have to do with an objective analogy between assemblages. The question is whether Little Hans can endow his own elements with the relations of movement and rest, the affects, that would make it become horse, forms and subjects aside. Is there an as yet unknown assemblage that would be neither Hans's, nor the horse's, but that of the becoming-horse of Hans? An assemblage, for example, in which the horse would bare its teeth and Hans might show something else, his feet, his legs, his peepee-maker, whatever? And in what way would that ameliorate Hans's problem, to what extent would it open a way out that had been previously blocked? When Hofmannsthal contemplates the death throes of a rat, it is in him that the animal "bares his teeth at monstrous fate." *This is not a feeling of pity,* as he makes clear; still less an identification. It is a composition of speeds and affects involving entirely different individuals, a symbiosis; it makes the rat become a thought, a feverish thought in the man, at the same time as the man becomes a rat gnashing its teeth in its death throes. The rat and the man are in no way the same thing, but Being expresses them both in a single meaning in a language that is no longer that of words, in a matter that is no longer that of forms, in an affectability that is no longer that of subjects. *Unnatural participation.* But the plane of composition, the plane of Nature, is precisely for participations of this kind, and continually makes and unmakes their assemblages, employing every artifice.

We wish to make a simple point about psychoanalysis: from the beginning, it has often encountered the question of the becomings-animal of the human being: in children, who continually undergo becomings of this kind; in fetishism and in particular masochism, which continually confront this problem. The least that can be said is that the psychoanalysts, even Jung, did not understand, or did not want to understand. They killed becoming-animal, in the adult as in the child. They saw nothing. They see the animal as a representative of drives, or a representation of the parents. They do not see the reality of a becoming-animal, that it is affect in itself, the drive in person, and represents nothing. There exist no other drives than the assemblages themselves. There are two classic texts in which Freud sees nothing but the father in the becoming-horse of Hans, and Ferenczi sees the same in the becoming-cock of Arpad. The horse's blinders are the father's eyeglasses, the black around its mouth is his mustache, its kicks are the parents' "lovemaking." Not one word about Hans's relation to the street, on how the street was forbidden to him, on what it is for a child to see the spectacle "a horse is proud, a blinded horse pulls, a horse falls, a horse is whipped ..." Psychoanalysis has no feeling for unnatural participations, nor for the assemblages a child can mount in order to solve a problem from which all exits are barred him: a *plan(e)*, not a phantasy. ... But to break the becoming-animal all that is needed is to extract a segment from it, to abstract one of its moments, to fail to take into account its internal speeds and slownesses, to arrest the circulation of affects. Then nothing remains but imaginary resemblances between terms, or symbolic analogies between relations. This segment refers to the father, that relation of movement and rest refers to the primal scene, etc. It must be recognized that psychoanalysis alone is not enough to bring about this breakage. It only brings out a danger inherent in becoming. ...

MEMORIES AND BECOMINGS, POINTS AND BLOCKS

What constitutes arborescence is the submission of the line to the point. ... A line of becoming is not defined by points that it connects, or by points that compose it; on the contrary, it passes *between* points, it comes up through the middle, it runs perpendicular to the points first perceived, transversally to the localizable relation to distant or contiguous points. A point is always a point of origin. But a line of becoming has neither beginning nor end, departure nor arrival, origin nor destination; to speak of the absence of an origin, to make the absence of an origin the origin, is a bad play on words. A line of becoming has only a middle. The middle is not an average; it is fast motion, it is the absolute speed of movement. A becoming is always in the middle; one can only get it by the middle. A becoming is neither one nor two, nor the relation of the two; it is the in-between, the border or line of flight or descent running perpendicular to both. If becoming is a block (a line-block), it is because it constitutes a zone of proximity and indiscernibility, a no-man's-land, a nonlocalizable relation sweeping up the two distant or contiguous points, carrying one into the proximity of the other – and the border-proximity is indifferent to both contiguity and to distance. The line or block of becoming that unites the wasp and the orchid produces a shared deterritorialization: of the wasp, in that it becomes a liberated piece of the orchid's reproductive system, but also of the orchid, in that it becomes the object of an orgasm in the wasp, also liberated from its own reproduction. A coexistence of two asymmetrical movements. . . .

BECOMING MUSIC

We find the same zigzag movement in the becomings-animal of music: Marcel Moré shows that the music of Mozart is permeated by a becoming-horse, or becomings-bird. But no musician amuses himself by "playing" horse or bird. If the sound block has a becoming-animal as its content, then the animal simultaneously becomes, in sonority, something else, something absolute, night, death, joy – certainly not a generality or a simplification, but a haecceity, this death, that night. Music takes as its content a becoming-animal; but in that becoming-animal the horse, for example, takes as its expression soft kettledrum beats, winged like hooves from heaven or hell; and the birds find expression in *gruppeti*, appoggiaturas, staccato notes that transform them into so many souls.[5] It is the accents that form the diagonal in Mozart, the accents above all. If one does not follow the accents, if one does not observe them, one falls back into a relatively impoverished punctual system. The human musician is deterritorialized in the bird, but it is a bird that is itself deterritorialized, "transfigured," a celestial bird that has just as much of a becoming as that which becomes with it. Captain Ahab is engaged in an irresistible becoming-whale with Moby-Dick; but the animal, Moby-Dick, must simultaneously become an unbearable pure whiteness, a shimmering pure white wall, a silver thread that stretches out and supples up "like" a girl, or twists like a whip, or stands like a rampart. Can it be that literature sometimes catches up with painting, and even music? And that painting catches up with music? (Moré cites Klee's birds but on the other hand fails to understand what Messiaen says about bird song.) No art is imitative, no art can be imitative or figurative. Suppose a painter "represents" a bird; this is in fact a becoming-bird that can occur only to the extent that the bird itself is in the process of becoming something else, a pure line and pure color. Thus imitation self-destructs, since the imitator unknowingly enters into a becoming that conjugates with the unknowing becoming of that which he or she imitates. One imitates only if one fails, when one fails. The painter and musician do not imitate the animal, they become-animal at the same time as the animal becomes what they willed, at the deepest level of their concord with Nature.[6] Becoming is always double, that which one becomes becomes no less than the one that becomes – block is formed, essentially mobile, never in equilibrium. ...

Becoming is never imitating. ... One does not imitate; one constitutes a block of becoming. Imitation enters in only as an adjustment of the block, like a finishing touch, a wink, a signature. ... As always, the same must be said of the animals themselves. For not only do animals have colors and sounds, but they do not wait for the painter or musician to use those colors and sounds in a painting or music, in other words, to enter into determinate becomings-color and becomings-sounds by means of components of deterritorialization. ...

Messiaen presents multiple chromatic durations in coalescence, "alternating between the longest and the shortest, in order to suggest the idea of the relations between the infinitely long durations of the stars and mountains and the infinitely short ones of the insects and the atoms: a cosmic, elementary power that ... derives above all from the labor of rhythm."[7] The same thing that leads a musician to discover the birds also leads him to discover the elementary and the cosmic. Both combine to form a block, a universe fiber, a diagonal or complex space. Music dispatches molecular flows. Of course, as Messiaen says, music is not the privilege of human beings: the universe, the cosmos, is made of refrains; the question in music is that of a power of deterritorialization permeating nature, animals, the elements, and deserts as much as human beings. The question is more what is not musical in human beings, and what already is musical in nature. Moreover, what Messiaen discovered in music is the same thing the ethologists discovered in animals: human beings are hardly at an advantage, except in the means of overcoding, of making punctual systems. That is even the opposite of having an advantage; through becomings-woman, -child, -animal, or -molecular, nature opposes its power, and the power of music, to the machines of human beings, the roar of factories and bombers. And it is necessary to reach that point, it is necessary for the nonmusical sound of the human being to form a block with the becoming-music of sound, for them to confront and embrace each other like two wrestlers who can no longer break free from each other's grasp, and slide down a sloping line: "Let the choirs represent the survivors ... Faintly one hears the sound of cicadas. Then the notes of a lark, followed by the mockingbird. Someone laughs ... A woman sobs ... From a male a great shout: WE ARE LOST! A woman's voice: WE ARE SAVED! Staccato cries: Lost! Saved! Lost! Saved!"[8]

*   *   *

Two years after the "Letter to the Father," Kafka admitted that he had "plunged into discontent" and did so "with all the means that [his] time and tradition gave [him]."[9] It turns out that Oedipus is one of these means – fairly modern, widespread since Freud's time, allowing many comic effects. All it takes is to exaggerate it: "Strange how make-believe, if engaged in systematically enough, can change into reality." But Kafka does not refuse the exterior influence of the father only in order to invoke an interior genesis or an internal structure that would still be Oedipal. "I cannot grant that the first beginnings of my unhappiness were inwardly necessitated; they may have indeed had a necessity, but not an inward one – they *swarmed down on me like flies* and could have been as easily driven off." In that lies the essential point: beyond the exterior or the interior, an agitation, a molecular dance, an entire limit-connection with an Outside that is going to disguise itself as an exaggerated Oedipus that is beyond all limits. ...

Thus, the too well-formed family triangle is really only a conduit for investments of an entirely different sort that the child endlessly discovers underneath his father, inside his mother, in himself. The judges, commissioners, bureaucrats, and so on, are not substitutes for the father; rather, it is the father who is a condensation of all these forces that he submits to and that he tries to get his son to submit to. The family opens onto doors, on which from the beginning there knock "'*diabolical powers' that rejoice from the fact that they will arrive soon.*"[10] What Kafka immediately anguishes or rejoices in is not the father or the superego or some sort of signifier but the American technocratic apparatus or the Russian bureaucracy or the machinery of Fascism. And to the degree that the familial triangle comes undone either in a single term or in its totality to the profit of those *powers* that are really its driving force, we could say that the other triangles that surge up behind it have something malleable, diffuse, a perpetual transformation from one triangle to another, either because one of the terms or points begins to proliferate, or because the sides of the triangle don't stop deforming. ... All children can understand this; they all have a political and geographic map with diffuse and moving contours if only because of their nursemaids, servants, employees of the father, and so on. ...

Yet, insofar as the comic expansion of Oedipus allows one to see these other oppressor triangles through the lens of the microscope, there appears at the same time the possiblity of an escape, a line of escape. To the inhumaness of the "diabolical powers," there is the answer of a becoming-animal: to become a beetle, to become a dog, to become an ape, "head over heels and away," rather than lowering one's head and remaining a bureaucrat, inspector, judge, or judged. All children build or feel these sorts of escapes, these acts of becoming-animal. And the animal as an act of becoming has nothing to do with a substitute for the father, or with an archetype. Because the father, as a Jew who leaves the country to settle in the city, is undoubtedly caught in a process of real deterritorialization; but he never stops reterritorializing, in his family, in his business, in the system of his submissions and of his authorities. As for the archetypes, these are processes of spiritual reterritorialization.[11] The acts of becoming-animal are the exact opposite of this; these are absolute deterritorializations, at least in principle, that penetrate deep into the desert world invested in by Kafka. ... To become animal is to participate in movement, to stake out the path of escape in all its positivity, to cross a threshold, to reach a continuum of intensities that are valuable only in themselves, to find a world of pure intensities where all forms come undone, as do all the significations, signifiers, and signifieds, to the benefit of an unformed matter of deterritorialized flux, of nonsignifying signs. Kafka's animals never refer to a mythology or to archetypes but correspond solely to new levels, zones of liberated intensities where contents free themselves from their forms as well as from their expressions, from the signifier that formalized them. There is no longer anything but movements, vibrations, thresholds in a deserted matter: animals, mice, dogs, apes, cockroaches are distinguished only by this or that threshold, this or that vibration, by the particular underground tunnel in the rhizome or the burrow. Because these tunnels are underground intensities. In the becoming-mouse, it is a whistling that pulls the music and the meaning from the words. In the becoming-ape, it is a coughing that "sound[s] dangerous but mean[s] nothing" (to become a tuberculoid ape). In the becoming-insect, it is a mournful whining that carries along the voice and blurs the resonance of words. Gregor becomes a cockroach not to flee his father but rather to find an escape where his father didn't know to find one, in order to flee the director, the business, and the bureaucrats, to reach that region where the voice no longer does anything but hum: " 'Did you hear him? It was an animal's voice,' said the chief clerk."

It is true that Kafka's animal texts are much more complex than we seem to be saying. Or, quite the contrary, much simpler. For example, in the "Report to an Academy," it is no longer a question of a becoming-animal of man, but a becoming-man of the ape; this becoming is presented as a simple imitation and if it is a question of finding an escape (an escape, and not "liberty"), this escape doesn't consist in fleeing – quite the contrary. Flight is challenged when it is useless movement in space, a movement of false liberty; but in contrast, flight is affirmed when it is a stationary flight, a flight of intensity ("No, freedom was not what I wanted. Only a way out; right, or left, or in any direction; I made no other demand"). On the other hand, the imitation is only superficial, since it no longer concerns the reproduction of figures but the production of a continuum of intensities in a nonparallel and asymmetrical evolution where the man no less becomes an ape than the ape becomes a man. The act of becoming is a capturing, a possession, a plus-value, but never a reproduction or an imitation. "[T]here was no attraction for me in imitating human beings; I imitated them because I needed a way out, and for no other reason." In fact, the animal captured by the man finds itself deterritorialized by human force, as the whole of the beginning of "A Report" tells us. But, in turn, the deterritori- alized animal force precipitates and intensifies the deterritorialization of the deterritorializing human force (if we can express it that way). "My ape nature fled out of me, head over heels and away, so that my first teacher was almost himself turned into an ape by it, had soon to give up teaching and was taken away to a mental hospital."[12] Thus, there is constituted a conjunction of the flux of deterritorialization that overflows imitation which is always territorial. It is in this way also that the orchid seems to reproduce an image of the bee but in a deeper way deterritorializes into it, at the same time that the bee in turn deterritorializes by joining with the orchid: the capture of a fragment of the code, and not the reproduction of an image. (In "The Investigations of a Dog," every idea of resemblance is even more energetically eliminated. Kafka attacks "the suspect temptations of resemblance that imagination proposes"; through the dog's solitude, it is the greatest difference, the schizo difference that he tries to grasp.)

Thus, we have two effects of the development or comic enlargement of Oedipus: the discovery *a contrario* of other triangles that operate beneath and, indeed, in the familial triangle, and the *a posteriori* outlining of paths of escape of the orphaned becoming-animal. No text seems to better show the connection of these two aspects than "The Metamorphosis." The bureaucratic triangle forms itself progressively. First, the director who comes to menace and to demand; then the father who has resumed his work at the bank and who sleeps in his uniform, demonstrating the external power that he is still in submission to as if even at home he was "only at the beck and call of his superior" and finally, in a single moment, the intrusion of the three bureaucrat lodgers who penetrate the family itself, taking up its roles, sitting "where formerly Gregor and his father and mother had taken their meals." And as a correlate of all of this, the whole becoming-animal of Gregor, his becoming beetle, junebug, dungbeetle, cockroach, which traces an intense line of flight in relation to the familial triangle but especially in relation to the bureaucratic and commercial triangle.

But at the very moment when we seemed to grasp the connections of a Going Beyond and a Falling Short of Oedipus, why are we farther than ever from a way out; why do we remain at an impasse? It is because there is always the danger of the return of Oedipal force. The amplifying perverse usage of Oedipus is not sufficient to guard against every new closure, every new reconstitution of the familial triangle that takes over other triangles such as the animal lines. In this sense, "The Metamorphosis" is the exemplary story of a re-Oedipalization. We would say that the process of Gregor's deterritorialization through his becoming-animal finds itself blocked for a moment. Is it the fault of Gregor who doesn't dare go all the way? To please him, his sister wanted to empty out the whole room. But Gregor refused to let go of the portrait of the lady in fur. He sticks to the portrait, as if to a last territorialized image. In fact, that's what the sister cannot tolerate. She accepted Gregor; like him, she wanted the schizo incest, an incest of strong connections, incest with the sister in opposition to Oedipal incest, incest that gives evidence of a nonhuman sexuality as in the becoming-animal. But, jealous of the portrait, she begins to hate Gregor and condemns him. From that point on, Gregor's deterritorialization through the becoming-animal fails; he re-Oedipalizes himself through the apple that is thrown at him and has nothing to do but die, the apple buried in his back. Likewise, the deterritorialization of the family through more complex and diabolical triangles has no room to develop; *the father chases away the three bureaucrat lodgers*, a return to the paternalistic principle of the Oedipal triangle, the family happily closes in on itself. And yet, it is not certain that Gregor was at fault. Isn't it rather that the acts of becoming-animal cannot follow their principle all the way through – that they maintain a certain ambiguity that leads to their insufficiency and condemns them to defeat? Aren't the animals still too formed, too significative, too territorialized? Doesn't the whole of the becoming-animal oscillate between a schizo escape and an Oedipal impasse? The dog, Oedipal animal par excellence, is often referred to by Kafka in his *Diaries* and his letters as a schizo beast, like the musical dogs of "The Investigations," or as the diabolical dog of "Temptation in the Village." In fact, Kafka's principal animal tales were written just before *The Trial* or at the same time as it, like a sort of counterpoint to the novel which liberates itself from all animal concern to the benefit of a much higher concern. ...

We are no longer in the situation of an ordinary, rich language where the word dog, for example, would directly designate an animal and would apply metaphorically to other things (so that one could say "like a dog").[13] *Diaries,* 1921: "Metaphors are one of the things that makes me despair of literature." Kafka deliberately kills all metaphor, all symbolism, all signification, no less than all designation. Metamorphosis is the contrary of metaphor. There is no longer any proper sense or figurative sense, but only a distribution of states that is part of the range of the word. The thing and other things are no longer anything but intensities overrun by deterritorialized sound or words that are following their line of escape. It is no longer a question of a resemblance between the comportment of an animal and that of a man; it is even less a question of a simple wordplay. There is no longer man or animal, since each deterritorializes the other, in a conjunction of flux, in a continuum of reversible intensities. Instead, it is now a question of a becoming that includes the maximum of difference as a difference of intensity, the crossing of a barrier, a rising or a falling, a bending or an erecting, an accent on the word. The animal does not speak "like" a man but pulls from the language tonalities lacking in signification; the words themselves are not "like" the animals but in their own way climb about, bark and roam around, being properly linguistic dogs, insects, or mice.[14] To make the sequences vibrate, to open the word onto unexpected internal intensities – in short, an asignifying *intensive utilization* of language. Furthermore, there is no longer a subject of the enunciation, nor a subject of the statement. It is no longer the subject of the statement who is a dog, with the subject of the enunciation remaining "like" a man; it is no longer the subject of enunciation who is "like" a beetle, the subject of the statement remaining a man. Rather, there is a circuit of states that forms a mutual becoming, in the heart of a necessarily multiple or collective assemblage. ...

Another component of Kafka's writing machine is the stories. They are essentially animalistic even though there aren't animals in all the stories. According to Kafka, the animal is the object *par excellence* of the story: to try to find a way out, to trace a line of escape. ... What Kafka does in his room is to become animal and this is the essential object of the stories. The first sort of creation is the metamorphosis. A wife's eyes shouldn't see that above all else, nor should the eyes of a father or mother. We would say that for Kafka, the animal essence is the way out, the line of escape, even if it takes place in place, or in a cage. *A line of escape, and not freedom. A vital escape and not an attack.* ... Let us remind ourselves, however, of several elements of the animalistic stories: (1) there is no possibility of distinguishing those cases where the animal is treated as an animal and those where it is part of a metamorphosis; everything in the animal is a metamorphosis, and the metamorphosis is part of a single circuit of the becoming-human of the animal and the becoming-animal of the human; (2) the metamorphosis is a sort of conjunction of two deterritorializations, that which the human imposes on the animal by forcing it to flee or to serve the human, but also that which the animal proposes to the human by indicating ways-out or means of escape that the human would never have thought of by himself (schizo-escape); each of these two deterritorializations is immanent to the other and makes it cross a threshold; (3) thus, what matters is not at all the relative slowness of the becoming-animal; because no matter how slow it is, and even the more slow it is, it constitutes no less an *absolute deterritorialization* of the man in opposition to the merely relative deterritorializations that the man causes to himself by shifting, by traveling; the becoming-animal is an immobile voyage that stays in one place; it only lives and is comprehensible as an intensity (to transgress the thresholds of intensity).[15]

There is nothing metaphoric about the becoming-animal. No symbolism, no allegory. Nor is it the result of a flaw or a malediction, the effect of some sort of guilt. As Melville says of the becoming-whale of Captain Ahab, it is a "panorama," not a "Gospel." It is a map of intensities. It is an ensemble of states, each distinct from the other, grafted onto the man insofar as he is searching for a way out. It is a creative line of escape that says nothing other than what it is. In contrast to the letters, the becoming-animal lets nothing remain of the duality of a subject of enunciation and a subject of the statement; rather, it constitutes a single process, a unique method that replaces subjectivity. However, if the becoming-animal is the object par excellence of the stories, we must in turn examine the insufficiencies of the stories. We might say that they are caught up in a choice that from both sides condemns them to defeat from the point of view of Kafka's project, no matter their literary splendor. On the one hand, the story will be perfect and finished but then will close in on itself. Or it will open but will open to something that could only be developed in a novel that would be itself interminable. In the first case, the story confronts a danger that is different from that of the letters, although somewhat analogous. The letters had to fear a sort of reflux directed against the subject of enunciation; the stories, on the other hand, bump up against a no-way out of the animal way out, an impasse of the line of escape (it is for this reason that they end when they erect this impasse). To be sure, the becoming-animal has nothing to do with a merely superficial sort of meaning, like that in the letters: however slow it may be, the deterritorial-ization of the becoming-animal is absolute; the line of escape is well programmed, the way out is well established. But this is only one side of the poles. In the same way that the egg, in its potentiality, contains two poles, the becoming-animal is a potentiality that is gifted with two equally real poles – a properly animal pole and a properly familial one. We saw how the animal oscil-lated between its own becoming-inhuman and an all-too-human familiarization. . . . To take another example: we saw how Gregor's metamorphosis was the story of a re-Oedipalization that leads him into death, that turns his becoming-animal into a becoming-dead. Not only the dog, but all the animals, oscillate between a schizo Eros and an Oedipal Thanatos. It is in this perspective alone that metaphor, with its whole anthropocentric entourage, threatens to come back on the scene. In short, the animalist stories are a component of the machine of expression. . . . Grasping the real, writing themselves within the real itself, they are caught up in the tension between two opposing poles or realities. The becoming-animal effectively shows a way out, traces a line of escape, but is incapable of following it or making it its own. . . .

ANIMAL BECOMINGS

James Urpeth

[A]nyone who likes cats or dogs is a fool (Deleuze and Guattari)

The theme of "becoming-animal" in the coauthored texts of Gilles Deleuze and
Félix Guattari is liable, at first glance, to be misinterpreted given the associations
it will evoke for many people. Perhaps Deleuze and Guattari's clear (but not
uncritical) endorsement in *Kafka*[1] and *A Thousand Plateaus*[2] of the process of
"becoming-animal" seeks to promote a naïve "primitivism" in which the reader
is invited to cast off all inhibition and celebrate the recovery of an unfettered
"state of nature." A contemporary "return to nature" doctrine would seem to be
advocated. Alternatively, the concept of "becoming-animal" might be considered,
especially given its application to a wide variety of works of art, to be indicative
of a reductive and functionalist approach, a "biologism" of some kind. Indeed,
the overtly "materialist" tenor – albeit of a very unfamiliar kind for many Anglo-
American readers – and "anti-humanist" tendency of the texts discussed here will
doubtless be considered by many readers to be their most challenging feature.

This essay aims to correct such misconceptions by indicating something of
the nature of the philosophical project within which the notion of "becoming-
animal" arises. In the extracts reprinted in this volume, Deleuze and Guattari
deploy the notion of "becoming-animal" as part of a critique of some of the basic
assumptions and values prevalent, not only in the philosophical tradition, but
also in a wide range of other disciplines, most notably, psychoanalysis, literary
theory, and biology. An overview of the key issues involved in these various
encounters will be attempted here. Finally, the very radical and distinctive
"political" implications of the theme of "becoming-animal" will also be briefly
considered. You might say that the theme of "becoming-animal" in Deleuze and
Guattari "puts the cat among the pigeons" in any number of fields.

Perhaps the key philosophical project discernible in the following texts is the
overcoming of the man/nature opposition – indeed dualisms in general –
through the elaboration of a *non-reductive* materialist ontology of difference and
multiplicity in which a "Spinozist" conception of power and affectivity are
particularly prominent. Through the development of such an ontology, Deleuze
and Guattari unfold a radically non-anthropomorphic (and thereby non-
theological) conception of "nature" within which the "human" is inscribed

without remainder.[3] This requires the expunging of all "moralism" (the source of negation) regarding individual or species identity, and the rejection of any pre-given transcendent form of nature or teleological trajectory. That is to say, Deleuze and Guattari are through notions such as "becoming-animal" seeking to think and affirm a radical order of *immanence*, a primordial ontological domain in which free-form creative synthesis operates unimpeded by the proprieties and boundaries of preset identities.

The extraordinary – and challenging – philosophical perspective at work in the texts included here can perhaps be best understood through an examination of Deleuze and Guattari's claim that "becoming-animal" is a *real* process. In their own words: "we believe in the existence of very special becomings-animal traversing human beings and sweeping them away, affecting the animal no less than the human" (*TP*, 237). Deleuze and Guattari insist that "becoming-animal" is not merely an act of imitation ("becoming is never imitating" [*TP*, 305]). To conceive of becoming in terms of imitation is to regard as primary and unassailable both human identity and that of the other animal involved in the process in question. "Becoming-animal" is not, therefore, a mere aping of animal behavior, perhaps for comic effect or due to a psychosexual pathology ("regression"), etc. While such processes doubtless take place, as we will see, Deleuze and Guattari do not think that they can be accurately described in terms of "becoming" or regarded as anything other than ontologically trivial. Such mimetic acts presuppose derivative phenomena such as species-identity, self-identity, literal language, the *telos* of heterosexual adulthood, etc. All such phenomena are, according to Deleuze and Guattari, less real than "becoming-animal," whose ontological primordiality, as an instance of "becoming-x," they seek to affirm. It will not be surprising that such a radical ontological perspective is at one with a critique of the claims to primary status of identity, signification, representation, the primacy of concept over affect, determined desire, etc.

Hence, a productive guiding question when reading Deleuze and Guattari on "becoming animal" can be formulated thus: What is presupposed *philosophically*, particularly with reference to ontology and logic, by the assertion that "becoming-animal" is a reality? A corollary question follows from this: What is implied, in terms of value, power and desire, by Deleuze and Guattari's overt advocacy of "becoming-animal"? Only once these ontological, logical, genealogical, and political issues are clarified can the credibility of the claims made concerning "becoming-animal," and the authors' positive evaluation of it, be adequately assessed.

As regards ontology, the theme of "becoming-animal" illustrates Deleuze and Guattari's insistence on the priority of becoming over being, of the kinetic and verbal over the static and nominal. Flux, change, and relation are, for them more real than permanence, stability, and identity. Indeed, Deleuze and Guattari pursue the Nietzschean task of conceiving being in terms of becoming. This requires a critique of the traditional claim to ontological primordiality of both substance and subject. Indeed, it contests the claims to primacy of any allegedly pre-given positivity or intentional agency that would presume to proceed and direct the diverse types of "becoming-x," which are, in Deleuze and Guattari's view, constantly contesting any supposedly originary self-identity. To argue for the primacy of becoming is to liberate it from all determination by the traditional synonyms for being. Pre-eminent in this respect are the notions of "origin" and "end," the terms and means traditionally employed to contain becoming by referring it to various surrogates of being.

This overcoming of the traditional hierarchical opposition of being and becoming is evident in the claim that "there is a reality of becoming-animal, even though one does not in reality become animal" (*TP*, 273). What we ordinarily take to be the "real" animal, namely, a classifiable, identifiable, bounded object, is described by Deleuze and Guattari in terms that reveal that such a stable, objectified "reality" is in fact a secondary phenomenon. "The 'real' animal is trapped in its molar form and subjectivity" (*TP*, 275). This ontological claim concerning the primacy of becoming over being underlies all of the themes found in the extracts on becoming-animal. For instance, Deleuze and Guattari's insistence that there is nothing metaphorical about the process of "becoming-animal," that it concerns a relation that cannot be adequately described in terms of resemblance or analogy, etc., are predicated on the claim that becoming is more real than being. Such a perspective entails that the metaphysics under-pinning the notion of the "literal" is flawed.

The key feature of this ontology is the theme of "immanence" – a reality that contains no negations or boundaries, but only differences and "thresholds," in which everything is implicated in everything else. This is clear in the color claim that "a fiber stretches from a human to an animal, from a human or an animal to molecules, from molecules to particles, and so on to the imperceptible" (*TP*, 249). Deleuze and Guattari develop the non-reductive nature of their materi-alism through the pursuit of "the magic formula we all seek – PLURALISM = MONISM" (*TP*, 20). This is illustrated in the following passage:

> each individual is an infinite multiplicity, and the whole of Nature is a multiplicity of perfectly individuated multiplicities. The plane of consis-tency of nature is like an immense Abstract Machine, abstract yet real and individual; its pieces are the various assemblages and individuals, each of which groups together an infinity of particles entering into an infinity of more or less interconnected relations. There is therefore a unity to the plane of nature, which applies equally to the inanimate and the animate, the artificial and the natural. (*TP*, 254)

Deleuze and Guattari conceive existence through the notion of "becoming-animal" from the sub-molecular to the most over-coded "molar" formation in terms of the radical immanence of the "plane of consistency." The materialist "plural monism" they propose commits them to the affirmation of "creative lines of escape" from the "human" into the impersonal terrain of material intensities shared with the animal (see *K*, 35–6). These key ontological presuppositions of the ontology of "becoming-animal" are formulated thus:

> What we are talking about is not the unity of substance but the infinity of the modifications that are part of one another on this unique plane of life. ... A fixed plane of life upon which everything stirs, slows down or accelerates. A single abstract Animal for all the assemblages that effectuate it. (*TP*, 254–5)

In logical terms the notion of "becoming-animal" challenges the primacy traditionally accorded to negation, a claim concerning the nature of thinking shared by both Aristotelian and Hegelian philosophy. The significance of such a displacement is clear if it is recalled that it is via negation that self-identity and indeed all distinctions in kind, including the opposition between "man" and "nature," are established. The complementary critique of being and negation implicit in Deleuze and Guattari's notion of "becoming-animal" is apparent in the following passage conjoining the theme of becoming with another important motif from the period in which the texts on becoming-animal were written, namely, the "rhizome." This term is contrasted with "arborescence," Deleuze and Guattari's term for philosophies that assume the primacy of and valorize identity, essence, origin, end, etc.

> A rhizome has no beginning or end; it is always in the middle ... *inter-mezzo*. The tree is filiation, but the rhizome is alliance. ... The tree imposes the verb "to be," but the fabric of the rhizome is the conjunction, "and ... and ... and ..." This conjunction carries enough force to shake and uproot the verb "to be" ... establish a logic of the AND ... do away with foundations, nullify endings and beginnings. (*TP*, 25)[4]

It is, therefore, Deleuze and Guattari's view that the ontologico-logical domain of becoming and conjunction precedes, and exceeds that of being and negation. Furthermore, the domain of becoming is constantly operative, contesting and eroding the order of identity and representation that is itself an effect of more profound differential and pre-oppositional generative processes or "forces." "Becoming-animal" is one – and by no means the most fundamental – of a number of instances Deleuze and Guattari identify in which immanence returns, a re-intensification (or "deterritorialization") of life takes place, and an undetermined and hyper-differentiated materiality repeats itself.

In order to explain the view that "there is a reality specific to becoming" (*TP*, 238), particularly in relation to the claim that "becomings-animal are neither dreams nor phantasies. They are perfectly real" (*TP*, 238), Deleuze and Guattari seek to establish the derivative ontological status – and diagnose the constitutive investments of power and desire involved – of the classificatory systems and theoretical concepts of the biological sciences insofar as these rest upon notions such as organism, species identification, evolutionary filiation, teleology, etc. These disciplines have, on balance, been predominantly concerned to impose such transcendences upon the material field of immanence, or "plane of consistency," which, for Deleuze and Guattari, constitutes the "transcendental" (see *TP*, 251).[5] To undergo a desire-flow of the "becoming-animal" variety is to be drawn back into a reality more fundamental than species and genera, organic classification, and evolution through filiation and descent. It is a process of "deterritorialization" that reasserts the ontological primordiality within any "territorialized," organized material or psychic totality of anonymous, undetermined, processes seeking "alliances" without regard to the interests of the organism or subject. Thus "becoming-animal" is an instance of a much wider "becoming-molecular," a positive process of "destratification" and "decodification" in which desires alien to all categorical representation (i.e., negation) or pre-given determination (e.g., Oedipus) begin to re-circulate as the unconscious produces itself in the exteriority that is its milieu.

Hence, rather than descent and filiation within allegedly homogeneous types, Deleuze and Guattari assert the priority of alliances between heterogeneous types, called "assemblages" (*TP*, 242), which form "blocks of becoming" (*TP*, 237). These involve "*symbioses* that bring into play beings of totally different scales and kingdoms, with no possible filiation" (*TP*, 238). On the basis of these claims, Deleuze and Guattari insist that "becoming is not an evolution" (*TP*, 238). Instead a notion of "involution" (*TP*, 238) is introduced to refer to such processes that entail a growth in differentiation and complexity. These points are summarized in the following passage.

> Becoming is a rhizome, not a classificatory or genealogical tree. Becoming is certainly not imitating, or identifying with something; neither is it regressing-progressing; neither is it corresponding, establishing corresponding relations; neither is it producing, producing a filiation or producing through filiation. Becoming is a verb with a consistency all its own. (*TP*, 239)

Deleuze and Guattari seek to clarify the notion of "becoming-animal" by distinguishing "Oedipal," "state," and "demonic" animals (*TP*, 240–1). "Becoming-animal" concerns the manner in which the third of these, namely, "pack or affect animals that form a multiplicity" (*TP*, 241), contest the first two formations, namely, "individuated animals, family pets," and "animals with characteristics or attributes; genus, classification ... animals as they are treated in the great divine myths" (*TP*, 241). Indeed, the concern here is less with the distinction between different kinds of animals than with the "different states according to which they are integrated into family institutions, State apparatuses" (*TP*, 243). This draws our attention to the fact that "there is an entire politics of becomings-animal" (*TP*, 247). This keen sense of the issue of an "ontological" politics concerning the critique of the investments of the ontology of any interpretation of nature, scientific or theological, is manifest throughout the texts above.[6] To affirm "becoming-animal" is to wrest nature back from its ingrained reduction to representation, truth, knowledge, function, etc., and to reassert the primacy of an undetermined, *anoedipal* conception of desire.[7] Deleuze and Guattari's non-moral, de-anthropomorphized vision of nature traversed by "becoming-animal" is evident in the following passage:

> We oppose epidemic to filiation, contagion to heredity, peopling by contagion to sexual reproduction. ... Unnatural participations or nuptials are the true Nature spanning the kingdoms of nature. Propagation by epidemic, by contagion, has nothing to do with filiation by heredity ... contagion, epidemic, involves terms that are entirely heterogeneous: for example, a human being, an animal, and a bacterium, a virus, a molecule, a micro-organism ... these combinations are neither genetic nor structural; they are interkingdoms, unnatural participations. That is the only way Nature operates – against itself. (*TP*, 241–2)

In order to develop an ontological vocabulary adequate to processes such as "becoming-animal," Deleuze and Guattari draw upon the Spinozist themes of "power" and "affect" (see *TP*, 253–60). Through such motifs they develop an ontology of thoroughly impersonal, abstract, yet real, "molecular" processes of becoming that precede the individuated subject or organism, and that are irreducible to form or function. It is at this primordial level far beneath the command of any intentionality that the symbioses of becoming operate. The key ontological criteria at this level of reality are "intensity" and "speed" or "tempo." This realm of anonymity has its own mode of individuation "very different from that of a person, subject, thing or substance" (*TP*, 261) for which Deleuze and Guattari retrieve the scholastic notion of "haecceity."[8] As Deleuze and Guattari state,

> you will yield nothing to haecceities unless you realize that that is what you are, and that you are nothing but that … a set of nonsubjectified affects … cease to be subjects to become events, in assemblages that are inseparable from an hour a season, an atmosphere, an air, a life. … Climate, wind, season, hour are not of another nature than the things, animals, or people that populate them, follow them, sleep and awaken within them. (*TP*, 262–3)

"Becoming-animal" is a "plunge into becomings-molecular" (*TP*, 272) involving "the relation of movement and rest of the animal particles" (*TP*, 274). The material realm of becoming constantly produces such "hacceities" at odds with the categories and values of being:

> between substantial forms and determined subjects, *between the two*, there is … a natural play of haecceities, degrees, intensities, events, and accidents that compose individuations totally different from those of the well-formed subjects that receive them. (*TP*, 253)

Hence, the realm of becoming is that of the "anorganic," the "asignifying" and the "asubjective" (*TP*, 279). Deleuze and Guattari ask us to "try to conceive of this world … peopled by anonymous matter, by infinite bits of impalpable matter entering into varying connections" (*TP*, 255). A similar point is made in the following extract.

> All children build or feel these sorts of escapes, these acts of becoming-animal. … To become animal is to participate in movement, to stake out the path of escape in all its positivity, to cross a threshold, to reach a continuum of intensities that are valuable only in themselves, to find a world of pure intensities where all forms come undone, as do all the significations, signifiers, and signifieds, to the benefit of an unformed matter of deterritorialized flux, of non-signifying signs. … There is no longer anything but movements, vibrations, thresholds in a deserted matter: animals, mice, dogs, apes, cockroaches are distinguished only by this or that threshold, this or that vibration, by the particular underground tunnel in the rhizome … these tunnels are underground intensities. (*K*, 12–3)

This passage contributes to an understanding of a key feature of the ontological presuppositions of "becoming-animal" that have been identified. It is Deleuze and Guattari's unequivocal rejection of the interpretation of "becoming-animal" as a "metaphorical" process and is of particular importance to the authors' reading of Kafka's "animal" stories. As they state, "there is nothing metaphoric about the becoming-animal" (*K*, 35). Deleuze and Guattari thereby reject the complacent ontological perspectives that would immediately translate the real processes occurring in Kafka's writing into phantasies and symbolic representations requiring a hermeneutic interpretation such as psychoanalysis. Rather, all accounts of becoming in terms of "mimesis" and resemblance are dismissed as "the becoming-animal of the human being is real" (*TP*, 238). To conceive becoming in terms of imitation would be to leave intact the "molar" formations it challenges, deny the contact it implies by keeping the relata at a distance from each other, and ignore the two-way directionality of all becoming. As Deleuze and Guattari insist, "there is neither imitation nor resemblance, only an exploding of two heterogeneous series on the line of flight composed by a common rhizome that can no longer be attributed to or subjugated by anything signifying" (*TP*, 10).

Rather than interpreting Kafka's animals as metaphors and symbols to be interpreted, Deleuze and Guattari instead find a "flux of deterritorialization that overflows imitation which is always territorial" (*K*, 14). Rather than the Oedipal interpretation of the "becomings-animal" of Kafka's texts, Deleuze and Guattari insist on the non-privative status of the "orphaned becoming-animal" (*K*, 14). This rejection of the metaphysics of identity and representation in favor of "affects" and "intensities" is strikingly formulated in the following terms:

> Kafka deliberately kills all metaphor, all symbolism, all signification, no less than all designation. Metamorphosis is the contrary of metaphor. There is no longer any proper sense or figurative sense, but only a distribution of states that is part of the range of the word. The thing and other things are no longer anything but intensities overrun by deterritorialized sounds or words that are following their line of escape. It is no longer a question of a resemblance between the comportment of an animal and that of a man. ... The animal does not speak "like" a man but pulls from the language tonalities totally lacking in signification. ... To make the sequences vibrate, to open the word onto unexpected internal intensities – in short, an asignifying *intensive utilization* of language. (*K*, 22)

If the ontologically flawed interpretation of the real in terms of the "literal" is accepted, then the only sense that can be made of the term "like" in statements concerning "becoming-animal" would be in terms of simile. Yet this conceals the fact that "haecceities" emerge through becoming, which entails that "the word 'like' is one of those words that change drastically in meaning and function when they are used in connection with haecceities, when they are made into expressions of becomings instead of signified states or signifying relations" (*TP*, 274).

Deleuze and Guattari devote considerable attention to clarifying the precise nature of "becoming-animal" in terms of the primacy within it of the *relation between* the human and the animal, displacing thereby the discrete entities that seem to precede and determine such a process. This displacement of the relata by the relation within "becoming-animal" is conceived as a process of mutual deterritorialization that determines both parties. As a "block of becoming," "becoming-animal" has precedence therefore over both human and animal, neither of which are either the origin or end of it. Becoming reveals the ontological primordiality of the "in-between" (*TP*, 293). However, Deleuze and Guattari's development of this "logic of relation" is clearly distinct from its deconstructive and phenomenological counterparts in both its decidedly materialist register and emphasis on the libidinal and affective. "The two becomings interlink and form relays in a circulation of intensities pushing the deterritorialization ever further" (*TP*, 10). Hence "becoming-animal" is always a mutual process. "Becoming is always double, that which one becomes becomes no less than the one that becomes" (TP, 305).

Deleuze and Guattari also devote considerable attention to formulating becoming as a process of "non-symmetrical double deterritorialization" in order to demonstrate that "one cannot draw a symbolic boundary between the human being and the animal. One can only compare powers of deterritorialization" (*TP*, 306–7). The process of mutual deterritorialization is described as follows:

> There is no longer man or animal, since each deterritorializes the other, in a conjunction of flux, in a continuum of reversible intensities … a circuit of states that forms a mutual becoming, in the heart of a necessarily multiple or collective assemblage … the metamorphosis is part of a single circuit of the becoming-human of the animal and the becoming-animal of the human … a sort of conjunction of two deterritorializations … each immanent to the other. (*K*, 22, 35)

Deleuze and Guattari are keen to deploy this radical ontology of relation in a critique of psychoanalytic interpretations of "becoming-animal" that they condemn as reductive attempts to re-appropriate and determine desire through its Oedipal entrapment. This feature is most brilliantly illustrated by the discussion of a specific case in which psychoanalysis encountered a "becoming-animal" in the "becoming-horse" of "Little Hans." According to Deleuze and Guattari, "Little Hans's horse is not representative but affective" (*TP*, 257), and they affirm the construction of the "rhizome" (i.e., "becoming-horse") that sweeps up both Hans and the horse. This is in stark contrast to the interpretation of psychoanalysis for which such creative syntheses are regarded as pathologies threatening the mastery of the ego and the proprietary claims of the family, along with its attempted triangulation of desire. Deleuze and Guattari start neither from little Hans nor from the horse, but from the more primordial "becoming-horse of little Hans." They ask: "Is there an as yet unknown assemblage that would be neither Hans's nor the horse's, but that of the becoming-horse of Hans?" (*TP*, 258). Deleuze and Guattari's alternative to psychoanalysis, namely, "schizoanalysis," develops a quite different agenda in such cases.[9] For Deleuze and Guattari, "becoming-animal" is not "the result of a flaw or a malediction" (*K*, 35) and thus is a reality that should be celebrated.

Unlike psychoanalysis, Deleuze and Guattari affirm the "becoming-animal of the human" (*TP*, 238). However, this is merely a preliminary and relatively modest voyage into the field of intensity and becoming.[10] Unlike arguably that of many of their deconstructionist and phenomenological contemporaries, Deleuze and Guattari's thought is both ontologically *and* genealogically radical. The notion of becoming as intrinsically self-differential dislocates and undermines negation before it can gain any purchase. It thereby resists dialectical appropriation as it cannot be reduced to negative determination. However, beyond such ontologico-logical concerns, Deleuze and Guattari's committed exploration and valorization of "becoming-animal" reveals a hostility to the threat of entrapment in the moribund, de-intensified domain of "interiority" that constitutes human subjectivity, synonymous in their texts with "reterritorialisation," the (inevitable) recapture of "lines of flight."

One of the most remarkable features of Deleuze and Guattari's thematization of "becoming-animal" is their identification of it with art. Indeed, a striking materialist aesthetics is implicit in their conception of art in non-mimetic terms as a process of reciprocal deterritorialization.[11]

> No art can be imitative or figurative. Suppose a painter "represents" a bird; this is in fact a becoming-bird that can occur only to the extent that the bird itself is in the process of becoming something else, a pure line and pure color. ... imitation self-destructs, since the imitator unknowingly enters into a becoming that conjugates with the unknowing becoming of that which he or she imitates. ... The painter and musician do not imitate the animal, they become-animal at the same time as the animal becomes what they willed, at the deepest level of their concord with Nature (*TP*, 304–5).

Deleuze and Guattari refuse to align art exclusively with the human for "it is not certain whether we can draw a dividing line between animal and human beings: Are there not, as Messiaen believes, musician birds and nonmusician birds?" (*TP*, 301). This remarkable rejection of ontological segregation in all its forms is clearly expressed in the following striking passage in *A Thousand Plateaus*:

> Music dispatches molecular flows ... music is not the privilege of human beings: the universe, the cosmos, is made of refrains; the question in music is that of a power of deterritorialization permeating nature, animals, the elements, and deserts as much as human beings. The question is more what is not musical in human beings, and what already is musical in nature ... human beings are hardly at an advantage, except in means of overcoding ... that is even the opposite of having an advantage ... nature opposes its power, and the power of music, to the machines of human beings, the roar of factories and bombers ... it is necessary for the nonmusical sound of the human being to form a block with the becoming-music of sound, for them to confront and embrace each other like two wrestlers who can no longer break free from each other's grasp. (*TP*, 309)

In conclusion, it is important to note that, beyond attempting to identify the conceptual content and comprehend the meaning of the above texts, Deleuze and Guattari's writings have a decidedly "performative" character. "Becoming-animal" is entirely an affective affair, a matter of desire, a process of "contagion" (*TP*, 239). Far more important than understanding *what* is being said in the texts above, it is crucial to feel oneself drawn, on a libidinal and affective level, into the processes that are not merely being described in them but are actually taking place by way of them.

If, upon completion, the reader remains none the wiser concerning the content of the extracts included here but feels oddly feral, perhaps inclined to whinny, bark, or howl joyously, then an understanding more profound than that which can be conceptualized will have been gained.

CHAPTER SEVEN: DERRIDA

THE ANIMAL THAT THEREFORE
I AM (MORE TO FOLLOW)*

Jacques Derrida

What animal? The other.

I often ask myself, just to see, *who I am* – and who I am (following) at the moment when, caught naked, in silence, by the gaze of an animal, for example the eyes of a cat, I have trouble, yes, a bad time overcoming my embarrassment.

Whence this malaise?

I have trouble repressing a reflex dictated by immodesty. Trouble keeping silent within me a protest against the indecency. Against the impropriety that comes of finding oneself naked, one's sex exposed, stark naked before a cat that looks at you without moving, just to see. The impropriety [*malséance*] of a certain animal nude before the other animal, from that point on one might call it a kind of *animalséance*: the single, incomparable and original experience of the impropriety that would come from appearing in truth naked, in front of the insistent gaze of the animal, a benevolent or pitiless gaze, surprised or cognizant. The gaze of a seer, visionary, or extra-lucid blind person. It is as if I were ashamed, therefore,

* This article represents the first part of a ten-hour address Derrida gave at the third Cerisy-la-Salle conference devoted to his work, in July 1997. The title of the conference was "L'animal autobi-ographique"; see *L'animal autobiographique: Autour de Jacques Derrida*, ed. Marie-Louise Mallet (Paris: Galilée, 1999); Derrida's essay appears on pages 251–301. Later segments of the address dealt with Descartes, Kant, Heidegger, Lacan, and Levinas, as note 1 explains and as other allusions made by Derrida suggest. The Lacan segment ("And Say the Animal Responded?") is included in Cary Wolfe, ed., *Zoontologies: The Question of the Animal* (Minneapolis: University of Minnesota Press, 2003), pp. 121–46.

The French title of Derrida's article is "L'animal que donc je suis (à suivre)." An obvious play on Descartes's definition of consciousness (of the thinking animal as human), it also takes advantage of the shared first-person singular present form of *être* (to be) and *suivre* (to follow) in order to suggest a displacement of that priority, also reading as "the animal that therefore I follow after." Throughout the translation "I am" has, very often, to be read also as "I follow," and vice versa. I have adopted the formula "I am (following)," except where the context, or demands of fluency, dictate a choice of one or the other possibility. – Trans.

naked in front of this cat, but also ashamed for being ashamed. A reflected shame, the mirror of a shame ashamed of itself, a shame that is at the same time specular, unjustifiable, and unable to be admitted to. At the optical center of this reflection would appear this thing – and in my eyes the focus of this incomparable experience – that is called nudity. And about which it is believed that it is proper to man, that is to say foreign to animals, naked as they are, or so it is thought, without the slightest inkling of being so.

Ashamed of what and naked before whom? Why let oneself be overcome with shame? And why this shame that blushes for being ashamed? Especially, I should make clear, if the cat observes me frontally naked, face to face, and if I am naked faced with the cat's eyes looking at me as it were from head to toe, just *to see*, not hesitating to concentrate its vision – in order to see, with a view to seeing – in the direction of my sex. *To see*, without going to see, without touching yet, and without biting, although that threat remains on its lips or on the tip of the tongue. Something happens there that shouldn't take place – like everything that happens in the end, a lapsus, a fall, a failure, a fault, a symptom (and *symptom*, as you know, also means "fall": case, unfortunate event, coincidence, what falls *due* [*échéance*], mishap). It is as if, at that instant, I had said or were going to say the forbidden, something that shouldn't be said. As if I were to admit what cannot be admitted in a symptom and, as one says, wanted to bite my tongue.

Ashamed of what and before whom? Ashamed of being as naked as an animal [*bête*]. It is generally thought, although none of the philosophers I am about to examine actually mention it,[1] that the property unique to animals and what in the final analysis distinguishes them from man, is their being naked without knowing it. Not being naked therefore, not having knowledge of their nudity, in short without consciousness of good and evil.

From that point on, naked without knowing it, animals would not, in truth, be naked.

They wouldn't be naked because they are naked. In principle, with the exception of man, no animal has ever thought to dress itself. Clothing would be proper to man, one of the "properties" of man. Dressing oneself would be inseparable from all the other forms of what is proper to man, even if one talks about it less than speech or reason, the *logos*, history, laughing, mourning, burial, the gift, and so on. (The list of properties unique to man always forms a configuration, from the first moment. For that reason, it can never be limited to a single trait and it is never closed; structurally speaking it can attract a nonfinite number of other concepts, beginning with the concept of a concept.)

The animal, therefore, is not naked because it is naked. It doesn't feel its own nudity. There is no nudity "in nature." There is only the sentiment, the affect, the (conscious or unconscious) experience of existing in nakedness. Because it *is* naked, without *existing* in nakedness, the animal neither feels nor sees itself naked. And it therefore is not naked. At least that is what is thought. For man it would be the opposite, and clothing derives from technics. We would therefore have to think shame and technicity together, as the same "subject." And evil and history, and work, and so many other things that go along with it. Man would be the only one to have invented a garment to cover his sex. He would only be a man to the extent that he was able to be naked, that is to say to be ashamed, to know himself to be ashamed because he is no longer naked. And knowing *himself* would mean knowing himself to be ashamed. On the other hand, because the animal is naked without consciousness of being naked, modesty would remain as foreign to it as would immodesty. As would the knowledge of self that is involved in that.

What is shame if one can be modest only by remaining immodest, and vice versa. Man could never become naked again because he has the sense of nakedness, that is to say of modesty or shame. The animal would be *in* nonnudity because it is nude, and man *in* nudity to the extent that he is no longer nude. There we encounter a difference, a time or *contretemps* between two *nudities without nudity.* This contretemps has only just begun doing us harm [*mal*], in the area of the science of good and evil.

Before the cat that looks at me naked, would I be ashamed *like* an animal that no longer has the sense of nudity? Or on the contrary, *like* a man who retains the sense of his nudity? Who am I therefore? Who is it that I am (following)? Whom should this be asked of if not of the other? And perhaps of the cat itself?

I must make it clear from the start, the cat I am talking about is a real cat, truly, believe me, *a little cat*. It isn't the *figure* of a cat. It doesn't silently enter the room as an allegory for all the cats on the earth, the felines that traverse myths and religions, literature and fables. There are so many of them. The cat I am talking about does not belong to Kafka's vast zoopoetics, something that nevertheless solicits attention, endlessly and from a novel perspective. Nor is the cat that looks at me, and to which I seem – but don't count on it – to be dedicating a negative zootheology, Hoffmann's or Kofman's cat Murr, although along with me it uses this occasion to salute the magnificent and inexhaustible book that Sarah Kofman devotes to it, namely *Autobiogriffures*, whose title resonates so well with that of this conference. That book keeps vigil over this conference and asks to be continually quoted or reread.

An animal looks at me. What should I think of this sentence? The cat that looks at me naked and that is *truly a little cat, this* cat I am talking about, which is also a female, isn't Montaigne's cat either, the one he nevertheless calls "my [pussy]cat" [*ma chatte*] in his *Apology for Raymond Sebond.*[2] You will recognize that as one of the greatest pre- or anti-Cartesian texts on the animal. Later we will pay attention to a certain evolution from Montaigne to Descartes, an event that is obscure and difficult to assign a date to, to identify even, between two configurations for which these proper names are metonymies. Montaigne makes fun of "man's impudence with regard to the beasts," of the "presumption" and "imagination" shown by man when he claims to assign them or refuse them certain faculties (*A*, 331, 330). Contrary to that he deems it necessary to recognize in animals a "facility" in forming letters and syllables. This capacity, Montaigne confidently assures us, "testifies that they have an inward power of reason which makes them so teachable and determined to learn" (*A*, 340). Taking man to task for "carv[ing] out their shares to his fellows and companions the animals, and distribut[ing] among them such portions of faculties and powers as he sees fit," he asks, and the question refers from here on not to the animal but to the naïve assurance of man:

How does he know, by the force of his intelligence, the secret internal stirrings of animals? By what comparison between them and us does he infer the stupidity that he attributes to them?

When I play with my cat [*ma chatte*], who knows if I am not a pastime to her more than she is to me? . . .

The 1595 edition adds: "We entertain each other with reciprocal monkey tricks. If I have my time to begin or to refuse, so has she hers." (*A*, 331)

Nor does the cat that looks at me naked, she and no other, the one I am *talking about here*, belong, although we are getting warmer, to Baudelaire's family of cats,[3] or Rilke's,[4] or Buber's.[5] Literally speaking at least, these poets' and philosophers' cats don't speak. "My" pussycat (but a pussycat never belongs) is not even the one *who speaks* in *Alice in Wonderland*. Of course, if you insist at all costs of suspecting me of perversity – always a possibility – you are free to understand or receive the emphasis I just made regarding "really a little cat" as a quote from chapter eleven of *Through the Looking Glass*. Entitled "Waking," this penultimate chapter consists of a single sentence: " – and it really was a kitten, after all"; or as one French translation has it: "and, after all, it really was a little black pussy cat" ["*et, finalement, c'était bel et bien une petite chatte noire*"].[6]

Although time prevents it, I would of course have liked to inscribe my whole talk within a reading of Lewis Carroll. In fact you can't be certain that I am not doing that, for better or for worse, silently, unconsciously, or without your knowing. . . .

If I say "it is a real cat" that sees me naked, it is in order to mark its unsubstitutable singularity. When it responds in its name (whatever *respond* means, and that will be our question), it doesn't do so as the exemplar of a species called cat, even less so of an animal genus or realm. It is true that I identify it as a male or female cat. But even before that identification, I see it as *this* irreplaceable living being that one day enters my space, enters this place where it can encounter me, see me, even see me naked. Nothing can ever take away from me the certainty that what we have here is an existence that refuses to be conceptualized. And a mortal existence, for from the moment that it has a name, its name survives it. It signs its potential disappearance. Mine also, and this disappearance, from that moment to this, *fort/da*, is announced each time that, naked or not, one of us leaves the room.

But I must also accentuate the fact that this shame that is ashamed of itself is more intense when I am not alone with the cat in the room. For then I am no longer sure before whom I am so numbed with shame. In fact, is one ever alone with a cat? Or with anyone at all? Is this cat a third person? Or an other in a face-to-face duel? We will return to these questions later. In such moments, on the edge of the thing, in the imminence of the best or the worst, when anything can happen, where I can die with shame or pleasure, I no longer know in whose or in what direction to throw myself. Rather than chasing it away, chasing the cat away, I am in a hurry, yes, in a hurry to have it appear otherwise. I hasten to cover the obscenity of the event, in short to cover myself. One thought alone keeps me spellbound: dress myself, even a little, or, which amounts to the same thing, run away – as if I were chasing⁷ myself out of the room – bite myself, bite my tongue for example at the very moment that I ask myself, Who? But, *Who* then? For I no longer know who I am (following) or who it is I am chasing, who is following me or hunting me. Who comes before and who is after whom? I no longer know where my head is. Madness: " 'We're all mad here. I'm mad. You're mad.' " I no longer know how to respond, or even to respond to the question that impels me or asks me who I am (following) or after whom I am (following) and the way I am running.

To follow and *to be after* will not only be the question and the question of what we call the animal. We shall discover further along the question of the question, that which begins by wondering what *to respond* means, and whether an animal (but which one?) ever replies in its own name. And by wondering whether one can answer for what "I am (following)" means when that seems to necessitate an "I am inasmuch as I am *after* [*après*] the animal" or "I am inasmuch as I am *alongside* [*auprès*] the animal."

Being *after*, being *alongside*, being *near* [*près*] would appear as different modes of being, indeed of *being-with*. With the animal. But, in spite of appearances, it isn't certain that these modes of being come to modify a preestablished being, even less a primitive "I am." In any case they express a certain order of the being-huddled-together [*être-serré*] (which is what the etymological root, *pressu*, indicates, whence are derived the words *près*, *auprès*, *après*), the being-pressed, the being-with as being strictly attached, bound, enchained, being-under-pressure, compressed, impressed, repressed, pressed-against according to the stronger or weaker stricture of what always remains pressing. In what sense of the neighbor [*prochain*] (which is not necessarily that of a biblical or Greco-Latin tradition) should I say that I am close or near to the animal and that I am (following) it, and in what type or order of pressure? Being-with it in the sense of being-close-to-it? Being-alongside-it? Being-after-it? *Being-after-it* in the sense of the hunt, training, or taming, or *being-after-it* in the sense of a succession or inheritance? In all cases, if I am (following) *after* it, the animal therefore comes before me, earlier than me (*früher* is Kant's word regarding the animal, and Kant will later be called as a witness). The animal is there before me, there close to me, there in front of me – I who am (following) after it. And also, therefore, since it is before me, it is behind me. It surrounds me. And from the vantage of this being-there-before-me it can allow itself to be looked at, no doubt, but also – something that philosophy perhaps forgets, perhaps being this calculated forgetting itself – it can look at me. It has its point of view regarding me. The point of view of the absolute other, and nothing will have ever done more to make me think through this absolute alterity of the neighbor than these moments when I see myself seen naked under the gaze of a cat.

What stakes are raised by these questions? One doesn't need to be an expert to foresee that they involve thinking about what is meant by living, speaking, dying, being and world as in being-in-the-world or being toward the world, or being-with, being-before, being-behind, being-after, being and following, being followed or being following, there where *I am*, in one way or another, but unimpeachably, *near* what they call the animal. It is too late to deny it, it will have been there before me who is (following) after it. *After* and *near* what they call the animal and *with* it – whether we want it or not and whatever we do about it.

I must once more return to the malaise of this scene. I ask for your forbearance. I will do all I can to prevent its being presented as a primal scene: this deranged theatrics of the *wholly other that they call animal, for example, a cat. . . .*

* * *

The animal, what a word!

The animal is a word, it is an appellation that men have instituted, a name they have given themselves the right and the authority to give to another living creature [*à l'autre vivant*].

At the point at which we find ourselves, even before I get involved, or try to drag you after me or in pursuit of me upon an itinerary that some of you will no doubt find tortuous, labyrinthine, even aberrant, leading us astray from lure to lure, I will attempt the operation of disarmament that consists in *posing* what one could call some hypotheses in view of theses; posing them simply, naked, frontally, as directly as possible, *pose* them as I said, by no means in the way one indulgently poses in front of a spectator, a painter of portraits, or a camera, but "pose" in the sense of situating a series of "positions."

First hypothesis: for about two centuries, intensely and by means of an alarming rate of acceleration, for we no longer even have a clock or a chrono-logical measure of it, we, we who call ourselves men or humans, we who recognize ourselves in that name, have been involved in an unprecedented trans-formation. This mutation affects the experience of what we continue to call imperturbably, as if there were nothing wrong with it, the animal and/or animals. I intend to stake a lot, or play a lot on the flexible separation of this *and/or*. This new situation can be determined only on the basis of a very ancient one. We must continuously move along this coming and going between the oldest and what comes of the exchange among the new, the "again," and the "anew" of a repetition. Far from appearing, simply, within what we continue to call the world, history, life, and so on, this unheard of relation to the animal or to animals is so new that it should oblige us to worry all those concepts, more than just problematize them. That is why I would hesitate to say that we are *living through* that (if one can still confidently call *life* the experience whose limits tremble at the bordercrossings between *bios* and *zoē*, the biological, zoological, and anthropological, as between life and death, life and technology, life and history, and so on). I would therefore hesitate just as much to say that we are living through a historical turning point. The figure of the turning point implies a rupture or an instantaneous mutation for which the model or the figure remains genetic, biological, or zoological, and which therefore remains, precisely, to be questioned. As for history, historicity, even historicality, those motifs belong precisely – as we shall see in detail – to *this* auto-definition, *this* auto-apprehension, *this* auto-situation of man or of the human *Dasein* with respect to what is living and with respect to animal life; they belong to this auto-biography of man that I wish to call into question today.

Since all these words, in particular "history," belong in a constitutive manner to the language, interests, and lures of this autobiography, we should not be overhasty in giving them credence or in confirming their pseudo-evidence. I will therefore not be speaking of an historical turning point in order to name a transformation in process, an alteration that is at the same time more serious and less recognizable than a turning point in the relation to the animal, in the being-with shared by man and by what man calls the animal: the *being* of what calls itself man or the *Dasein with* what he himself calls, or what we ourselves call, what we still dare, provisionally, to name in general but in the singular, *the animal.* However one names or interprets this alteration, no one could deny that it has been accelerating, intensifying, no longer knowing where it is going, for about two centuries, at an incalculable rate and level.

Given this indetermination, the fact that it is left hanging, why should I say, as I have more than once, "for about two centuries," as though such a point of reference were rigorously possible in speaking of a process that is no doubt as old as man, as old as what he calls his world, his knowledge, his history, and his technology? Well, in order to recall, for convenience to begin with and without laying claim to being exact, certain preexisting indices that allow us to be heard and understood and to say "us" here today. Limiting ourselves to the most imposing of these indices we can refer to those that go well beyond the animal sacrifices of the Bible or of ancient Greece, well beyond the hecatombs (sacrifices of one hundred cattle, with all the metaphors that that expression has since been charged with), beyond the hunting, fishing, domestication, training, or traditional exploitation of animal energy (transport, plowing, draught animals, the horse, ox, reindeer, and so on, and then the guard dog, small-scale butchering, and then animal experiments, and so on). It is all too evident that in the course of the last two centuries these traditional forms of treatment of the animal have been turned upside down by the joint developments of zoological, ethological, biological, and genetic *forms of knowledge* and the always inseparable *techniques* of intervention with respect to their object, the transformation of the actual object, its milieu, its world, namely, the living animal. This has occurred by means of farming and regimentalization at a demographic level unknown in the past, by means of genetic experimentation, the industrialization of what can be called the production for consumption of animal meat, artificial insemination on a massive scale, more and more audacious manipulations of the genome, the reduction of the animal not only to production and overactive reproduction (hormones, genetic crossbreeding, cloning, and so on) of meat for consumption but also of all sorts of other end products, and all of that in the service of a certain being and the so-called human well-being of man.

All that is well known; we have no need to dwell on it. However one interprets it, whatever practical, technical, scientific, juridical, ethical, or political consequence one draws from it, no one can deny this event any more, no one can deny the *unprecedented* proportions of this subjection of the animal. Such a subjection, whose history we are attempting to interpret, can be called violence in the most morally neutral sense of the term and even includes a certain interventionist violence that is practiced, as in some very minor and in no way dominant cases, let us never forget, in the service of and for the protection of the animal, most often the human animal. Neither can one seriously deny the disavowal that this involves. No one can deny seriously, or for very long, that men do all they can in order to dissimulate this cruelty or to hide it from themselves, in order to organize on a global scale the forgetting or misunderstanding of this violence that some would compare to the worst cases of genocide (there are also animal genocides: the number of species endangered because of man takes one's breath away). One should neither abuse the figure of genocide nor consider it explained away. For it gets more complicated here: the annihilation of certain species is indeed in process, but it is occurring through the organization and exploitation of an artificial, infernal, virtually interminable survival, in conditions that previous generations would have judged monstrous, outside of every supposed norm of a life proper to animals that are thus exterminated by means of their continued existence or even their overpopulation. As if, for example, instead of throwing people into ovens or gas chambers (let's say Nazi) doctors and geneticists had decided to organize the overproduction and overgeneration of Jews, gypsies, and homosexuals by means of artificial insemination, so that, being more numerous and better fed, they could be destined in always increasing numbers for the same hell, that of the imposition of genetic experimentation or extermination by gas or by fire. In the same abattoirs. I don't wish to abuse the ease with which one can overload with pathos the self-evidences I am drawing attention to here. Everybody knows what terrifying and intolerable pictures a realist painting could give to the industrial, mechanical, chemical, hormonal, and genetic violence to which man has been submitting animal life for the past two centuries. Everybody knows what the production, breeding, transport, and slaughter of these animals has become. Instead of thrusting these images in your faces or awakening them in your memory, something that would be both too easy and endless, let me simply say a word about this "pathos." If these images are "pathetic," if they evoke sympathy, it is also because they "pathetically" open the immense question of pathos and the pathological, precisely, that is, of suffering, pity, and compassion; and the place that has to be accorded to the interpretation of this compassion, to the sharing of this suffering among the living, to the law, ethics, and politics that must be brought to bear upon this experience of compassion. For what has been happening now for two centuries involves a new experience of this compassion. In response to the irresistible but unacknowledged unleashing and the organized disavowal of this torture, voices are raised – minority, weak, marginal voices, little assured of their discourse, of their right to discourse and of the enactment of their discourse within the law, as a declaration of rights – in order to protest, in order to appeal (we'll return to this) to what is still presented in such a problematic way as *animal rights*, in order to awaken us to our responsibilities and our obligations with respect to the living in general, and precisely to this fundamental compassion that, were we to take it seriously, would have to change even the very basis (and that basis is what I wish to discuss today) of the philosophical problematic of the animal.

It is in thinking of the source and ends of this compassion that about two centuries ago someone like Bentham, as is well known, proposed changing the very form of the question regarding the animal that dominated discourse within the tradition, in the language of both the most refined philosophical argument and everyday acceptation and common sense. Bentham said something like this:

the question is not to know whether the animal can think, reason, or talk, something we still pretend to be asking ourselves. (From Aristotle to Descartes, from Descartes, especially, to Heidegger, Levinas, and Lacan, this question determines so many others concerning *power* or *capability* [*pouvoirs*] and *attributes* [*avoirs*]: being able, having the power to give, to die, to bury one's dead, to dress, to work, to invent a technique, and so on, a power that consists in having such and such a faculty, thus such and such a power, as an essential attribute.) Thus the question will not be to know whether animals are of the type *zoōn logon echon*, whether they *can* speak or reason thanks to that *capacity* or that *attribute* implied in the *logos*, the *can-have* [*pouvoir-avoir*] of the *logos*, the aptitude for the *logos* (and logocentrism is first of all a thesis regarding the animal, the animal deprived of the *logos*, deprived of the *can-have-the-logos*: this is the thesis, position, or presupposition maintained from Aristotle to Heidegger, from Descartes to Kant, Levinas and Lacan). The *first* and *decisive* question will rather be to know whether animals *can suffer*.

"Can they suffer?" asks Bentham simply yet so profoundly.

Once its protocol is established, the form of this question changes everything. It no longer simply concerns the *logos*, the disposition and whole configuration of the *logos*, having it or not, nor does it concern more radically a *dynamis* or *hexis*, this having or manner of being, this *habitus* that one calls a faculty or "power," this can-have or the power one possesses (as in the power to reason, to speak, and everything that that implies). The question is disturbed by a certain *passivity*. It bears witness, manifesting already, as question, the response that testifies to a sufferance, a passion, a not-being-able. The word *can* [*pouvoir*] changes sense and sign here once one asks "can they suffer?" The word wavers henceforth. As soon as such a question is posed what counts is not only the idea of a transitivity or activity (being able to speak, to reason, and so on); the important thing is rather what impels it towards self-contradiction, something we will later relate back to auto-biography. "Can they suffer?" amounts to asking "can they *not be able*?" And what of this inability [*impouvoir*]? What of the vulnerability felt on the basis of this inability? What is this nonpower at the heart of power? What is its quality or modality? How should one account for it? What right should be accorded it? To what extent does it concern us? Being able to suffer is no longer a power, it is a possibility without power, a possibility of the impossible. Mortality resides there, as the most radical means of thinking the finitude that we share with animals, the mortality that belongs to the very finitude of life, to the experience of compassion, to the possibility of sharing the possibility of this nonpower, the possibility of this impossibility, the anguish of this vulnerability and the vulnerability of this anguish.

With this question – "can they suffer?" – we are not standing on the rock of indubitable certainty, the foundation of every assurance that one could, for example, look for in the *cogito*, in *Je pense donc je suis*. But from another perspective we are here putting our trust in an instance that is just as radical, however different it may be, namely, what is undeniable. No one can deny the suffering, fear or panic, the terror or fright that humans witness in certain animals. (Descartes himself was not able to claim that animals were insensitive to suffering.) Some will still try – this is something else we will come to – to contest the right to call that *suffering* or *anguish,* words or concepts that they would still reserve for man and for the *Dasein* in the freedom of its being-toward-death. We will have reason to problematize that discourse later. But for the moment let us note the following: the response to the question "can they suffer?" leaves no doubt. In fact it has never left any room for doubt; that is why the experience that we have of it is not even indubitable; it precedes the indubitable, it is older than it. No doubt either, then, for the possibility of our giving vent to a surge of compassion, even if it is then misunderstood, repressed, or denied, held in respect. Before the *undeniable* of this response (yes, they suffer, like us who suffer for them and with them), before this response that precedes all other questions, the problematic changes ground and base. Perhaps it loses all security, but in any case it no longer rests on the old, supposedly natural (its ground) or historic and *artifactual* (its base) foundation. The two centuries I have been referring to somewhat approximately in order to situate the present in terms of this tradition have been those of an unequal struggle, a war being waged, the unequal forces of which could one day be reversed, between those who violate not only animal life but even and also this sentiment of compassion and, on the other hand, those who appeal to an irrefutable testimony to this pity.

War is waged over the matter of pity. This war probably has no age but, and here is my hypothesis, it is passing through a critical phase. We are passing through that phase and it passes through us. To think the war we find ourselves waging is not only a duty, a responsibility, an obligation, it is also a necessity, a constraint that, like it or not, directly or indirectly, everyone is held to. Henceforth and more than ever. And I say "to think" this war, because I believe it concerns what we call "thinking." The animal looks at us, and we are naked before it. Thinking perhaps begins there.

Here now, in view of another thesis, is the *second hypothesis* that I think must be deduced without hesitation. It concerns or puts into effect another logic of the limit. I will thus be tempted to inscribe the subject of this thesis in the series of three conferences that, beginning with "*Les Fins de l'homme*" and followed by "*Le Passage des frontières,*" have been devoted to a properly *transgressal* if not transgressive experience of *limitrophy.* Let's allow that word to have both a general and strict sense: what abuts onto limits but also what feeds, is fed, is cared for, raised, and trained, what is cultivated on the edges of a limit. In the semantics of *trephō, trophē,* or *trophos,* we should be able to find everything we need to speak about what we should be speaking about in the course of these ten days devoted to the autobiographical animal: feeding, food, nursing, breeding, offspring, education, care and keeping of animals, training, upbringing, culture, living and allowing to live by giving to live, be fed, and grown, autobiographically. *Limitrophy* is therefore my subject. Not just because it will concern what sprouts or grows at the limit, around the limit, by maintaining the limit, but also what *feeds the limit,* generates it, raises it, and complicates it. Whatever I will say is designed, certainly not to efface the limit, but to multiply its figures, to complicate, thicken, delinearize, fold, and divide the line precisely by making it increase and multiply. Moreover, the supposed first or literal sense of *trephō* is just that: transform by thickening, for example, in curdling milk. So it will in no way mean questioning, even in the slightest, the limit about which we have had a stomachful, the limit between Man with a capital M and Animal with a capital A. It will not be a matter of attacking frontally or antithetically the thesis of philosophical or common sense on the basis of which has been built the relation to the self, the presentation of the self of human life, the autobiography of the human species, the whole history of the self that man recounts to himself, that is to say the thesis of a limit as rupture or abyss between those who say "we men," "I, a man," and what this man among men who say "we," what he *calls* the animal or animals. I won't take it upon myself for a single moment to contest that thesis, nor the rupture or abyss between this "I–we" and what we *call* animals. To suppose that I, or anyone else for that matter, could ignore that rupture, indeed that abyss, would mean first of all blinding oneself to so much contrary evidence; and, as far as my own modest case is concerned, it would mean forgetting all the signs that I have sought to give, tirelessly, of my attention to difference, to differences, to heterogeneities and abyssal ruptures as against the homogeneous and the continuous. I have thus never believed in some homogeneous continuity between what calls *itself* man and what *he* calls the animal. I am not about to begin to do so now. That would be worse than sleepwalking, it would simply be too asinine [*bête*].[8] To suppose such a stupid memory lapse or to take to task such a naïve misapprehension of this abyssal rupture would mean, more seriously still, venturing to say almost anything at all for the cause, for whatever cause or interest that no longer had anything to do with what we claimed to want to talk about. When that cause or interest begins to profit from what it simplistically suspects to be a biologistic continuism, whose sinister connotations we are well aware of, or more generally to profit from what is suspected as a geneticism that one might wish to associate with this scatter-brained accusation of continuism, the undertaking in any case becomes so aberrant that it neither calls for nor, it seems to me, deserves any direct discussion on my part. Everything I have suggested so far and every argument I will put forward today stands overwhelmingly in opposition to the blunt instrument that such an allegation represents.

For there is no interest to be found in a discussion of a supposed discontinuity, rupture, or even abyss between those who call themselves men and what so-called men, those who name themselves men, call the animal. Everybody agrees on this, discussion is closed in advance, one would have to be more asinine than any beast [*plus bête que les bêtes*] to think otherwise. Even animals know that (ask Abraham's ass or ram or the living beasts that Abel offered to God; they know what is about to happen to them when man says, "Here I am" to God, then consent to sacrifice themselves, to sacrifice their sacrifice or to forgive themselves). The discussion is worth undertaking once it is a matter of determining the number, form, sense, or structure, the foliated consistency of this abyssal limit, these edges, this plural and repeatedly folded frontier. The discussion becomes interesting once, instead of asking whether or not there is a discontinuous limit, one attempts to think what a limit becomes once it is abyssal, once the frontier no longer forms a single indivisible line but more than one internally divided line, once, as a result, it can no longer be traced, objectified, or counted as single and indivisible. What are the edges of a limit that grows and multiplies by feeding on an abyss? Here is my thesis in three paragraphs:

1. This abyssal rupture doesn't describe two edges, a unilinear and indivisible line having two edges, Man and Animal in general.
2. The multiple and heterogeneous border of this abyssal rupture has a history. Both macroscopic and microscopic and far from being closed, that history is now passing through the most unusual phase in which we find ourselves and for which there is no scale. Indeed, one can only speak here of history, of an historic moment or phase, from one of the supposed edges of the said rupture, the edge of an anthropocentric subjectivity that is recounted or allows a history to be recounted about it, autobiographically, the history of its life, and that it therefore calls *History*.
3. Beyond the edge of the *so-called* human, beyond it but by no means on a single opposing side, rather than "the Animal" or "Animal Life," there is already a heterogeneous multiplicity of the living, or more precisely (since to say "the living" is already to say too much or not enough) a multiplicity of organizations of relations between living and dead, relations of organization or lack of organization among realms that are more and more difficult to dissociate by means of the figures of the organic and inorganic, of life and/or death. These relations are at once close and abyssal, and they can never be totally objectified. They do not leave room for any simple exteriority of one term with respect to another. It follows from that that one will never have the right to take animals to be the species of a kind that would be named the Animal, or animal in general. Whenever "one" says, "the Animal," each time a philosopher, or anyone else says, "the Animal" in the singular and without further ado, claiming thus to designate every living thing that is held not to be man (man as *rational animal*, man as political animal, speaking animal, *zoōn logon echon*, man who says "I" and takes himself to be the subject of a statement that he proffers on the subject of the said animal, and so on), each time the subject of that statement, this "one," this "I" does that he utters an *asinanity* [*bêtise*]. He avows without avowing it, he declares, just as a disease is declared by means of a symptom, he offers up for diagnosis the statement "I am uttering an *asinanity*." And this "I am uttering an *asinanity*" should confirm not only the animality that he is disavowing but his complicit, continued and organized involvement in a veritable war of the species. Such are my hypotheses in view of theses on the animal, on animals, on the word *animal* or *animals*. Yes, *animal*, what a word!

Animal is a word that men have given themselves the right to give. These humans are found giving it to themselves, this word, but as if they had received it as an inheritance. They have given themselves the word in order to corral a large number of living beings within a single concept: "the Animal," they say. And they have given themselves this word, at the same time according themselves, reserving for them, for humans, the right to the word, the name, the verb, the attribute, to a language of words, in short to the very thing that the others in question would be deprived of, those that are corralled within the grand territory of the beasts: the Animal. All the philosophers we will investigate (from Aristotle to Lacan, and including Descartes, Kant, Heidegger, and Levinas), all of them say the same thing: the animal is without language. Or more precisely unable to respond, to respond with a response that could be precisely and rigorously distinguished from a reaction, the animal is without the right and power to "respond" and hence without many other things that would be the property of man.

Men would be first and foremost those living creatures who have given themselves the word that enables them to speak of the animal with a single voice and to designate it as the single being that remains without a response, without a word with which to respond.

That wrong was committed long ago and with long-term consequences. It derives from this word or rather it comes together in this word *animal* that men have given themselves at the origin of humanity and that they have given themselves in order to identify themselves, in order to recognize themselves, with a view to being what they say they are, namely men, capable of replying and responding in the name of men.

I would like to try and speak of a certain wrong or evil that derives from this word, to begin with by stammering some chimerical aphorisms.

The animal that I am (following), does it speak?

That is an intact question, virginal, new, still to come, a completely naked question. . . .

*   *   *

Ecce animot – that is what I was saying before this long digression. In order not to damage French ears too sensitive to spelling and grammar I won't repeat the word *animot* too often. I'll do it several times but each time that, henceforth, I say the animal [*l'animal*] or the animals [*animaux*] I'll be asking you to silently substitute *animot* for what you hear. By means of the chimera of this singular word, the *animal*, I bring together three heterogeneous elements within a single verbal body.

1. I would like to have the plural of animals heard in the singular. There is no animal in the general singular, separated from man by a single indivisible limit. We have to envisage the existence of "living creatures" whose plurality cannot be assembled within the single figure of an animality that is simply opposed to humanity. This does not of course mean ignoring or effacing everything that separates humankind from the other animals, creating a single large set, a single great, fundamentally homogeneous and continuous family tree going from the *animot* to the *homo* (*faber, sapiens*, or whatever else). That would be an *asinanity*, even more so to suspect anyone here of doing just that. I won't therefore devote another second to the double stupidity of that suspicion, even if, alas, it is quite widespread. I repeat that it is rather a matter of taking into account a multiplicity of heterogeneous structures and limits. Among nonhumans and separate from nonhumans there is an immense multiplicity of other living things that cannot in any

way be homogenized, except by means of violence and willful ignorance, within the category of what is called the animal or animality in general. From the outset there are animals and, let's say, *l'animot*. The confusion of all nonhuman living creatures within the general and common category of the animal is not simply a sin against rigorous thinking, vigilance, lucidity, or empirical authority; it is also a crime. Not a crime against animality precisely, but a crime of the first order against the animals, against animals. Do we agree to presume that every murder, every transgression of the commandment "Thou shalt not kill" concerns only man (a question to come) and that in sum there are only crimes "against humanity"?

2. The suffix *mot* in *l'animot* should bring us back to the word, namely, to the word named a noun [*nomme nom*]. It opens onto the referential experience of the thing *as such*, as what it is in its being, and therefore to the reference point by means of which one has always sought to draw the limit, the unique and indivisible limit held to separate man from animal, namely the word, the nominal language of the word, the voice that names and that names the thing *as such*, such as it appears in its being (as in the Heideggerian moment in the demonstration that we are coming to). The animal would in the last instance be deprived of the word, of the word that one names a noun or name.

3. It would not be a matter of "giving speech back" to animals but perhaps of acceding to a thinking, however fabulous and chimerical it might be, that thinks the absence of the name and of the word otherwise, as something other than a privation.

Ecce animot, that is the announcement of which I am (following) something like the trace, assuming the title of an autobiographical animal, in the form of a risky, fabulous, or chimerical response to the question "But me, who am I?" that I have bet on treating as that of the autobiographical animal. Assuming that title, which is itself somewhat chimerical, might surprise you. It brings together *two times two* alliances, as unexpected as they are irrefutable.

On the one hand, the title gives rise to the thought, in the informal form of a playful conversation, a suggestion that would take witty advantage of idiom, that quite simply there are those among humans, writers, and philosophers whose character implies a taste for autobiography, the irresistible sense of or desire for autobiography. One would say, "(s)he's an autobiographical animal," in the same way that one says, "(s)he's a theatrical animal, a competitive animal, a political animal," not in the sense that one has been able to define man as a political animal but in the sense of an individual who has the taste, talent, or compulsive obsession for politics: he who likes that, likes doing that, likes politics. And does it well. In that sense the autobiographical animal would be the sort of man or woman who, as a matter of character, chooses to indulge in or can't resist indulging in autobiographical confidences. He or she who works *in* autobiography. And in the history of literature or philosophy, if it can be suggested in such a summary manner, there are "autobiographical animals," more autobiographical than others, animals for autobiography: Montaigne more than Malherbe, similarly Rousseau, the lyrical and romantic poets, Proust and

Gide, Virginia Woolf, Gertrude Stein, Celan, Bataille, Genet, Duras, Cixous; but also (the matter is structurally more rare and more complicated when it comes to philosophy) Augustine and Descartes more than Spinoza, Kierkegaard, playing with so many pseudonyms, more than Hegel, Nietzsche more than Marx. But because the matter is really too complicated (it is our theme after all) I prefer to end the list of examples there. With the problems it poses this connotation of the autobiographical animal must certainly remain present, even if tangential, to our reflections. It will weigh on them with its virtual weight.

But, *on the other hand*, I was not thinking of that usage of the expression "autobiographical animal" in the last instance and in order to get to some bottom of the matter, if there is such a thing. It happens that there exist, between the word *I* and the word *animal*, all sorts of significant connections. They are at the same time functional and referential, grammatical and semantic. Two general singulars to begin with: the *I* and the *animal* designate an indeterminate generality in the singular and by means of the definite article. The *I* is anybody at all; *I* am anybody at all and anybody at all must be able to say "I" to refer to herself, to his own singularity. Whosoever says "I" or apprehends or poses him- or herself as an "I" is a living animal. On the other hand, animality, the life of the living, to the extent that one claims to be able to distinguish it from the inorganic, from the purely inert or cadaverous physico-chemical, is generally defined as sensibility, irritability, and *auto-motricity*, a spontaneity that is given to movement, to organizing itself and affecting itself, marking, tracing, and affecting itself with traces of its self. This *auto-motricity* as auto-affection and relation to itself is the characteristic recognized as that of the living and of animality in general, even before one comes to consider the discursive thematic of an utterance or of an *ego cogito*, more so of a *cogito ergo sum*. But between this relation to the self (this Self, this ipseity) and the *I* of the "I think," there is, it would seem, an abyss.

The problems begin there, we suspect, and what problems they are! But they begin where one attributes to the essence of the living, to the animal in general, this aptitude *that it itself* is, this aptitude to being itself, and thus the aptitude to being capable of affecting itself, of its own movement, of affecting itself with traces of a living self, and thus of *autobiograparaphing* itself as it were. No one has ever denied the animal this capacity to track itself, to trace itself or retrace a path of itself. Indeed the most difficult problem lies in the fact that it has been refused the power to transform those traces into verbal language, to call to itself by means of discursive questions and responses, denied the power to efface its traces (which is what Lacan will do, and we will come back to everything that that implies). Let us set out again from this place of intersection between these two general singulars, the animal (*l'animot*) and the "I," the "I"s, the place where in a given language, French for example, an "I" says "I." Singularly and in general. It could be anyone at all, you or I. So what happens there? How can I say "I" and what do I do thereby? And in the first place, me, what am I (following) and who am I (following)?

"I": by saying "I" the signatory of an autobiography would claim to point himself out physically, introduce himself in the present [*se présenter au présent*] (*sui*-referential deictic) and in his totally naked truth. And in the naked truth, if there is such a thing, of his or her sexual difference, of all their sexual differences. By naming himself and responding in his own name he would be saying "I stake and engage my nudity without shame." One can well doubt whether this pledge, this wager, this desire or promise of nudity is possible. Nudity perhaps remains untenable. And can I finally show myself naked in the sight of what they call by the name of animal? Should I show myself naked when, concerning me, looking at me, is the living creature they call by the common, general and singular name of the animal? Henceforth I will reflect (on) the same question by introducing a mirror. I import a full-length mirror [*une psyché*] into the scene. Wherever some autobiographical play is being enacted there has to be a *psyché*, a mirror that reflects me naked from head to toe. The same question then becomes whether I should show myself but in the process see myself naked (that is reflect my image in a mirror) when, concerning me, looking at me, is this living creature, this cat that can find itself caught in the same mirror? Is there animal narcissism? But cannot this cat also be, deep within her eyes, my primary mirror?

The animal in general, what is it? What does that mean? Who is it? To what does that "it"[9] correspond? To whom? Who responds to whom? Who responds in and to the common, general and singular name of what they thus blithely call the "animal?" Who is it that responds? The reference made by this what or who regarding me in the name of the animal, what is said in the name of the animal when one appeals to the name of the animal, that is what needs to be exposed, in all its nudity, in the nudity or destitution of whoever, opening the page of an autobiography, says, "here I am."

"But as *for* me, who am I (following)?"

THINKING WITH CATS

David Wood

Few readers will be surprised at what Derrida can tease out from the experience of being looked at by his cat. But can it all be taken in? Is it his distrust of the logic of sacrifice that prevents him from poking out his own eyes when he finally grasps the truth? Or is it the very impossibility of grasping the truth that protects him? "The Animal That Therefore I Am (More to Follow)" is a brilliant sequel to his "Eating Well" interview with Jean-Luc Nancy,[1] one that opens onto extended readings of the treatment of the animal by Descartes, Kant, Heidegger, Lacan, and Levinas,[2] and one that reconstitutes his whole work as a zoopilosophy. This recasting of his own past is no accident – it is Derrida's contribution to the third Cerisy conference [1997] devoted to his work, entitled "L'animal autobiographique." Instead of confessing his truth to St. Peter at the pearly gates, Derrida is provoked more profoundly by the request of an earthly companion, once a god to the Egyptians, to be let out the door. This paper is a hard act to follow.[3] Nonetheless, my aim here is to lay out a number of its principal concerns, to show why it represents one of the most *indépassable*, critical engagements of our time, and along the way to weave a response that continues the conversation.

Derrida's original published paper, from which we include a selection here,[4] starts a number of hares, and manages to track most of them with his usual elegance. I try, in various ways both to affirm and contest Derrida's extraordinary contribution to a rethinking of the animal question. I affirm various strands of his diagnosis: (1) the intimate connection between our thinking about animals, and our self-understanding; (2) how our carnivorous and other exploitative practices need to be called what they are: violence and genocide; (3) how our experience of the other animal opens in various ways onto "abyssal ruptures" of any happy domesticated conceptualization; and (4) the importance of the logic of sacrifice in understanding why we act as we do. I also suggest that something of the abyssal dimension of our relation to animals is set aside once we fill out more fully our historical engagements with different animals and species of animals. This would give the experience with a pet or companion a limited, if special significance. Finally, I argue for expanding our horizons away from a focus on the individual animal to broader environmental concerns, especially thinking through our role in the imperiled future of the web of life on the planet.

1. THE OTHER'S LOOK: LOOKING FOR THE OTHER

"Hallo!" said Piglet, "what are you doing?" ...

"Tracking something," said Winnie-the-Pooh very mysteriously.

"Tracking what?" said Piglet, coming closer.

"That's just what I ask myself. I ask myself, What?"

"What do you think you'll answer?"

"I shall have to wait until I catch up with it," said Winnie-the-Pooh. "Now, look there." He pointed to the ground in front of him." What do you see there?"

"Tracks," said Piglet. "Paw-marks." He gave a squeak of excitement. "Oh, Pooh! Do you think it's a – a – a Woozle?" (A. A. Milne)[5]

"A cat may look at a king," said Alice. "I've read that in some book, but I don't remember where." (Lewis Carroll)

While, quite properly, Derrida resists claiming for it the status of a primal scene, the event from which he sets out and to which he repeatedly returns, is that of an encounter with his cat.[6] Derrida fastens not on his own awareness of the cat, but on the experience of being seen by his (female) cat, who, moreover sees him naked, focused, we are told, on his sex. As with Hitchcock's rearing-up camera angles, this scene allows Derrida to open an abyssal dimension to the most domestic of scenes. Unlike Nagel's bat, for example,[7] where something alien (the bat uses sonar) obstructs the work of empathy from the beginning, the cat is a "familiar," a close companion, a creature one shares a space, even a life with. And yet ...

Derrida is of course opening up at least two questions at once – the question of our relationship to "animals" (and to specific individual animals), and the question of who "I" am, the truth of my being, the "autobiographical" question. We may admit that the "other" has a role to play in determining who I am. I cannot be an author unless others read, or at least buy, my books. But the look of a cat threatens to interrupt fatally what Ricoeur would call the constructive detour through the other.

2. LOOKING BACK TO SARTRE AND LEVINAS

The look which the eyes manifest, no matter what kind of eyes they are, is a pure reference to myself. What I apprehend immediately when I hear the branches crackling behind me is not that *there is someone there*; it is that I am vulnerable, that I have a body which can be hurt ... in short that I *am seen*. (Sartre)[8]

To manifest oneself as a face is to impose oneself ... without the intermediary of any image, in one's nudity, that is, in one's destitution and hunger. (Levinas)[9]

The phenomenology of the look, of being looked at, does not of course begin with Derrida and his cat, and it is instructive to remind ourselves what powerful work it does for both Sartre and Levinas before him. In Sartre's classic analysis,[10] the look of the other affects an intentional reversal in which I experience myself objectified, even "devoured" by the other's gaze. Specifically, I experience my own subjectivity and freedom withering in the presence of the other. What this experience shows to Sartre is the struggle for ascendancy latent in human interaction, the instability that arises from the meeting of two subjects each projecting a world. Sartre's other is not limited to the actual presence of the another human. A *No Smoking* sign, crackling branches, or a creak on the stairs can make me blush. He does not, to my knowledge, give the animal's gaze a status comparable to that of man. But the reason for this exclusion may be stranger than it seems. For there is no better model for the objectifying gaze than that of the predator weighing up dinner. There are many kinds of look or gaze – that of love, adoration, pride, envy, pity, etc. The reductive focus of the modality of the look Sartre chooses suggests a fatal interweaving of that freedom which, for Sartre (after Hegel), distinguishes man from the animal, with the inability fully to recognize that freedom in the other. Where the other *is* an animal, we may suppose that at least the dialectical instabilities do not arise, and we can get on with the everyday business of subjugation.

For Levinas, too, the experience of the other is incomplete without the experience of being addressed by the other. The face-to-face relation *means* "Don't kill me" – it *is* an address. Again there is a reversal or blockage of our normal intentional stance, and the displacement of the primacy of the subject. The "abyssal" dimension of this experience *with* the other consists not in the fact that the other (as with Nagel) is cognitively allusive or recessive, generating for example "the problem of other minds" – but rather that the other, by addressing me, invokes an obligation, an infinite obligation, that exceeds knowledge "as such." The "abyss" is not so much my unfathomably deep ignorance of what it might be like to be you but rather the incalculable gap between knowledge as such and responsibility.

Now for Levinas we might imagine that the animal would be a godsend, illustrating his thesis in an exemplary way. Strangely this is not so. When asked about the animal as other, he insists that the animal has a face only by analogy with the human. And it quickly becomes clear that Levinas adheres to a very traditional account of the great chain of being, doubting, for example, that a snake could have a face. He writes:

> I cannot say at what moment you have the right to be called 'face.' The human face is completely different, and only afterwards do we discover the face of an animal. ... The human breaks with pure being, which is always a persistence in being. That is Darwin's idea. The being of animals is a struggle for life. A struggle for life without ethics.[11]

It is tempting to suggest that in his poem "The Snake" D. H. Lawrence is being more Levinasian than Levinas:

> A snake came to my water-trough
> On a hot, hot day, and I in pyjamas for the heat
> To drink there. ...

Someone was before me at my water-trough
And I, like a second comer, waiting.
He lifted his head from his drinking, as cattle do,
And looked at me vaguely, as drinking cattle do,
And flickered his two-forked tongue from his lips, and mused a moment."[12]

We know that Levinas takes for granted some sort of connection between face
and language, so it is especially significant that Derrida will speak of the cat
"addressing" me. But as we noted in the case of Sartre, there may be a strange
structural reason why the animal is given a derivative ethical status. Levinas's
entire focus on the ethical is an antidote to what he believes to be man's fundamentally murderous natural disposition. Subscribing in this way to Tennyson's
"Nature red in tooth and claw" means that "the animal" already has a place in
Levinas's philosophy, as the condition that man must overcome – long before
there is any meeting with cat, bat, or snake.[13] And it may be that the scene of a
man's or woman's encounter with an animal is, all too often even for philosophers, the site of a ritual reenactment of a problematic internal relation to our
own "animality."

All this suggests that Derrida's cat scene is far from an innocent one. Rather
it has been tracked back and forth many times before. But if Derrida is indeed
walking in the footsteps of others, perhaps the point of his invocation of this
domestic scene is precisely to resist these teleological operations, by finding the
unheimlich (uncanny) even where we feel most at home.

Derrida marks this methodological resistance by pointing out the twin
dangers that beset us here: (1) to declare the animal (the cat) unknowable, and
(2) to appropriate the cat (388). His focus on the cat's looking at me is meant
to help us avoid such a choice. At the same time, as we have seen, if the cat is
given a role in determining who *I* am, this experience also serves as a cautionary
brake on my own self-understanding. This is the profound lesson of A. A.
Milne's metaphysical tales, disguised as children's stories. The band of Woozles
that Pooh and Piglet are "tracking" round and round in the same circle is in fact
themselves. Piglet does not so much have a moment of insight about this as
remember something else he needs to do. When Lewis Carroll's Lion asks Alice
"What's this? ... Are you animal – or vegetable – or mineral?," and the Unicorn
replies (before Alice can) "It's a fabulous monster!," we find a similar cautionary
mechanism in play.

3. FOLLOWING THE TRAIL OF LANGUAGE

To follow and to *be after* will not only be the question and the question of
what we call the animal. We shall discover further along the question of the
question, that which begins by wondering what *to respond* means, and
whether an animal (but which one?) ever replies in its own name. (Derrida)[14]

The title of this paper plays on the ambiguity of "je suis," both "I am" and "I
follow," effecting a certain disturbance of the clarity and autonomy of "*Je pense
donc je suis.*" With a light touch of words, Derrida is re-enacting the move from

the Cartesian subject, to Heidegger's being-in-the-world, to Nancy's attention to being-with. And the various semantic resources of "following" promise to allow a multi-faceted exploration of the complex interface of "man" and "animal." The wordplay proposes that what it is to be me and what it is to be human are precisely not to be discovered in the kind of evidentiary moment that Descartes announced. As we will see, Derrida will rework the sense of the indubitable when laying out the dimensions of our violence against animals. A play on the French *suis* is only an enabling device, allowing us to thicken the existential plot, much as Heidegger deployed the semantic resources of *es gibt* (there is, but *literally* "it gives") to suggest a certain receptivity in our relation to being. The idiosyncrasies of a natural language can provoke us to explore pathways that can later be seen to have a conceptual significance that goes beyond that singular origin. But Derrida follows up this linguistic play with a more direct critique of the linguistic landscape in which we encounter animals. We may suppose that the damage, if any, done by using the word "leaf" – this is Nietzsche's example – to apply to all leaves, is damage done to us, to our cognitive capacity,[15] not to the leaves. But the use of the word "animal" or "the animal" to refer to any and all living creatures is a conceptual violence that expeditiously legitimates our actual violence. Derrida is not quite right to suppose that no philosopher has ever made this point before,[16] but he is right to draw attention to it again. Derrida toys with the idea that there is a deep connection between naming and death, that naming already anticipates the absence of something, the need to be able to refer to it after it is gone. In naming, we might say, is the beginning of mourning. He importantly distances himself from that whole view of nature (including "animals") that would have it veiled in sadness, in loss – a view he attributes both to Heidegger and to Benjamin – but the advent of language does not unambiguously bring loss onto the scene.[17] Unless, as he seems to suggest, the "loss" is that of the gift of death (389).

But I have doubts about this. The violence lodged in the word animal is not the product of naming. We do not *name* the creatures of the world "animal" or "the animal." Rather "animal" is a category, one of the same order as "man." To call it a category rather than a name is important. Categories are gross ways in which we (humans) carve up the world. Violence arises at two levels. First, these categorial distinctions (man/animal, man/woman) are affirmations of the very kinds of distinctions that would block the extension of consideration (for example, from man to animal). For it is no accident that these categorial distinctions are actually wielded by only one of each pair. (Unless we go Wari' [see below], it is only men who designate animals as such, and not vice versa.) Second, these categories *can* be deployed nominally and descriptively so that such violence can be applied to this or that specific animal. "Animal," in other words, is one of the ways we say "Other."[18]

Foucault begins *Madness and Civilization* with a quote from Dostoievsky's *Diary of a Writer.* "It is not by confining one's neighbor that one is convinced of one's own sanity." Of course the implication is precisely that we do believe this. And what this argues, as I suggested earlier, is that the way we treat animals is deeply caught up with the ongoing need for symbolic reaffirmation of our own humanity.

Derrida negotiates the issue that I have dealt with in terms of categories and names in connection with the question of the continuity or discontinuity between humans and animals. He is suspicious of continuity theses, but his affirmation of discontinuity (an abyssal rupture) is one that holds between "we men" and "what *we call* animals" (my emphasis). (Echoing Nietzsche,[19] he writes that humans are those who have assigned to themselves the right to use the word "animal" [400].) This careful formulation ("what *we call* animals") opens up a whole can of worms. Let me just a make a couple of comments: (1) Derrida seems to be worried about continuity theses because of the biologistic reductionism often associated with them. But perhaps instead we should be more cautious in supposing that "biology" has the best handle even on the description of *animal* life.[20] And does not the Benthamite reference to suffering ("The question is – do they suffer?") that Derrida quotes approvingly suggest precisely a fundamental continuity? (2) It is surely true that between "we men" and "what *we call* animals," there is an abyss, but that is not surprising if these are oppositional categories legitimating violent discrimination. But do "we" need to "endorse" the practice of calling them all "the animal," "animals," etc.? And if we did not, would the abyss remain?

Derrida attempts to make a pet out of a word-bird that landed on his shoulder while writing; he must have hoped it would work the same magic as *trace* and *différance* once did. The word is *animot*, in which he attempts to speak the plural of animals in the singular, and continually to remind us of how language is affecting our access to this complex world. It is an attempt to displace "animals" or "the animal" in our linguistic habit structure with a term that would disrupt the pattern of homogenization. It *is* a delightful word, but that may be the problem. We may precisely need tough new habits, reflecting all that is now visible of the horizon of violence stretching out before us, not a dainty new *indécidable*.

4. ANIMAL TALK

If a lion could talk, we could not understand him. (Wittgenstein)[21]

Standardly, attempts have been made to bridge the man/animal gap (or to reinforce it), by focusing not on the language we use to deal with animals, but on whether it is precisely language that distinguishes us from animals. It would be something of an irony if the most notable example of our distinction here were a linguistic opposition that licensed violence, suggesting perhaps that language might ultimately serve ends not so different from those we typically attribute to our "animal origins." The question of animal language has a long history that I shall not reprise here. But Derrida makes the interesting point that in thinking about animal language we need not focus on the level of cognitive sophistication possessed by this or that animal. We might instead consider the ethical issue – whether we could be "addressed" by an animal. Philosophers, Derrida writes, "have taken no account of whether what they call animal could *look at* them and *address* them from down there, from a wholly other origin" (382). The point is that addressing and being addressed are modes of communication, of responsibility, that, while often interwoven with what we humans call a "natural language" (such as English or French), are separable from such a capacity. Derrida could be said to be taking the leap that Levinas was unable to take when he doubted that the snake had a face. Derrida's reference to being addressed "from down there" seems an obvious response to Levinas's seemingly theologically impregnated reference to the Other, as "the most high."

5. SILENCE IS (NOT) CONSENT

If I can be called, addressed (accused, requested, ignored) by an animal, it is as if speech-act theory is being given a second life. First it saved some (mostly analytic) philosophers from limiting language to propositions. Now it offers us a way of getting into better focus something of our contact with animals.

But it is worth revisiting the general claim about the connection between language and violence. Understanding "animal" as a category rather than (just) a name allowed me to offer an explanation somewhat different from Derrida's of the violence this word licenses. It is equally important to stress the general ambivalence attached to naming, and to the naming of animals in particular.[22] For, on the whole, even if a name anticipates death and absence, the absence of a name can mean that death and violence are not even registered, let alone anticipated. The countless animals we kill to eat each day are recorded, at best, as numbers. The tags can be reused, and there is no other locus of memory. Giving a name to a favorite farm animal is a sentimental interruption of a process that will have to be overcome, usually with tears. But the true pathos of the absence of the name is perhaps best captured by the fact that in the sixth major period of global species extinction that we are currently witnessing, most of the 27,000 species that become extinct each year die out before even having been discovered, let alone named.[23] It is hard to mount a campaign to protect faceless and nameless creatures;[24] even an endangered lesser spotted bandersnatch has a better chance. As we have seen, Derrida points to a general version of this ambivalence when he speaks of the twin dangers – of appropriating the other (e.g., the animal) and of leaving it in silence (388). It is one of the greatest achievements of deconstruction to have drawn our attention to the fact that thinking (and responsible action) typically consists not in resolving ambivalences, but in "going through the undecidable," finding "productive" ways of acknowledging and responding to conflicting considerations.

And what is true of naming – that its relation to violence and death is ambivalent – is equally true of silence (and speaking out). Silence can preserve possibilities that articulation would prematurely close off, but, in many political contexts, silence is construed as consent, and can be fatal. Few animals are actually silent, though not many have a voice in decisions that affect their future. Animal rights advocates can be understood to be lending them a voice, enabling them at least notionally to be represented.[25]

We may imagine that ideally those who represented the interests of animals and spoke up for them would somehow smuggle themselves into their client's lives, and allow their specific silence to be captured in appropriate words.[26] Before Derrida's doubts, it was Wittgenstein who remarked about a big cat that

"If a lion could talk, we could not understand him." Understanding is not just propositional, but involves a reference to a form of life, unspoken background conditions, or being-in-the-world. Wittgenstein is fishing in Derrida's abyss.

6. THE ABYSSAL RUPTURE

There is an "abyssal rupture" between "we men" and "what we call animals" – and this formulation is very deliberate. That there is such a rupture is not in dispute, Derrida claims firmly. Rather we can more productively focus on "determining the number, form, sense or structure, the foliated consistency of this abyssal limit, these edges, this plural repeated, folded structure" (399). The game has moved on. It is here that Derrida announces his three-part thesis:

1. that this abyssal rupture does not simply have two edges (such as Man and Animal);
2. this folded border has a history, told from one side, the one we take to be ours;
3. what we take to be "animal life" is "a heterogeneous multiplicity of the living," or better "a multiplicity or organizations of relations between living and dead." This complexity of relations can never be objectified (399).

I want to pursue here the references to history. For, of course, time and history can always be counted on to skew a simple linear boundary. In particular, our relationship to this cat, or this snake, rides on the whole human record of our dealings with animals. For the sake of simplicity, I want to gesture first in the direction of our practical involvement with animals and then, briefly, our symbolic relationship. It will be my contention that Derrida's experience of being seen, even addressed, by his cat, requires some reference to this background to be understood. First, it is clear that the key stages in the development of human civilization have been marked by transformations in our relations to animals, and hence in our dominant attitudes. For hunters, on the one hand, animals are a wild, often unmanaged resource of food, clothing and even tools (as well as a source of wisdom!). For the farmer, on the other hand, animals compete for the crops he grows, they are put to work in the fields, and used for food, transportation, security, and clothing. Household pets – in particular cats and dogs – have no less practical a history, and one parallel to the development of the home. Dogs have long been hunting companions, but also house guards, and alarm units. And cats began their domestic life patrolling the boundaries of the house against poisonous snakes (Egypt) and against vermin (Europe) that would destroy food stores and carry disease. I point – "gesture" would be more accurate – in the direction of these background conditions because it suggests that being looked at by one's cat may be something of a special case. It is not clear, for example, whether this creature does any work around the Derrida household, whether she is an adored princess – in short what kind of life she has. Compare the "look" of a sheepdog, intensely alert, waiting for a precise signal that he will know exactly what to do with. And more generally, recall Vicki Hearne's work on animals, in which she argues that we can unlock through training – especially dogs and horses – what would otherwise be unrealized possibilities in animals (much as a mentor might do for a student).[27]

7. SHAPING THE ABYSS

Nowhere in a zoo can a stranger encounter the look of an animal. At the most the animal's gaze flickers and passes on. . . . That look between animal and men . . . has been extinguished. (John Berger)[28]

After dark, all cats are leopards. (Native American Proverb [Zuni])

Our response to Wittgenstein's claim that if a lion could speak, we could not understand him, surely depends on the kind of life that lion is leading. The question then would be: does not the manifold shape of the abyssal rupture between "we men" and "what we call animals" depend to a great extent on our mode of mutual engagement – either directly, or indirectly, even through the use of evocation and imagination? This is true even for those animals who are our companions – mostly dogs and cats. For there is something right about the stereotypes we have of dogs and cats – that dogs are more actively concerned to share a life, every bit of it, while cats train us just enough to serve their inscrutable needs. To reformulate this point – I am suggesting that the question of the abyss is inseparable from the question of the kind of relationship that obtains between a man and an animal.[29] The reason this is so is surely that what we mean by an abyss is inseparable from a failure of representation, and histori-cally embedded forms of life are just what is hard to reduce to a "representation." Though if the cat that looks at me is a hungry mountain lion sitting in a tree on the side of a narrow trail, I do not know quite where the abyss is to be found. We might conclude that the situation is perfectly transparent to each party – if, that is, I see the cat looking at me in time.

A systematically worked out elaboration of this point can be found in the Wari' understanding of their relation with another cat – the jaguar.[30] The Wari' are a South American tribe who used to practice funerary cannibalism, and who pride themselves on their hunting abilities. Their word for "jaguar" literally means "one who kills to eat," and jaguars are the most dangerous predators in the Amazonian rainforest. So far so good. But the Wari' don't just note the parallel between themselves as hunters and the jaguar. They have a fully blown perspectivism.

> [H]uman and jaguar perspectives on reality are mirror images of each other. . . . Wari', of course, perceive themselves as people and see jaguars as animals. For their part, however, jaguars perceive themselves as people, and see Wari' as jaguars. . . . when a jaguar attacks a person . . . an ordinary person . . . sees the jaguar as a feline with claws and teeth walking on all fours. . . . the jaguar, however, sees himself as a man walking upright and carrying a bow and arrows. . . . When this jaguar/hunter meets a person, to the jaguar's eyes, he looks like a jaguar, so he shoots it.[31]

We could of course argue that this belief is simply a way of covering up the real abyss between man and jaguar. But the Wari'/jaguar identification is based both on a common being-in-the world (hunting), and the fact that each is prey for the other. For the Wari', if a jaguar could speak, of course we could understand him. All too well. And this sense of broad equality and reciprocity of a being-in-common between humans and animals exhibited by Wari' beliefs is less exotic than it might seem, reflecting the shared assumptions of pre-industrial, pre-urban cultures everywhere.

We have expanded the cat category to make the point that the character of the abyss is altered by the quality of the man/animal relationship. We might think that the deepest abysses would arise where we have very little engagement with other life-forms. And yet despite Derrida's distrust of homogeneous biological continuities, the way he amplifies our understanding of animal life in the third part of his thesis on the abyssal rupture surely offers us a surprising glimpse of some sort of bridge over the abyss. His first characterization of animal life is "a heterogeneous multiplicity of the living." This gets refined into "a multiplicity of organizations of relations between living and dead." And yet surely this formulation opens the possibility of a real continuity among other life-forms, and between that multiplicity and ourselves. For this account is *no longer biological.* It applies equally to ... writing, to "culture" in general, perhaps to philosophy itself. Would Plato have balked at the suggestion that philosophy "mediated relations between life and death"? No, he would have asked for an acknowledgment. Derrida himself has taken the lead in demonstrating this. The irony would be that it is precisely a non-biological discourse of life that could apply equally to the human and the nonhuman, problematizing somewhat the idea of an abyssal rupture.[32]

If a consideration of our long history of our many different practical engagements with animals problematizes the idea that there is any global structure of the abyss, however complexly folded, this is no less true for the symbolic role of animals in human society. Rather than pursue this enormous topic here (it encompasses much of the anthropological literature, as well as Western folkloric tradition) allow me to make an observation: that many animals are symbolically deployed as boundary negotiating operators, servants themselves, that is, of *an* abyss at least. Coyote, fox, spider, cat, jackal, jaguar[33] – have all been given this work to do – educating men, bringing fire, mediating the transition between life and death, etc. We perhaps learn more about how humans project onto animals than anything about these animals themselves, although, as we mentioned with "the domestic cat and dog," the boundary being managed is a very concrete one – the human dwelling. But it might be just this symbolic/projective dimension that we need to have in view when trying to understand that central practice many humans engage in – that of eating meat, underdetermined, as most admit, by our need for protein. The driving force of Hegel's account of the life-and-death struggle is each party's demonstration to the other that there is something they value more than life itself, by being willing to risk their life. Might not the legitimacy of meat-eating rest, albeit precariously, not on our clear superiority to "the animal," but on our need to demonstrate this over and over again?

8. A CULT OF SACRIFICE

Derrida's analysis of this issue is profound. In a breathtaking analysis drawing together the shame and nudity of Adam and Eve, Cain's sense of fault and crime, Bellepheron's modesty, and Prometheus' compensatory gift of fire to an otherwise naked and vulnerable man, Derrida argues that what unites both biblical and Greek myth is a distinctive way of understanding the proper privilege of man over the animal, a way perhaps characteristic of the West. The invariable schema is that

> what is proper to man, his superiority over and subjugation of the animal ... his emergence out of nature, his sociality, his access to knowledge and technics ... all that is proper to man would derive from this originary fault, indeed from this default in propriety – and from the imperative that finds in it its imperative and resilience. (413)

This passage is the key to the "conceit" of the whole paper, that the question of autobiography is that of my *truth*, and that the question of truth in general, and *my* truth in particular is also structured by this logic of restitution, paying back, making good, putting right, correcting an original fault. Man is distinctive in knowing he is naked, needing to be clothed, supplemented with technics (like fire, and, we might add, writing and even philosophy), aware of his lack. The animal sadly, blindly, just lives in or lives out its impoverished position. This is the key to the primal scene with the cat, in which the animal sees my nakedness. There is an implication parallel perhaps with Nietzsche's recognition that while men project an imperturbable silence onto women, those white-sailed ships on the horizon, women know better – that on board it is all chatter and confusion.[34] That women have often been taught to sacrifice themselves for men suggests that a parallel logic continues. God's preference for Abel over Cain has to do, it is said (and perhaps this is some of the point of the story of Abraham and Isaac), with his willingness to engage in animal sacrifice. And the point of that, as I understand it, is that it is an affirmation of our distinctive privilege over the animal's mere fullness of being, and more broadly of our non-natural status. Animals, then, are slaves and sacrificial offerings to our need for ritual symbolic confirmation of our peculiar self-understanding.

We may surmise that the (external) animal we eat stands in for the (internal) animal we must overcome. And by eating, of course, we internalize it! On this reading, our carnivorous violence towards other animals would serve as a mark of our civilization, and hence indirectly legitimate all kinds of other violence. If we are to target anything for transformation it would be this culture (or should we say cult) of fault and sacrifice. Derrida's brilliance lies in tracking it along the finest filaments.

Finally, to the extent that animals have been deployed mythologically as category mediators – the Egyptian jackal god Anubis presided over the embalming of the dead – we perhaps find anticipations of the concerns of philosophy itself. For much of the work of philosophy has been to relieve the damage done to our thinking by the rigid treatment of oppositions (treating categories as descriptive) – such as life/death, mind/body, self/other.

As in *Specters of Marx*[35] where he lists ten plagues of the contemporary world,[36] Derrida does not hesitate in this selection to list many of the horrific ways in which we treat animals (394–5), even using the word genocide.[37] "No one can deny the unprecedented proportion of this subjection of the animal. Such a subjection ... can be called violence in the most morally neutral sense" (394).[38] "Everybody knows this," he repeats rhetorically. His point (going back to the title of the essay) is that we have here something quite as indubitable as Descartes's cogito. Indeed, as he puts it, "it precedes the indubitable" (397), even though it occupies the opposite relational pole (oriented to the other, not the self). But he is *also* insisting that we need to see the deeper picture reflected in this litany of anguish. His answer is that two hundred years ago when Bentham insisted that the real question was not whether animals could think or speak, but "Can they suffer?" – everything changed. Bentham inaugurated a reversal from considering animals in terms of their powers, to considering their passivity.

> What we have witnessed is a war waged over the matter of pity ... a war ... between those who violate animal life but even and also this sentiment of compassion, and ... those who appeal to an irrefutable testimony to this pity. (399)

Derrida insists we need "to think" this war, that it is passing through a critical phase, and that thinking this war is an obligation for each of us.

9. THE DIVIDED LINE

> Getting back to Descartes, I would only want to say that the discontinuity he saw between animals and human beings was the result of incomplete information. (Coetzee)[39]

However dangerous it might be to admit them, it would be just as foolish to dismiss the many "continuities" between humans and animals. It is telling that in the fifth of his *Cartesian Meditations*,[40] Husserl addresses the question of the other by reference to my "animate organism."[41] And it could well be argued that much compassion we feel for the physical pain of other humans is directly extendable *without translation* to other mammals.[42] Is not Derrida's firm stand against "homogeneous continuity" at least in tension with the organismic under-pinnings of that compassion? Perhaps the point is that we must try not to allow our moral imagination to end with those creatures who seem to function like us. And that it is where obvious continuities break down that the ethical begins. To be morally embraced it should not be necessary to be furry (like a cat). The cat is the exemplary object of compassion – an expressive, cuddly, warm-blooded mammal. There are cat-shelters in many parts of the world. Cat books are a publishing phenomenon. But compassion has its limits – marked perhaps by Levinas's doubts about the face of the snake. Perhaps we could propose instead an *objective* compassion, which tries, as far as possible not to be limited by our actual capacity for fellow-feeling, and recognizes "life itself," in each of its forms, as addressing us. This is also to register a concern that being able to "address the human," in the personal way available to Derrida's cat, might be too high a bar for being protected against violence.

10. PITY AND THE BIG PICTURE

Only connect. (E. M. Forster)

Derrida lists our many abuses of animals, and then frames this two-century saga in terms of a "war on pity." It is worth noting, however, that even if "everyone knows" each of the items on the list (394–5) (and, in fact, many are ignorant of the ongoing march of mass species extinction), very few put all this together at one time. It is just not clear that we all have such a full picture, whatever interpretation we subsequently make. The fact that there is no strong popular vision of another way forward is also critical. As a supplement to thinking the war on pity, we are perhaps at a time at which two broad processes are moving in opposite directions: the first is the growing importance of *interconnected phenomena* (in its extreme form the "global environmental crisis"), and the second is the *growth of an increasingly administered society* in which the kind of knowledge needed for global citizenship has little local value, and political power is used to shelter our wide-eyed enclaves of ignorance and irresponsibility from the immediate consequences of their folly.

It is important to note here a dramatic shift in the political value of what might broadly be called the postmodern, where that is identified with the critique of grand narrative, a certain irreducible perspectivism, and anti-realism. For it gives a field day to those with a genuine appetite for world-historical domination. Derrida has never been a postmodernist. The productive tension in his work is now between a genuinely multi-folded constructivism, in which various logics interweave and play themselves out within a broadly materialist history (logic of the gift, logic of sacrifice, logic of shame, guilt and fault, etc.), and what I would call a methodological skepticism, which would Socratically seek out the back-room deals, the abyssal cracks in any and every consensual complacency. Perhaps between these two paths, we should not choose, even if we thought we could.

Do animals need our pity? The "war on pity" is surely much greater in scope than the animal world. Certainly in the US, where child poverty rates average over 20 percent, higher than any European countries, alongside a greater GNP than any country in the history of the world, this war extends to the poor and to racial minorities. The role of race in limiting pity seems clear enough when we look at the selective basis for international military intervention. Rwanda no, Bosnia yes.

One of the complicating factors in the "war on pity" is that most people have a well-developed sense of pity; it's just that we collude with each other to veil from ourselves the occasions that would surely solicit it. Much of the barbaric interface occurs behind closed doors – in abattoirs, laboratories, agro-industrial production units, at the end of long driveways. This suggests that we need a war on "deception," on "self-deception," and, yes, on the ignorance that knows many things but does not connect them.

11. CALCULATING PITY

If the question of pity is understood individualistically, as first it must be, it is even then immediately drawn up into a calculation that it would prefer to have avoided.[43] The classic dilemma here is that of the buffalo that falls through the winter ice at Yellowstone National Park. The rangers *could* rescue it, but in doing so would deprive the local bears (and cubs) of food. More broadly this points to a genuine conflict between animal rights advocates (such as Singer and Regan) and environmentalists (such as Callicott and Holmes Rolston III). The former focus largely on practices affecting denumerable individual animals, usually those under human control or management. The latter deal with ecosystems, with ways of promoting healthy balances between different species, etc. This has reproduced ancient splits between individualism and holism to such a point that political objections have been raised against strong versions of any such holism. Aldo Leopold, a justly famous pioneer of the land ethic once wrote: "A thing is right when it tends to preserve the integrity, stability, and beauty of the biotic community. It is wrong when it tends otherwise."[44] Some have responded with the charge of eco-fascism,[45] for the apparent willingness to sacrifice some animals (even humans!) to the greater good.[46] It is clear enough that environmental concerns cannot be dealt with just by individual compassion. It should be recalled that the same Bentham who said that "The question is: Can they suffer?" had as his motto not a question but an exhortation: *Calculemus* ("Let us calculate!"). As a utilitarian, he bought into trade-offs from the outset. What Derrida sees as the moment of "passivity" (moving from a power to the capacity to suffer) is immediately objectified. Just as the *third* enters Levinas's face-to-face dyad, so the question of comparison, judgment, calculation is always on the horizon. The cases in which compassion is not followed by comparison are exceptions. If there is a war on pity, it is, I believe, a consequence of what, under existing historical conditions (massive human population expansion and "development"), is a necessary commodification. And that war cannot be fought without addressing its underlying causes. Environmentalism is perhaps another owl flying at dusk.

Not all environmentalists share the concern for balance and harmony. Some stress the value of change, even dramatic change, and see the planet as a dynamic, turbulent place. But the logical conclusion of this is that the species Man might be, as Foucault put it (in a slightly different sense), "erased like a face drawn in sand at the edge of the sea."[47] If we send two-thirds of the species on the planet into extinction, then die out ourselves, we can assume that evolutionary forces would continue, and perhaps a new dominant species, less predisposed to violence, would emerge in a few million years. One would have to be very patient, and very detached to acquiesce in a process with such an outcome. When one reflects on what exactly is being lost by this dramatic disposal of the fruits of evolution, and where one comes by the values in play in protesting such a loss, the answers that emerge seemingly unbidden are surprising and interesting. We seem to value diversity for its own sake, but also for the sake of the developmental possibilities it maximizes. A diverse gene pool enhances the chances for individual adaptation and survival. And that seems to promote increasingly complex organisms, and relationships between them. We value these things without specific reference to the human – that is, we can imagine valuing another life-system that had these properties without it including *Homo sapiens*. If anything we are grateful for our capacity to appreciate these things, but what we are appreciating seems to have an intrinsic value. Rather than just casting aside this unfashionable thought, we might consider one possible explanation for this – that it is not so much that this *buoyant* nature has intrinsic value, but rather that some such exuberant productivity lies at the heart of value itself.[48]

If indeed our environmental "problems" are not just an adventure in difference, but symptoms of a coming crisis, and we were to look around for the source of the imbalance we would find little until we looked down at the ground on which we are standing – the explosive growth in the human population. It is that, more than anything, that forces the zero-sum choices in which we gain, and other animals (indeed entire species) lose. And here I am not convinced that Derrida's cat has a meow (or teeth) strong enough to address the scale of such a problem.

12. FINALLY, WE ALMOST CATCH THE WOOZLE . . .

As I promised, I have strongly supported Derrida's position, and vigorously, I hope, entered into critical dialogue with it. I trust this is the kind of response he was calling for. It was also a response to all animals who have looked to us humans for relief, and a response to those who have not and never will address us. One of my concerns is that there is, if only in a residual way, a certain hubris, in insisting on being addressed by an animal (once we have discovered that this is possible!). Much of that to which we do violence has no name, will never know our name, and does not address us. We must perhaps begin with the ruptures in the familiar, with the uncanny we find at home. But we must also step off the porch and reflect on the violence that is being done in our name, without our knowing it, and the violence happening behind the back of history merely as an aggregated consequence of the individually reasonable things we do.

Violence is not, I believe, a natural human disposition. Or if it is, it can be civilized, and the conditions on which it thrives starved of sustenance. The threat of violence-upon-violence both for humans and other animals, comes largely from increasing competition for scarce resources, driven by our own unprecedented expansion of numbers. There are optimists who argue that the human population will level off – the affluent want fewer children. But affluence currently construed would put greater pressure than ever on the planet's limited resources.

It is tempting to call for a disinterested repudiation of our narrow anthropocentric selfishness, to argue for moral evolution beyond a species tribalism. But pacifism cannot be relied on to prevent war. Instead we need to come to recognize that our inter-est, our inter-esse, our being-connected, being-related, is in need of enlightenment even for the sake of our own survival. We need to come to recognize that dependency – and inter-dependency – is the name of the game. And then we need not fear the impurity of motive that would save ourselves along with the planet.

In the end the "war on pity" tells only part of the story. We need a war on the culpable blindness that hides from us the sites at which compassion is pathologically suppressed. And we need a war on the environmental destruction that is multiplying the occasions calling for such pity as we may still possess. Environmentalism is the owl of Minerva for our time. Its screech from on high is clear: if we do not hang together, we will surely hang separately. Following our own tracks is a road to nowhere.

CHAPTER EIGHT: FERRY

NEITHER MAN NOR STONE

Luc Ferry

The photograph shows a bull being followed by a disturbing crowd. It is immediately apparent that he is going to die. But as the scene evokes a lynching ritual, we sense that the road to this final liberation will be long and painful. This strange drama unfolds in our time, in Spain, in a little village called Coria. It is a game, of course, the rules of which are extremely simple: at four in the morning, a bull is set loose on the streets, where he is riddled with darts, first in the eyes and most sensitive parts. Four hours later, the animal is beaten until he dies of his wounds. In the picture, he looks like a pin cushion. The little white dots are so close together he almost looks snow-covered. Two men are pointing at him, smiling. One of them holds a banderilla which he will plant, several seconds later (as appears in another photo), in the animal's anus. The entire population participates in the festival ...

This game has nothing, or almost nothing, to do with bullfighting. No particular talent is required to participate, and no one would dream of comparing it to an art. It is simply an enactment, solely for entertainment, of the reality of animal suffering. And people find this suffering captivating. The proof being that this type of entertainment, in which crowds gather to see the intensity of the pain preceding the killing, has its equivalent in every, or almost every, country and at every period. In France, during the Restoration, people sought entertainment in open-air cafes near the gates of Paris:[1] here a rooster is stoned to death, there an archery match is held in which the target is a live rat nailed to a wooden plank. In our day, in Australia, the rabbit population becomes a real scourge from time to time. But is it necessary to organize baseball games in which the animal, replacing the ball, literally explodes on impact with the bat, to the vast enjoyment of large, enthusiastic crowds?

People like to talk about the cruelty of Chinese markets, where chicks and kittens are "cleaned," placed on a spit and grilled alive, snakes are cut into slices while being kept alive for days on end to better preserve their flesh, heads of monkeys are drilled open in order that one may enjoy the warm brain as the animal continues weakly to struggle ... Literally and figuratively, there is nothing prohibiting us today from continuing to torture "nonhuman beings," since they are merely unimportant heaps of matter. And if, for one reason or another, they are unlucky enough to be classified as "vermin," their "destruction" even becomes a legitimate and useful exercise. The final prohibitions fall away, and any means become valid to arrive at ends condoned by both the public authority and the ambiant Cartesianism. The animal caught in a trap, captured alive, will not end his days sweetly: alone against man, who possesses all rights over it, custom has it that it will pay dearly for belonging to the realm of those considered noxious to the masters of the earth.

Even in the case of stock farming, the mere fact that the animal is destined to be killed for consumption is almost always enough to ensure that it will have a bad time of it, *because as mere raw material, it is deprived of all dignity.* Thus the chickens plucked alive, the live frogs whose legs are removed, the rabbits whose eyes are pulled out for bleeding, the pigs who are beaten before being slaughtered ("it makes them taste better"), if possible slowly and painfully ... Certain peasants are kind enough to kill them first, but they are less common than one thinks, and in any case they are not obliged to do so. I still have a cookbook, published in France between the wars, which specifies that for a certain recipe to be successful "the hare must be skinned alive." A strange requirement indeed ...

We cannot help but wonder: Why so much hatred if animals are only things?

To answer this, we need a phenomenology of the enigmatic nature of animals and of the contradictory sentiments it evokes in us, particularly in a modern world in which the hierarchies between beings have grown hazy. Psychoanalysis has no doubt taught us a great deal about the nature of sadism as a disposition of the subject. It has taken less interest, on the other hand, in the *objects* upon which this sadism most readily alights, the first among them being the living body of the animal.

Here is why, I believe, its enigmatic nature so fascinates us.

We are, at least since Descartes, authorized to treat animals as simple *things* devoid of the slightest ethical significance. The Grammont law protected *domestic* animals against cruelty inflicted *in public.* But the legislation, which is still fundamentally Cartesian, doesn't even mention wild animals or private brutality. This is to suggest that they have no moral status and that in treating them "like animals" our "super-ego," or whatever stands in place of it, is safe. But what pleasure (or what terror), what unavowable private quiver would come over us if we were *really* only dealing with machines? Maupertuis already said it, speaking against Descartes in a famous letter: "If animals were pure machines, to kill them would be a morally indifferent but ridiculous act: like smashing a watch."

The remark is more profound than it seems. Animals are neither automata, nor plants with roots "in the belly," as the Cartesians had it. The truth is we know they suffer. And even if we cannot evaluate the exact nature of their pain, the degree of consciousness attached to their cries, the signs are sufficiently visible, the symptoms sufficiently transparent for there to be no doubt as to their similarity to those of humans.

Now, the spectacle of suffering cannot leave one entirely indifferent, whether it is a matter of a pig or a rabbit. For it is, according to a certain conception of life, the ultimate symbol of not belonging to the world of things: it is *finalized,* it induces reactions, such as flight, which is evidence of a *significance.* At the end of the eighteenth century, life was apt to be defined as "the faculty to act according to the representation of a goal" – which is why it was believed that plants, which cannot move "because they have their stomachs in the earth," were not living beings. This definition no longer has a place within the structure of contemporary sciences. It nonetheless continues to have meaning from the perspective of a phenomenology of the signs of freedom: finalized movement, or action if one prefers, remains for us the visible criteria of animal nature, what distinguishes it from unorganized matter, but also from the vegetable world – which is why the intermediaries, anemones or carnivorous plants, are still somewhat mysterious to us. And it is because of this capacity to act in a non-mechanical fashion, oriented by a goal, that the animal, *analogon* of a free being, appears to bear a certain relationship to us, whether we like it or not. Its suffering is evidence of this. *Thus considered in nonutilitarian fashion, this suffering furnishes a synthesis between the idea that one must respect animals in order not to debase man and the idea that animals possess intrinsic rights.* This is the significance of the *analogy.*

Thus it is not a matter of returning to and contesting the fundamental difference established by Rousseau between animal-kind and humankind. The animal remains a creature of nature. Yet how can we help but account for that part of it that is not merely a thing? How can we deny its enigmatic nature? In this respect, suffering is but one of many signs that allow us to see that the animal and the automaton cannot be included in the same classification of beings.

This is no doubt why animals can arouse both sadism and compassion in us – sentiments that appear to be the two faces of a same psychic disposition. The animal is the *dreamed* object. We should recall here what Freud teaches us about "waking dreams": they are the stories one tells oneself in order to satisfy, at least in an imaginary fashion, certain desires left unsatisfied in reality. Hence the banal yet embarrassing nature of these "castles in Spain" in which the hero, which is to say oneself, is overwhelmed by the success denied him in the real world. Money, power, love: he has everything, almost to excess. As the saying goes: "The neurotic builds castles in Spain, the psychotic lives in them, the psychiatrist collects the rent ..."

In dreams, then, the plot corresponds to our desires. But when these desires are forbidden, because they are reputed to be immoral or inappropriate – and Lord knows this is common – one has to cheat: the storyline must be "elaborated upon," sufficiently deformed, encoded, for our moral standards to lose their bearings – yet clear enough, of course, for our desires to be fulfilled. Thus, dreams evade the vigilance of the superego to more calmly address the libido. This is what accounts for their strange obscurity.

Whether this theory is "true" or not is largely irrelevant here. It offers a model that allows us to understand the enigmatic nature of animals and, with it, the complexity of the sentiments of sadism or compassion it evokes: by asserting that animals are things, simple mechanisms, we evade the prohibitions that weigh upon possible sadistic impulses. By acting in this fashion, we do more than legitimize the impulses: we eliminate them, since there is no such thing as sadism toward inanimate objects. But since we are more or less covertly aware that in truth animals are not entirely things, that as luck would have it they suffer, the tortures we inflict remain interesting.

If we raise our sights from the phenomenology of feelings to philosophy, should humanism itself not be incriminated? Are we not justified in discerning in it a formidable ideological enterprise aimed at legitimizing, by way of "rationalization," the colonization of "brute" nature and more, of the living in all its "prehuman" forms? Is it not humanism that dictates that compassion toward animals must be ridiculed at any price and qualified as infantile "sentimentality?" The question cannot be rejected out of hand but warrants closer examination.

IS HUMANISM ZOOPHOBIC?

The hypothesis of a secret complicity between humanism, which is necessarily anthropocentric, and the exploitation of nature does not seem particularly original. Within the context of contemporary thought, it is a standard argument among critics of modernity. There are neo-Marxist versions of it in Adorno's and Horkheimer's *Dialectic of Enlightenment*, and neo-Heideggerian versions are even easier to find. It is this second path that Elisabeth de Fontenay chose to follow in an exemplary article entitled "La bête est sans raison."[2] In it she develops three theses, which I will present by moving from the general to the particular:

1. The essence of modernity, since Descartes, is nothing but *Ratio*, which can be defined either as the functional rationale of capitalism in its quest for economic profitability (Marxist version), or as the "world of technology" devoting man's energies to the domination of the earth (Heideggerian version). This vocation, which emerged with Cartesianism, came to fruition with the ideology of the Enlightenment and its belief in progress. Thus there is "an irrevocable ontological complicity between the founding subjectivity and the mechanism," since, once the subject is established as the sole and unique pole of meaning and value, nature can no longer be conceived as anything but a gigantic reservoir of neutral objects, or raw materials destined for human consumption.
2. From this perspective, in which rationality becomes the *absolute* norm of all evaluation, that which is without reason can only be devoid of value. Foucault had already applied a similar grid to his reading of the history of madness, defined as "*déraison*," unreason. Elisabeth de Fontenay chose another object, the animal: "Because the very essence of this *Aufklärung*, which we translate as *Ratio*, is technology, the Cartesian theory of the animal-machine in its paradoxical self-evidence became the centerpiece of classical science." In the same way one could "deconstruct" the modern representation of the "primitive," the "marginal," or of women, who, according to machinist ideologies, are reputed to be more "intuitive" than "rational." But let's stick to animals ...
3. From here, technoscience could unabashedly and unreservedly wage a veritable campaign of violence against animals. The proof lies in the close link between experimentation and vivisection, an extreme form of legitimized torture:

The great affair of our times is thus to force life to give up its secret. "When one speaks of vivisection," writes Georges Canguilhem, "one speaks of the demand that life be maintained as long as possible." Isn't that the very definition of torture? A terrorist theory, a violent vision, an armed eye, an unflinching hand, an implacable collaboration between the scalpel and the microscope: curiosity kills slowly, pleasurably, strong in the knowledge that it is at the service of truth, drunk with consulting so many pulsating breasts. The Enlightenment may have fulfilled rather than abolished the heritage of Christianity by devoting itself to this impassive manipulation of the animal.

Foucault said that "reason is a torture whose subject is the agent." Similarly, Elisabeth de Fontenay speaks of "rational despotism," free of all compassion, of the "work of the *Ratio* under the surveillance of the *Cogito*" for which "nature is nothing but the substratum of domination."

It is unfortunate that the analysis, being too "applied," too unilateral, so obviously underestimates the complexity of the modern universe. ... An entire tradition of "humanitarian" republicanism, from Michelet to Hugo, revolted, *in the name of the Enlightenment*, against the cruelty of men. From a simple empirical point of view, it is most often scientists who, in their professional capacities, are interested in the fate of nature and wish to limit vivisection, or militate among the ranks of the ecologists. To associate contemporary science with Cartesianism results, I'm afraid, from a misconception which the Heideggerian philosophers are the last not to have abandoned. Instead they would have us believe that it is necessary to "deconstruct" humanism at all costs in order to respond to the threat of a metaphysical anthropocentrism. We are given a choice, so to speak, between Descartes on the one side, and Heidegger, Derrida, or Foucault on the other. The strategy is too clunky, the connections too obvious to still be convincing today. We have to get beyond this, we mustn't give in so readily to alternatives that run counter to the diversity of the Enlightenment heritage, which cannot be identified solely with the forces of instrumental or technical reason. Humanism cannot be reduced to the dimensions of a Cartesian "metaphysics of subjectivity" anymore than the rights of man are the "superstructure" of the bourgeoisie.

All the more reason to remain vigilant and avoid the traps humanism sets for itself when it appears to legitimize, in the name of the separation of humankind and the animal kingdom, an imperious domination of the latter. Here is another example worth considering.

HUMANISM TO THE RESCUE OF BULLFIGHTING?

In an article entitled "L'esprit de la corrida" ["The Spirit of Bullfighting"], Alain Renaut, who is what I believe one calls an *aficionado*, endeavors to give these "games" an aesthetic, if not ethical, justification, in order to facilitate defending their existence against ritual attacks by zoophiles.[3] Right from the start his text has the merit of avoiding the trap of arguing for tradition. To seek to legitimize an institution by the simple fact "that it has existed for a long time" is a senseless enterprise: on these grounds, one could call for the preservation of slavery or *just primae noctis* in countries where these practices have subsisted "uninterrupted" for centuries, to repeat the terms of the law on bullfighting. This seems obvious, yet it mustn't be forgotten that it is in the name of this parody of an argument, contrary to all our republican principles, that French legislation continues, to this day, to exempt bullfighting from the laws protecting animals from public cruelty.

Retracing the history of Madrilenian bullfighting, examining and dismissing the sociological and psychoanalytic interpretations of its latent or unconscious meanings one by one, Renaut ultimately concludes that only a philosophical approach can enable one to grasp its true *spirit*. More concerned with *understanding* than with *explaining*, Renaut traces the lines of his own interpretation based on the remarks of matadors such as Paquirri, the "hero," so it seems of the 1970s, who in 1984 was to fall victim to a little black *toro* named Avispado: "What I really like is educating the beasts. All they know is how to attack. Sometimes slowly, sometimes viciously. They're like children starting school. You have to teach them everything, from b, to a, to ba, to the whole alphabet. You have to discover their potential ..."

I'm tempted to say he wouldn't be my choice of a babysitter. But let us avoid cheap shots and instead follow our guide in this matter in order to understand this strange confession. Here is what Alain Renaut makes of it:

> Less shocking than naïvely blundering in its choice of images, Paquirri's admission makes clearly apparent the significance the fight held for a *matador* who conceived of his profession as the will to affirm the superiority of reason: because the *toro* represents brute force, because it incarnates all that is not human, bullfighting symbolizes man's combat with nature – a nature that is constantly threatening to engulf him from without and from within, while he attempts to break away from it by countering violence and aggressivity with reason and calculation.

As in Rousseau or Kant, man is defined by this "breaking away" from a natural state to which the animal remains prisoner – and it is the enactment of this difference, the foundation of modern humanism, that we are witnessing at a bullfight. Hence, according to Renaut, its aesthetic quality: it is one of the tangible, visible illustrations of the humanistic idea par excellence, as he indicates in a passage that summarizes the heart of his argument. Here, according to him, is what happens in the arena:

> In barely twenty minutes, a savage force is subjected to the will of man, who manages to slow, channel, and direct its attacks. The submission of brute nature (which is to say violence) to man's free will, the victory of freedom over nature, elicits an aesthetic emotion in the spectator. Not that the goal of tauromachy is to create beauty through elegant and successfully executed maneuvers, but fighting in the bullring means commanding the course of the bull, triggering its direction with one's voice or gesture, altering its trajectory

with a simple movement of the wrist, determining as much as possible where the animal will move and where, pass after pass, he will be subjected to the toreador's control: herein resides the true aesthetic dimension of bullfighting, on the basis of which it no longer seems absurd to consider it an art, if it is true that artistic creation is in some way connected to the submission of unreasoning matter to a will that gives it form.

The interpretation is seductive: it has the advantage of furnishing a plausible reading for cultural aspects of a game which does indeed attract more than just sadistic, bloodthirsty crowds. Nonetheless, I cannot share the idea that the love of bullfighting corresponds to a philosophical commitment to humanism. This is not a simple empirical or personal question. It is true that bullfighting interests me very little and that I have some trouble understanding the pleasure others derive from it. But the very fact that I am indifferent means that I am not militantly hostile toward it either. The question lies elsewhere: it has to do with the nature of humanism, an illustration of which Renaut sees or believes he sees in bullfighting. I would like to show in what follows that it still remains Cartesian ("non-Kantian" – just as one says "non-Euclidean") while the object to which it is applied (the living being) is "non-Cartesian."

From a strictly philosophical point of view, the stakes of this debate are far from small: it is a matter of knowing whether a position one claims to be the expression of a "theoretical humanism" implies that nature, in this case the living being, is relegated to the status of an object to be dominated or "civilized." If this were the case, I must admit that the "nonmetaphysical" humanism, whose principles I have attempted to elaborate for the past fifteen years in each of my books, would make little sense to me. I say this because it would mean that there would no longer be a significant difference between the Cartesian goal of making ourselves "masters and possessors of nature" and the Kantian goal of a humanism concerned with respecting *the diversity of the orders of reality*. I say this, too, because the Heideggerian deconstruction of modernity which we have constantly denounced as unilateral would finally be justified: it would rightfully be able to show, in very Cartesian fashion, how humanism *in all its forms* leads to justifying what one would be forced to call a "colonization of nature."

Everyone knows or ultimately finds out that ecology, or at least the ecology movement, possesses some questionable roots, and that the musty smell of the Petainist obsession with one's native soil often lingers in its wake. Must we conclude that the love of man necessarily implies the hatred of nature? Must one give in, because "ecologists can be fascists," to the polemical construction that makes the proof of one's humanity depend on one's degree of disdain toward plants and animals? I don't think so, although I already know, ideological confrontations being what they are, that in the years to come the debate on ecology will increasingly take this caricatural form. Nothing prevents us from anticipating this tendency.

But let's get back to bullfighting. In what way does Renaut's interpretation bring into play a humanism that is still *Cartesian*?

Let us return to the essential element, the element without which the entire argument would make no sense: the fight must take place against a *living* being and not a simple machine. That the bull incarnates brute force, which is "civilized" by the toreador, as Renaut argues, is not in question here (though the idea of "civilization" suggested is somewhat problematic). But clearly it is necessary that this force be neither mechanical, nor entirely natural: no fight is possible against a locomotive (a machine conducted and constructed by men), or against the waves of the ocean (a simple material event). The toreador is not Don Quixote: he must master a living force, which is to say a force that is *mobile, finalized, and, to some extent at least, however small, unpredictable.* Without this condition there could *never* be a victory of the animal over man, and the game would be entirely without interest.

Thus human freedom must prevail, not over brute force in general but over a *living being.* I maintain that, given these conditions, the aesthetic satisfaction derived from the spectacle of the bullfight cannot be based on the fact that the latter illustrates or "enacts" a nonmetaphysical idea of humanism. It is clear, in effect, that this type of domination of the living being, which is perfectly satisfying from a Cartesian perspective, is unacceptable within the broader Kantian perspective which Renaut in fact claims as his own. Not at all out of "sentimentality," as fools might say, but because, for anti-Cartesian philosophical reasons which must be examined, *the reduction of an animal to the state of a thing* (its killing) cannot be the object of a *game.* It may, in some instances, be a necessity, but never entertainment for those who are attentive to the *diversity of the orders of reality.* And no one can pretend that the "killing" (or even the animal's suffering) is not essential to bullfighting, for as we know it was on this precise point that the legislation, which since the mid-nineteenth century had forbidden fighting with or among animals, had to be changed, following long and heated debates.

We know Kant's own position: animals have no rights (as zoophiles would have it), but on the other hand we do have certain, indirect duties toward them, or at least "on their behalf" ("*in Ansehung von,*" says Kant). The justification for this "behalf" may be deemed insufficient. Why would there be duties "on behalf" of animals if there were not *within them* some *intrinsic* particularity worthy of respect? Kant suggests a path for reflection when he writes the following: "Because animals are an *analogue* of humanity, we observe duties toward humanity when we regard them as analogous to humanity, and thus we satisfy our obligations toward it." Why? Simply because, as opposed to what Descartes and his automata makers thought, the living being is not a thing, the animal is not a stone, nor even a plant. So what, one may ask? So life, defined as "the faculty to act according to the representation of a goal," is an *analogue of freedom. As such* (that is to say in its highest forms) and because it maintains a relationship of analogy with that which makes us human, it is (or should be) the object of a *certain* respect, a respect which, by way of animals, we *also* pay ourselves.

It is not by chance if Kant links up here with one of Judaism's most profound intuitions: man is an antinatural being, a being who lives by law (this, in fact, is what prohibits both the Kantian tradition and Judaism from identifying with radical ecology). He can thus dispose of plants and animals *to a certain degree* – but not at will (*nach Belieben*), not by *playing* at killing them, even if within the rules of art and as testimony to his humanity. According to the Pentateuch, slaughtering is to be practiced not only without cruelty but in moderation. There is great wisdom and depth here, *for this position is not accompanied by the "naturalist" and vitalist principles that ordinarily justify zoophile arguments.* There is no possible confusion here between man and animal in the great cosmic order. No reduction, either, of the dignity of one or the other to the simple calculating logic of pleasure and pain. Instead, attention is paid to the enigmatic uniqueness of animals which the Cartesian machinery, entirely devoted to the domination of the earth, casts unreservedly on the side of things.

This friendly disagreement brings three further reflections to mind.

The first is that the *philosophical* status of the living being apparently has yet to be considered, stymied as we still are by the powerful antinomy between the (Cartesian) mechanism and (romantic, then Nietzschean) vitalism. Rousseau, Kant, and Fichte have pointed toward paths for reflection. As we have seen, they never reduced animals to simple mechanisms. When Rousseau described animals as being governed by the code of instinct, he granted that they enjoyed the privilege of affectivity and even of thought in the same breath. In a course during the winter semester of 1929–1930, the "first" Heidegger, who was closer to Kant than is ordinarily believed, had also attempted to elucidate the meaning of animal ambiguity through his analysis of the proposition: "The stone is without world, the animal is poor in world, man is creator of world (*Weltbildend*)." "Poor in world" means it is "less" than man, no doubt, who can "exist," *transcend* natural cycles to rise to the consideration of questions that no longer bear only on intraworldly facts but on the world's existence itself. It is nonetheless "more" than the stone, which attains no representation and is endowed with no finalized movement. However, Heidegger emphasizes that the terms "more" and "less" are misleading here: they suggest a continuity between orders of reality, whereas these orders are qualitatively different. Which doesn't mean that no *analogies* can be made between them, in particular in the case of the latter two: let's not forget that many things have been done against/to animals, *exactly as many things have been done against/to humans.* Here the expression "it's not by chance . . ." is appropriate.

Faced with the reproach to the humanist tradition, that it is nothing but anthropocentrism, a "metaphysics of subjectivity," the verification of which can be seen in the devastation of the earth and the torture of animals at the heart of a "technological world," it is time to show that a non-Cartesian humanism evades the absurd alternative to which radical ecology condemns us: the "step backward" or barbarity. And since the philosopher is occasionally asked to elaborate on the concrete consequences of the distinctions he establishes, here is one that clearly indicates the dividing line with Cartesianism: I am speaking of what takes place in Canada, where "animal ethics committees," working in university hospitals, are responsible for monitoring, and if need be modifying, the protocol of experiments in which animal suffering is involved. Why, after all, should we passively accept the right of irresponsible scientists to indulge in the most improbable experiments in the privacy of their laboratories? I am not claiming that this is the general rule – though every year countless experiments are performed in which great suffering is inflicted on thousands, even millions of animals, without the slightest benefit. And yet rules of deontology are no doubt already in effect among most scientists. I see nothing wrong, however, with the idea of ensuring that these rules are observed in practice, and that one not be allowed to do anything at all, not only "on behalf" of animals but to them.

I had an opportunity to closely examine the report of the meetings of the University of Quebec's animal ethics committee: I must admit that in several hundred pages, I saw only intelligent remarks and useful advice. All things considered, once I got over my initial reactions I became convinced that there was nothing ridiculous about prescribing a certain type of analgesic or insisting on a less painful manner of killing an animal to be dissected – rather than considering that there is no matter for reflection here and that anything and everything should be allowed.

* * *

One may object that respect for animals is a "projection" in the psychoanalytic sense of the word – which is why it is characteristic of children. In a sense, this is true. Still it should be noted that if man cannot help but see himself, to some extent, in the enigmatic nature of *animals*, it is not only due to a psychological projection but also to a *philosophical* one, because the *analogue* of freedom can never leave entirely cold one whom the eighteenth century would have called "a man of taste." Freud said that the latter must renounce, even if regretfully, the pleasure of puns. To which I will add the enjoyment of bullfights and other games of that order. What we need is a synthesis between the Heideggerian *Gelassenheit,* or "letting be," and the imperious "civilizing" activity of the Cartesians. For perhaps the circumscribed respect we owe animals, far from being inscribed in nature or a burden placed upon us by civilization, is in this sense a matter of *politeness* and *civility.*

MANLY VALUES: LUC FERRY'S ETHICAL PHILOSOPHY

Verena Conley

For centuries Western philosophers have been debating the differentiation between animals and humans. Montaigne celebrated the superiority of animals in his *Apologie de Raymond Sebond* before Descartes reduced them to soulless machines. By equating animals with things, Descartes paved the way for 300 years of metaphysical humanism that asserted the superiority of culture over nature and of humans over animals.

Growing criticism of the foundations of Cartesian humanism since the nineteenth century culminated in France in the decades following the events of May 1968. Philosophical arguments, combined with research in other disciplines, led to a renewed and spirited debate on the respective status of animals and humans. A stringent critique of Cartesian metaphysics inspired many thinkers, often by way of psychoanalysis, to retrace the line of demarcation between humans and animals. Philosophers and writers discover the animal in themselves and rethink their relation to nature at the very moment of its disappearance. In Nietzsche's wake, Freud, Carroll, Kafka, Cixous, Derrida, Irigaray, Deleuze-Guattari, Michel Serres and others give the age-old dilemma a new twist. They complicate philosophy by their appeal to psychoanalysis. Their conclusions are further reoriented by recent findings in biology that invalidate older modes of classification and distinctions at the basis of Cartesian humanism.

Luc Ferry, a French philosopher of a generation younger than that which emerges from 1968, joins the debate with the publication of *The New Ecological Order* (1992).[1] The book, locating the dilemma of differentiation of humans from animals within larger concerns about humanism, democracy and ecology, was awarded the prestigious Medicis Prize for best essay in 1992. Ferry reduces the dilemmas to three major points of argument: the superiority of man over the animal; that of rational, democratic man over deep ecologists; finally, that of a new humanism over the poststructuralist philosophies of difference. He praises a new humanism while debunking differential thinking, from Derridean deconstruction to Deleuzian or Foucauldian constructions. Ferry traces these philosophers' appurtenance to leftism but also to rightism that includes Nazism. He is intent on rehabilitating a non-metaphysical, rational humanism that would avoid the romantic excesses of his elders who strayed on paths that led them to identify with Nietzsche and Heidegger. Ferry appeals to a democratic process and a culture that would not lose itself in what he considers to be regressive speculations about the erasure of the limit between humans and animals or in sociobiological analyses of culture.

Dismissing postmodernism equated with "posthumanism," he denounces any return to a premodern vision of the world in which nature would be given legal status. Writing most probably against Bruno Latour's *We Have Never Been Modern* that appeared in French in 1991, Ferry declares in his introduction to *The New Ecological Order:* "We are still modern" (xix). To whom, a reader quickly asks, does the ubiquitous "we" refer? The pronoun remains equivocal. It is never quite clear whether it refers to all humans, to French citizens, or to the enlightened new French democratic philosophers who distinguish themselves from the French poststructuralists lumped together with German and Anglo-Saxon deep ecologists from Hans Jonas to Aldo Leopold, and who, closer to a fusion with nature, are said to be on the verge of fascism.

Ferry rejects the arguments of those who want to accord legal rights to animals and reduce culture to nature. The modern day, rational French citizen, he declares, defends himself against the onslaught of those who want to give moral significance to nonhuman beings (xix), of those utilitarians who seek to relieve universal suffering, and, even worse, of those who give the biosphere a value superior to that of human activities (xxiv). Ferry locates what he calls nonsensical reasoning in many thinkers from the generation of 1968. He finds it at the heart of Michel Serres's *Natural Contract* – one of the favorite targets in the essay – and others out to criticize the "West" in a "politically correct way" (xxiv). Why, exclaims Ferry in a statement that he might well wish to retract today, does the Third World not worry about ecological destruction or the limit between humans and animals? (xxv) Against some of his elders, he proposes a reformist ecology based on an internal criticism of modernity in "highly democratic" fashion (xxvii). Man, he concludes, is an anti-natural being par excellence. That is what distinguishes *Homo sapiens* from the animal kingdom (xviii).

Ferry has a marked preference for man and kingdoms, a penchant shown by the gender-neutral nominations in the gist of his discourse. Thus, there are few women or queens in his human or animal worlds unless, like American ecofeminists, they are viewed critically. Though the French word *l'homme* does not have the same resonance as the English "man," it is noteworthy that Ferry avoids using the adjectival noun *humain* that has been coined to avoid expressions of a relation of power that make men the masters of women or humans the colonizers of a world they believe a manly "God" (always "He") has bequeathed to them. He denounces the erasure of the distinction between humans and animals that he sees at work in radical politics to the right and the left. Rather than putting in question the limit between the two terms by rethinking the concept of man, Ferry decides to elevate the animal and resituate it within a philosophy of consciousness. The animal is no longer a machine or a thing. It is a living being endowed with a certain amount of freedom but lacks "ethical reciprocity."

The essay is rhetorically persuasive. Ferry begins with what he calls a phenomenology of feelings to show that the animal is a living being. It suffers. From there, he moves to the realm of philosophy proper, specifically to the debate about the status of humanism. He decries those who argue that an anthro-pocentric humanism with its objective science leads to a colonization of nature. Mocks Ferry:

> they would have us believe that it is necessary to deconstruct humanism at all costs in order to respond to the threat of metaphysical anthropocen-trism. We are given a choice between Descartes on one side, Heidegger, Foucault and Derrida on the other. The strategy is too clunky, the connec-tions too obvious to still be convincing today. (49)

Throughout the essay, the debate about animals becomes a pretext for Ferry to undermine his intellectual "adversaries" by pretending that they are united in an effort to eradicate contemporary enlightened citizens.

Still problematic for Ferry is the essay by one of his own friends, Alain Renaut, whom he takes to task for seeing in bullfighting a symbolic enactment of the separation between nature and culture. Man would tear himself away from nature by killing the animal. By way of Freud, Ferry makes the point that some traditions must die and that human sensibilities change for the better. The suffering of animals is unacceptable. Renaut, Ferry concludes, is stuck in Cartesian humanism though he claims to be Kantian. This assertion enables the philosopher to make his major point: there is more than one kind of humanism. Instead of Descartes's model, we need to espouse that of Kant. If there were not a crucial difference between the two, Ferry declares, the "'non-metaphysical' humanism" he has elaborated for the past 15 years would make no sense. The Heideggerian deconstruction of modernity that he has denounced as unilateral would be justified since "humanism *in all its forms* would lead us to a 'colonization of nature'" (52).

The brand of humanism Ferry proposes would be a third term between Cartesianism and a poststructuralism, here somewhat unilaterally seen as a blend of post-Nietzschean vitalism, neo-Heideggerian naturalism, utilitarianism, and deep ecology. He takes another swipe at ecology by linking it with Pétainism through its revalorization of the soil, that is, of race, blood relations, and immanence over mobility and transcendence. After freely spending "isms" of every kind in his argument, he ushers in existential concepts to declare that human "freedom" cannot prevail over brute force. It can only reside in sentient beings (63). Domination of others – as it remained implied in Renaut's remarks on bullfighting – may be acceptable from a Cartesian, but no longer from a Kantian point of view. Contra those whom he somewhat condescendingly calls "zoophiles," Ferry repeats that animals have no rights. With Kant, he underlines the necessity of a "diversity of reality." To respect this diversity, humans have to appeal to ethics. The Heideggerian *Gelassenheit* or letting be, predicated on a fusion with nature, is detrimental to modern democratic culture.

Worthy of a Cornelian hero, Ferry speaks of indirect duties that humans have on behalf of animals. Animals are an analogue of humanity; humans observe duties toward humanity; they satisfy a duty when killing an animal. Humans must show respect to animals and, indirectly, to themselves. Appealing to Judaism, Ferry writes that man must live by law and dispose of animals only according to rules, without cruelty and in moderation. These ethical duties, for Ferry, are connected to biblical and symbolic laws.

The philosophical status of the animal then appears to be caught in the antinomy between Cartesianism and naturalism. For Ferry, a non-Cartesian humanism would avoid the absurd alternative to which radical ecology condemns "us": the step backward, the move toward barbarism (55). Humans need not rid themselves of humanistic culture and revert to nature. Thanks to their enlightened sense of ethics, democratically inclined neo-Kantian humanists will respect and protect animals. This is, Ferry concludes, what is taking place in Canada in hospitals with animal ethics committees (56). In the synthesis between "letting be" on the one hand and the civilizing activity of Cartesians on the other, of importance is the respect of animals as a matter of civility (56).

The real difference between men and animals, for Ferry, goes through ethics. Animals lack what, in a more recent critique of animal rights, he calls "reciprocal responsibility."[2] To develop his non-metaphysical humanism, Ferry wants to return to the eighteenth century and to Kant. However, much has happened since the eighteenth century. Not only has science revised many of the earlier humanistic assumptions but also demographics and a general acceleration of the world through technologies have contributed further to change the status of humans and animals. It is often the very disappearance of animals that informs the debate on the concept of "man" and erases many of the Cartesian distinctions. The philosophy of consciousness at the basis of Ferry's thought has been reevaluated as a short parenthesis or accident in the history of the world. Its Eurocentrism has been denounced. Not only do other, non-European, cultures have very different relations to animals but also, under the impact of cybernetics, science has pushed humans from center stage. No longer functioning against a natural backdrop, humans are now thought to be a part of the environment understood in terms of open, self-organizing systems. It is through science and technology – and not only *Gelassenheit* – that humans have been seen as part of a nature that has, however, been entirely reassessed. As N. Katherine Hayles argues, humans have de facto become "posthuman."[3]

This kind of posthumanism differs from that which Ferry criticizes. It is not in conflict with poststructuralism from which it draws and which, in turn, it also inflects. It is not a Cartesianism either. Benefiting from the presence of science and technology in contemporary culture, it points to the interrelatedness of humans, animals, and the world, while cautioning against any attempt at unilateral domination. At the same time, it points to the ubiquitous and irreversible presence of technologies that have infiltrated all areas of the world and make all humans de facto into cyborgs. Nature and culture cannot be separated. Here is where we could situate philosophers like Deleuze and Guattari who are somewhat summarily dismissed when Ferry grafts them freely onto American ecofeminists. In a world of open systems, the difference between humans and animals is often couched in language, a dimension that remains absent from Ferry who hinges it entirely on culture, democracy, the more abstract notion of "freedom," and ethics.

Today, when demographic pressures threaten the existence of many animals, from loss of habitat to over-consumption, and when imbalances add to the production of more "nuisance" animals – geese, pigeons, gulls, deer – in endless stretches of suburban space, it is less a question either of "letting be" or of acting out of "respect" and "duty." Humans have to be made aware of a functioning of the world that is no longer Cartesian. To replace Descartes with Kant might not be a sufficient correction. On the one hand, science is constantly reevaluating humans' knowledge of the world. On the other, symbolic laws associated with traditional authority are being replaced by legal rights. We may wonder whether sacred laws are sufficient in a culture where, as Ferry himself states, religion is disappearing (149). Without giving animals themselves legal status, as in the Renaissance trial of a colony of crawlers, a case history that Ferry uses compellingly in the preface to his book, laws are necessary to protect animals from humans above and beyond ethics that are too often the first casualty in today's world. Several decades ago Lévi-Strauss, commenting on ecological problems, the plight of humans and animals, urged the French government to implement laws of protection.[4] Ethics and respect have to be accompanied by laws and by a novel understanding of the world beyond that of the enlightened, rational citizen philosopher. Ferry's noble ethical ideal may well belong to an older *polis* – celebrated by Henri Lefebvre in *The Production of Space* (1974) – that existed between the sixteenth and nineteenth century and that was pushed out by modernization and industrialization. Ferry's non-metaphysical humanism will have difficulties existing in today's hegemony of global consumer culture. The question whether animals have rights in terms of having legal status might be secondary to that of the existence of laws that protect them for their own sake but also for that of the functioning of the world.

Ferry alludes to a variety of animals. He moves from pets, whose oedipal status in Western society has been effectively decried by Deleuze and Guattari (though they are abandoned by humans by the hundred of thousands to be euthanized every year in the state of Massachussetts alone), to laboratory animals and to the rest of the zoological "kingdom." He barely distinguishes between the so-called wild animals, those which exist on the fringes of civilization and whose habitat is threatened by the encroachment of civilization, or those which, like many species of fish, are on the verge of extinction because of human overconsumption. Calling attention to these rather massive problems can hardly be dismissed as "zoophilic."

The thorny part of the essay concerns less the contested legal status of animals – itself also a major issue in the United States – than the way in which Ferry frames the question. On the one hand, he somewhat glibly dismisses those philosophers he perceives as his rivals. On the other, he rather unproblematically makes the case for a return to Kant and the eighteenth century. In defense of some of those he accuses of "barbarism," one could show how Ferry himself establishes continuities where there are none. He associates rather freely all poststructuralist thinkers and lumps them indiscriminately with deep ecologists and American eco-feminists, Nazis and Pétainists. To criticize anthropocentrism in Cartesian humanism is not equivalent to granting animals legal status. To debunk a culture advocated by his rivals and barbaric ecologists, Ferry seems to twist the arguments of others.

The world today is threatened by the eradication of species and a general loss of biodiversity. Can this be dealt with through a philosophy of ethics alone?

When rethinking the limit between humans and animals, it might be more productive to note some of the changes made possible by science and technology. Many philosophers affiliated with poststructuralists heeded the influence of other disciplines on philosophy much more than Ferry in *The New Ecological Order*. It is only in a conversation with a scientist, Jean-Didier Vincent, in their co-authored book, *Qu'est-ce que l'homme* that Ferry addresses preemptively a vague charge of "philosophism."[5] Reduction of a world replete with its messy complications to easy binarisms lends to his writings a strong didactic and pedagogical value. The universal concepts that make up his rhetoric appear to predispose him to a public career in politics and education. It comes as no surprise that he would be named to the distinguished post as French Minister of Education. Since the publication of *The New Ecological Order*, in addition to *Qu'est-ce que l'homme*, Ferry has co-edited with Claudine Germé, a volume entitled *Des Animaux et des hommes*, on the animal in French thought from the fifteenth century to the present that still does not include Montaigne's *Apologie de Raymond Sebond*.[6] Again, Ferry asks the question from the point of view of "man" in his relation to God and animals. Does respect for nature suffice, or should animals be given legal status by way of animal rights? Still, what disturbs is not so much the rather legitimate question that Ferry raises as the way he contextualizes it.

The text is more about the promotion of Ferry's brand of non-metaphysical humanism than about the welfare of animals. This promotion is based on a philosophical "regime change" that will be rid of all those perceived as rivals. Ferry repeatedly claims that the debate on animal rights is couched in crude terms, between Cartesianism and romantic Nietzscheanism. We can quote Ferry against himself and say that his argument made out to be between new humanists and barbarians is equally "clunky." While we cannot but agree with Ferry about some of the excesses of a movement like deep ecology that wants to go back in time and maintain an impossible status quo, as well as some of the ecological resonances in Nazism, all ecological thought that comes out of poststructuralism is far from barbaric. If Nietzsche and Heidegger play a decisive role in philosophical elaborations that reevaluate the division between nature and culture, animal and human, so do many other types of knowledge, in particular those derived from the biological and physical sciences that inform much poststructuralist thought. These developments, and the shift from an analog to a more digital world, enable humans to reconfigure the limit between humans and animals.

Instead of a non-metaphysical humanism, one could conceive of another kind of metaphysics. Ferry's gesture of elevating the animal toward man can be read backwards. One can conceive of a movement in the other direction, that is, toward immanence. Rather than focusing on what sets humans apart from animals, we could look for what brings them closer together. As biologists would have it, over the last century this difference has become much smaller. Such a way of perceiving and conceiving the world makes it possible to argue for an interdependence between humans, animals and the rest of the natural world that is not one of fusion. Few will dispute that a "natural equilibrium" does not exist and possibly never has. As some scientists will argue, every system is always "off center." Yet the impact of human implementations of technology have accelerated this course. Though we are now aware that unilateral Cartesian domination does not work, little is done to stop it. Many philosophers have argued for "other ways of domesticating the earth," ways that would not be based on unilateral domination but on the recognition of mutual interdependence of all elements of the biosphere through ongoing negotiation. This has to be done in today's conditions. Paradoxically, it is through technology that humans have become more aware of an interdependence between themselves, animals and nature. Michel Serres's words ring true when, in *The Natural Contract,* he argues that, far from being menacing, nature has become fragile and is in need of protection. The changed status of nature is also reflected in the perception of wild animals. The "ferocious beasts" of nineteenth-century tales are perceived as "endangered" and far from "savage."

Yet the sensitivity of which Ferry speaks is not very widespread. The animal world has deteriorated significantly since Ferry wrote his essay in the 1990s. Thousands of species have become extinct and many links in the food chain have been broken. People may become emotionally invested in the fate of a pet, a cat, a dog, or an animal raised for the fur industry but they will still not see the larger consequences due to an interrelation between humans, animals, and nature that is distinct from that heralded by deep ecology. At the same time, the political movements that Ferry thinks threaten democracy are very marginal in the world at large. In view of many government decisions, often under the pressure of all-powerful lobbies that affect animals and the environment quite negatively, the philosopher's fears seem misplaced.

With its insistence on "manly" values, Ferry's philosophical discourse has a somewhat antiquated ring. It may be more adequate for a smaller, more immediately democratic society less under the sway of the media. In today's world where soaring demographics, information, telematics, and consumerisms of all kind prevail, the democratic ideals of a distant era are severely challenged. Like many animals, Ferry's ethical "man" may have become an endangered species. It appears difficult to appeal to ethics alone in an era where there is no belief, especially in the future of the planet. Another third term – or another metaphysics – is needed to reinstate belief in the world. It will have to be based on a novel understanding of relations between humans, animals, and nature that goes *through* technologies. It will have to construct and compose a world by means of heterogeneous affiliations. It will, hopefully, use new modes of knowing in order to develop other ways of being and of sharing the world between humans and animals.

CHAPTER NINE: CIXOUS

BIRDS, WOMEN AND WRITING

Hélène Cixous

I am interested in a chain of associations and signifiers composed of birds, women, and writing. This may sound funny, it may sound gratuitous, but it is not. We only have to read the chapter in Leviticus in the Bible to realize that it is deadly serious. The chapter gives Moses and humanity in general laws on eating: dictating what is edible and what is not. In English the distinction is between meats that are *clean* and meats that are *unclean*. I need the French: in French *unclean* is *immonde*, which comes from the Latin *immundus*; it is the same word in Brazilian – *immundo* – and I'll need this later.

> And these are they which you shall have in abomination among the fowls, they shall not be eaten, they are an abomination, the eagle and the ossifrage and the vulture. And the owl and the nighthawk, and after his kind; and the little owl, and the great one; and the swan and the pelican, and the deer eagle. The stork, the heron and the lapling and the bat. All fowls that creep, going on all fours, shall be an abomination unto you.[1]

So this is what we are not supposed to eat. These are abominable. Why are they abominable? While there are others one can eat: for example:

> The locust and after his kind, and the bull locust after his kind. The beetle after his kind and the grasshopper after his kind. But all the creeping things which have four feet shall be an abomination unto you. And for these you shall be unclean.[2]

We can dream round the mystery of the stork's "immundity." We can have all kinds of reveries regarding the swan and the swan's abomination. And of course, if we were childlike enough, we'd worry; or, if we were Percival, we'd wonder why there are birds that are abominable. And we would have to accept the law's answer: Because. It is what the Bible says.

In *The Passion According to G. H.*, G. H., a woman reduced to her initials, encounters in complete solitude, face to face – even eye to eye – a cockroach, an abominable cockroach.[3] In Brazilian the word for cockroach is *barata*, and it is feminine. So a woman meets a barata, and it becomes the focus for a type of fantastic, total, emotional, spiritual, and intellectual revolution, which, in short, is a crime. The revolution leads G. H. to completely revise her clichéd way – our clichéd way – of thinking: our relations to the world in general and to living things in particular. She must deal with the phobia, with the horror we have of so-called abominable beings. I will now quote from a chapter in the middle of the book, after G. H. has had an initially ordinary reaction to the barata: that is, she has almost "killed" it by crushing it. A kind of white paste spurts out of the barata, which is nonetheless immortal. G. H. comes into contact with this paste; she starts thinking about what the white paste is and how to relate to it. This is what she says at one point:

I had committed the forbidden act of touching something impure.[4]

In Brazilian "impure" is *immundo*.

And so impure was I [so *immonde* was I], in my sudden indirect moment of self- knowledge, that I opened my mouth to call for help.[5]

The American translation continues:

They proclaim, the Bible does, but if I understand what they proclaim, they will call me crazy. People like me had proclaimed that understanding them would be my destruction. "But you shall not eat the impure, the eagle, the griffon, and the hawk." Nor the owl, nor the swan, nor the bat, nor the stork, nor the entire tribe of crows.[6]

Now let me correct that translation. Actually G. H. does not say: "They proclaim, the Bible does ..."

E tao imunda estava eu, naquele meu subito conhecimento indirecto de mim, que abri a boca para pedir socorro. *Eles dizem tudo, a Biblia, eles dizem tudo* – mas se eu entender o que eles dizem, eles mesmos me chamarao de enlouquecida.[7] Pessoas iguais a mim haviam dito, no entanto entende-las seria a minha derrocada.
"Mas nao comereis das impuras: quais sao a aguia, e o grifo, e o esmer-ilhao." E nem a coruja, e nem o cisne, e nem o morcego, nem a cegonha, e todo o gênero de corvos.[8]

What Clarice actually suggests is that the Bible is a masculine "they."
One might have translated it like this: "Those He-Bible, those Bible, they say everything." It sounds awkward, but it is the way Clarice writes, awkwardly, roughly, and as truly as possible to what she wants us to feel.
So those He-Bible, it is *they* who tell us what is unclean and abominable. Clarice Lispector is a writer who has dealt throughout her work, among other questions, with this notion of the abominable in our lives, in all its forms. Let those birds be "abominable": I associate women and writing with this abomi-nation. I do this, of course, half playfully, half seriously. It is my way of indicating the reserved, secluded, or excluded path or place where you meet

those beings I think are worth knowing while we are alive. Those who belong to the birds and their kind (these may include some men), to writings and their kind: they are all to be found – and a fair company it is – outside; in a place that is called by Those Bible, those who are the Bible, abominable.

Elsewhere, outside, birds, women, and writing gather. *Not all* women however: quite a number of this kind linger inside, as we realize daily, and identify with "those-He-Bible" and their kind. Outside we shall find *all* those precious people who have not worried about respecting the law that separates what is and is not abominable according to Those Bible.

I have deliberately included Genet among those writers I have chosen to meet today. I wanted you to have the French version and the English translation, which is both correct and misleading. Genet is particularly difficult to translate: he inhabits a verbal land that resists all attempts at "naturalization" as we say in French. One has to travel to his elsewhere, that is meet him on his own idio-grounds and read along his specific paths in order to become acquainted with his universe.

This is like the writing of Clarice Lispector and those writers with whom I have a deep and everlasting love affair: Anna Akhmatova, Marina Tsvetaeva, Ingeborg Bachmann, Ossip Mandelstam. They all – without having decided to, without having met, without having read one another – inhabit what Genet calls in French: "les domaines inférieurs" (the nether realms).[9] They dwell somewhere in that most evasive of countries without a precise address, the one that is most difficult to find and work with, and where it is even difficult to live without effort, danger, risk. This risky country is situated somewhere near the unconscious: to reach it you have to go through the back door of thought.

If I gather these beings to talk about them in the same way, if I am worried by the fate of birds and women, it is because I have learned that not many people – unfortunately – or perhaps fortunately – can really love, tolerate, or understand a certain kind of writing; I am using women and birds as synonyms.

This is what Clarice Lispector wisely says at the beginning of *The Passion according to G. H.*[10] The translation says: "To potential readers." It should say: "To possible readers."

The translation says: "This is a book just like any other book" (106), so be reassured. But this is what Clarice Lispector says: "This book is like any other book."[11]

The translation goes on: "But I would be happy if it were read only by people whose outlook is fully formed."[12]

I don't know what "outlook" is, so let me tell you what Clarice says: "But I would be pleased if it were read only by persons whose souls are already mature."

And so I continue:

Those who know that the approach to anything is done progressively and painfully – and includes as well passing through the opposite of what is being approached. These people and they alone will understand very slowly that this book takes nothing away from anyone. To me, for example, the character G. H. gradually gave a difficult joy; but it is called joy.[13]

This is how you are greeted when you open the book. You are told that this book is a book like others. Then you must ask yourself whether you are one of those persons whose souls are already mature. It is threatening, disquieting. Asking yourself: "Is my soul already mature" might sound prohibitive, but it isn't. The moment you read the next sentence you are either in or outside what is approaching. You must at least once in your life have realized you were undergoing the opposite of what was coming. I suppose this to be the case, but if it has not yet happened it will.

What comes next is most important: after having been severe Clarice says: "But this book does not take anything from anybody. To me, for example, the character G. H. gradually gave a difficult joy." In writing this Clarice Lispector wisely and emphatically sides with us readers: she is not the author, she is like us before the book. She too is reading it and has to deal with the character who comes to her in the book and gives her all kinds of emotions. Yet it is a warning that this book will give us pain, which is of course a joy. What about the book not *taking away* anything from anyone: the writing moves fast, and you might not even notice the remark, though I believe this to be one of the keys to our lives together. Each one of us – the whole of mankind, irrespective of sexual difference – must deal with the feeling of things being *taken away* from us. What is interesting is that birds, writing, and many women are considered abominable, threatening, and are *rejected*, because others, the rejectors, feel something is taken away from them. But let me leave women aside for today, since this is a controversial issue, and keep only birds and writing. Neither birds nor writing take anything away, yet people feel that some forms of writing do take something from us. Clarice Lispector has never been a feminist, Genet is not a feminist, though theirs are writings that may hurt, may dissatisfy, and give the feeling that something is taken away.

This is exactly (and I have chosen this example in order to make things clear) what happened to Gandhi. I imagine you believe he was for the most part adored; in fact he was hated and he is still hated today. Hatred is still alive in India and he died of it. Those who were for Gandhi were mostly from what is called the scheduled castes, those who belong to the gutters with whom he had sided. Yet he did not ask anything of anyone; he simply went his own way. He did not ask people to change. He did what he felt he had to do. When people approached, he never asked, he never exacted anything from them, he never demanded anything from the people who approached him, not even his close friends: they went on living the way they wanted to live. But the simple fact that he lived according to his own law – which was ascetic and demanding of himself – was something that people could not tolerate. There are ways of writing that are perceived in the same way as Gandhi was perceived by the Indians.

Clarice Lispector had to deal with this perception, as did Ingeborg Bachmann and Tsvetaeva. Fortunately, there is always a small group who love such writings. But the majority are "those Bible."

Now what about what is called in French *l'immonde*, in Brazilian *imundo*, and in English *the unclean*? This is what Clarice says:

I was knowing that the Bible's impure animals are forbidden because the imund is the root.[14] For there are things created that have never made themselves beautiful, and have stayed just as they were when created, and only they continue to be the entirely complete root, they are not to be eaten. The fruit of good and evil, the eating of living matter, would expel me from the paradise of adornment and require me to walk forever through the desert with a shepherd's staff. Many have been those who have walked in the desert with a staff.

To build a possible soul, a soul whose head will not devour its own tail, the law commands that one uses only what is patently alive. And the law commands that whoever partakes of the imund, must do so without knowing; for, he who partakes of the imund knowing that it is imund, must also come to know that the imund is not imund. Is that it?[15]

She quotes the Bible:

"And everything that crawls on the ground and has wings shall be imund, and shall not be eaten."

I opened my mouth in fright to ask for help. Why? Because I did not want to become imund like the cockroach. What ideal held me from the sensing of an idea? Why should I not make myself imund? Exactly as I was revealing my whole self, what was I afraid of? Being imund? With what? Being imund with joy.[16]

That is my theme for today: to be "imund," to be unclean with joy. *Immonde,* that is, out of the *mundus* (the *world*). The monde, the world, that is so-called clean. The world that is on the good side of the law, that is "proper," the world of order. The moment you cross the line the law has drawn by wording, verb(aliz)ing, you are supposed to be out of the world. You no longer belong to the world.

Out there we shall be in the company of swans, storks, and griffons. Imagine this list on the other side, celebrated by someone like Dante. Dante loves birds, and in *Paradise* he has visions of birds like letters in the sky. So why are those birds imund? Because. As you know, this is the secret of the law: "because." This is the law's logic. It is this terrible "because," this senseless fatal "because" that has decided people's fate, even in the extremity of the concentration camps. People were divided, some were sent to gas chambers while others were "spared" for a later date, "because." It is this *because* that rules our lives. It pervades everything. It can even reach the fragile world of translation.

Now Clarice says explicitly that what is imund is joy. They are synonymous. Joy is imund, it is *not unclean*: if you use the English expression *unclean* you lose the necessary meaning "out of the world." Joy is out-of-the-world – this is what Clarice wants us to understand. It is true that what is really forbidden is enjoyment, jubilation. As Clarice says, with a stroke of genius, the point for Those Bible is that joy, jubilation, birds are forbidden because they are the root.

So the purpose of Those Bible is to forbid the root. This is what I wanted to bring to the surface, though we will not remain here; instead our ladder will grow down into the earth.

Writing is not put there, it does not happen out there, it does not come from outside. On the contrary, it comes from deep inside. It comes from what Genet calls the "nether realms," the inferior realms (*domaines inférieurs*). We'll try to go there for a time, since this is where the treasure of writing lies, where it is formed, where it has stayed since the beginning of creation: down below. The name of the place changes according to our writers. Some call it hell: it is of course a good, a desirable hell. This is what Clarice calls it: *inferno*. She does not always use the word hell but all kinds of parallel denominations ("*the other side*" cited in *The Stream of Life* is Tsvetaeva's abyss).[17] It is deep in my body, further down, behind thought. Thought comes in front of it and it closes like a door. This does not mean that it does not think, but it thinks differently from our thinking and speech. Somewhere in the depths of my heart, which is deeper than I think. Somewhere in my stomach, my womb, and if you have not got a womb – then it is somewhere "else." You must climb down in order to go in the direction of that place. But as I said yesterday, this sort of descent is much more difficult to achieve, much more tiring, much more physically exacting (*physically* because the soul is body), than climbing up. It is a climb, but it requires the whole strength of everything that is you – which I don't want to call "body," since it is more complex than the body – to go through the various doors, obstacles, walls, and distances we have forged to make a life. I know besides that what also prevents us in our society from going there is not our inability – because *all of us* are able – but our cowardice, our fear. Our fear, since we know perfectly well that we will reach the dangerous point where those who are excluded live – and we hate exclusion. This is our emotional, our personal, and political problem, the fact that we can't bear exclusion. We are afraid of it, we hate to be separated, that is why we are apt to commit all kinds of small crimes, self-denials, and treachery.

But one has to choose between losing what is mund and losing the best part of ourselves that is called imund. Since we are shaped by years and years of all kinds of experiences and education, we must travel through all sorts of places that are not necessarily pleasant to get there: our own marshes, our own mud. And yet it pays to do so. The trouble is we are not taught that it pays, that it is beneficial. We are not taught the pain nor that in pain is hidden joy. We don't know that we can fight against ourselves, against the accumulation of mental, emotional, and biographical clichés. The general trend in writing is a huge concatenation of clichés. It is a fight one must lead against subtle enemies. Our personal enemies in this fight are those Kafka denounced as preventing our return to paradise. Kafka insists paradise is not lost, it is there. But we are lazy and impatient. If we were neither lazy nor impatient we would be back in paradise. But we have to deal with this laziness and impatience. And of course with all the representatives of "Those Bible." There is a whole list of institutions, media, and machines that make for the banishment of birds, women, and writing. We are mistaken if we think *aparatchik* is a Russian word. Aparatchiks exist in all countries, especially in France; they are powerful against birds, i.e., women, i.e., writing, and people are afraid of them.

What is forbidden is unfortunately the best and that is joy. We are told by the law, "Thou shalt not eat of those birds, and thou shalt not read those books," i.e.: Thou shalt not eat of those books that are joy. Thomas Bernhard told us in "Montaigne" how when he was a child his family would say to him: if you go to the library and take a book you will go mad, insane; it is bad, wrong, rotten, vicious. Reading is a wonderful metaphor for all kinds of joy that are called vicious.

Tsvetaeva died early: she was a very strong, powerful, rebellious woman, much too powerful and full of joy to be allowed to survive. In a long poem called "The Poem of the End" there is a short line where she suddenly strikes out and says: "All poets are Yids."[18] The word is extremely insulting; it is a synonym of imund. Poets are unclean, abominable in the same way women are abominable. When Tsvetaeva used this word in the context of Russian society, the most abominable of the abominable at that time, poets, she felt, were *yids*. It was equivalent to all the other abominables. In another text she suggests that the abominable-she-loved, the abominable with whom she identified, was the nigger. So in the same line of substitutions you find: Jews, women, niggers, birds, poets, etc., all of them excluded and exiled. Exile is an uncomfortable situation, though it is also a magical situation. I am not making light of the experience of exile. But we can endure it differently. Some exiles die of rage, some transform their exile into a country. I understand those who die of (out)rage. It is what happened to Sakharov. Recently I met his wife, Elena Bonner, who is utterly mad with rage. She suffers day and night because all she feels is a desperate rage, which I do understand. Some exiles can draw joy from rage; those who are able to benefit from this strange experience relearn, recapture what we have lost. This was our experience as children, but we have lost the taste of bread, since, as Clarice Lispector says, we have eaten lobster in the meantime. We have lost the taste of hands, of the touching of hands. We have lost all the small and great secrets of joy. But the country of exile is not unattainable. It is even easier to go to that country, Exile, than it sometimes is to cross the border of a country like the United States.

THE WRITING OF THE BIRDS, IN MY LANGUAGE

Stephen David Ross

She is sitting at a desk, the woman ... bird, the bird ... woman. She is writing, perhaps drawing, with her right hand – and yes, it is a hand. She has a left and a right hand, left and right feet. She is a bird with human feet, a woman with hands and feet covered in skin, with fingers and toes. The rest of her body is covered with pale green-brown feathers, including the top of her head. Her intent eyes are wide and circular, owl eyes, somehow human, a birdwoman's eyes. The lower half of her face is a woman's face – distinctly a woman's, not a bird's, and not a man's. Her face is a woman's face with a woman's mouth, chin, and nose. She does not have a beak, though the contours of her face and the room follow the curves of a beak. She does not present herself as a bird, with a beak or talons. She is lovely as a bird and as a woman, both and neither. She is beautiful and yet neither birds and women nor perhaps writers would insist on her beauty. Her work overcomes any insistence.

She is writing with her right hand, the birdwoman, womanbird. The bird-who-is-a-woman-who-is-a-bird is holding a pen, perhaps a brush, in her right hand, drawing, painting a bird on paper or canvas. The woman-bird is writing or drawing or painting with her right hand. In her left hand she holds a triangular instrument that catches the rays of light from a star, rays that pass through the glass instrument to fall on the canvas or paper or painted bird. And the bird, or the one just drawn before, is magically, alchemically, scientifically, or naturally transformed into a bird who flies from the canvas into the air.

She is looking downward, focused upon her work. She does not seem to see the bird that flies, the bird who is flying off. Her work is to create, to create the bird. Where and how the bird flies away is not her task, not her concern. She loves the bird in her hand, in her brush, her pen. She loves the touch of the bird. The flight of the bird is its love for her, for light and air, for sky and world. Her creation is love.

The room is a medieval stone room filled with alchemical and hermetic mysteries. The bird comes to life in the mystery of drawing-painting-writing. The birdwoman is filled with mystery, fills the room with mystery, catches the mysteries of the stars and releases them as if they were living birds. The womanbird is mistress of mystery, sorceress witch. The room is filled with mystery. And love. The birds are lovely. The birdwoman is lovely, in her green brown feathery body. The birds are loved. The birds are joy.

The desk is a writing desk, perhaps a drawing table or laboratory bench on which experiments are performed. She is sitting as if she were writing, as if she were drawing, painting, writing, as if she were examining, gazing, liberating the energies of life and flight, as if the forces of nature were inseparable from the mysteries of writing and painting, as if she – woman, bird, painter, poet, biologist, creatrix, aviatrix – crossed them all in her joy. Her love of knowledge is love for birds. Her quest for truth is creation. Her work is poiēsis.[1]

In *Three Steps on the Ladder of Writing*, Hélène Cixous (*HC*) asks us, her readers, to ascend the ladder H by descending, to go up by going down.[2] *HC* writes of Clarice Lispector (*CL*) who writes of the passion according to *GH* and of the passion of the cockroach *GH* almost kills – although *HC* says it is immortal.

> And our condition is accepted as the only one possible since it is what exists and none other. And since the experience of it is our passion. The human condition is Christ's passion.[3]

The human condition is our passion, the *barata-cafard*-cockroach's suffering. At least in our Judeo-Christian tradition, if you will. If it is yours and mine.

HC asks us to go up the ladder by going down. According to her name, perhaps: *ci-sous* – though she calls her name *insignificant* and *impossible*. Perhaps her name goes up by going down, like writing, ascending by descending, split by the letter *chi*. Three steps on the ladder, three schools: *The School of the Dead, The School of Dreams, The School of Roots*. Three schools, three steps – *pas*: perhaps not steps, unsteps, unclean, *immonde* steps. Not beyond.

The School of Roots begins with "Birds, Women, and Writing." At the beginning of what she calls *the most advanced, the highest, the deepest* step, *HC* asks us to think of three figures up and down: birds, women, and writing. If they are figures, if they are three, if they are not one. If they can fly.

> If I gather these beings to talk about them in the same way, if I am worried by the fate of birds and women, it is because I have learned that not many people – unfortunately – or perhaps fortunately – can really love, tolerate, or understand a certain kind of writing; I am using women and birds as synonyms.[4]

Perhaps they are both up and down, one and many. Perhaps birds and women and writing – a certain kind of writing – are inseparable, up and down and elsewhere, other to themselves. A certain kind of writing and a certain kind of reader, described by *CL* as "persons whose souls are already mature" (114). I don't know what mature souls are but I do know that *HC* is serious.

> We only have to read the chapter in Leviticus in the Bible to realize that it is deadly serious. The chapter gives Moses and humanity in general laws on eating: dictating what is edible and what is not. (111)

The Bible here, for *HC* and *CL*, is not the anonymous, God-given Bible, but the He-bible written by those He-men. "So those He-Bible, it is they who tell us what is unclean and abominable" (113). Birds, women, and writing are linked by *HC* in memory of the men who wrote the Bible telling us what is abominable and what is unclean: *immonde* in French, *immundo* in Brazilian, *immundus* in Latin, impossible to say in English. Eagles, owls great and small, storks, and bats are an abomination.[5] I would recall that birds fly, that eagles and owls soar and swoop, that upward is flight for birds. It is not birds that creep – perhaps against the heavens where birds belong. Some of the most glorious birds are abominable, *immonde* in French. Abominable after their kind.

I would recall *GH*'s passionate words, "the first step in relation to the other is to find in oneself the man of all men. Every woman is the woman of all women, every man is the man of all men."[6] Perhaps every eagle and swan and bat may be the man and woman and bird and word of all men and women and birds and writing.

I would recall that women are sometimes beautiful, and sometimes cruel, that, like birds, they have been kept in cages as if that were home, as if their home might be behind walls instead of soaring in the sky or face to face with other women or birds. To write of women and animals together, to gather them in one place, is to put them back in a cage, together, kitchen or cage, where they have been unclean, impure, un-worldly. They have been kept out of the world in the name of their unworldliness, women, birds, and writing. *HC* imagines that a certain kind of writing, from its unworldliness, might redeem the unworldliness of women and of animals: abominable, unclean, impure, polluted, contaminated: *immonde*, improper. *GH* imagines that eating from its unworldliness might save her from her purity, might be *imund*.

This cannot be said in English. The meaning *HC* wants is not abominable, unclean, impure, but *immonde*, un-worldly, not-worldly, un-real, improper, not having a proper place in the world. *GH* says that what is unclean, impure, forbidden, abominable, is declared to be that by men, in the He-book written by those He-men. Not by birds or women. Written to set down the law of the world, not to be *immonde* – or for that matter *l'immonde*, the improper of a certain kind.

And as for *imund*, *GH* adds, it is the root. The not-earth, un-law – birds, women, and writing outside, beyond the law – is the root.

> I was knowing that the Bible's impure animals are forbidden because the imund is the root. And the law commands that whoever partakes of the imund, must do so without knowing; for, he who partakes of the imund knowing that it is imund, must also come to know that the imund is not imund. Is that it?[7]

Is that it? An *imund* question. A question of questions in and out of the world. The law commands that we – birds and women, perhaps some men – live in the propriety of the *mundus*. *GH* comes to know, as we may know, by partaking of the *imund* that it is not *imund*.

HC writes "I was knowing" where the English translation of *The Passion according to G.H.* says "I know," and writes "the imund is the root" where the translation says "the impure is the root." She notes that "I was knowing" sounds unclean, incorrect, *imund*, and for that reason she will write it. Writing and knowing what is incorrect in love and joy is what we are called to at the root. To come to know that the impure is not impure, not unclean, is at the root. To be impure with what? With joy and love.

> to be "imund," to be unclean with joy. *Immonde*, that is, out of the *mundus* (the *world*). The monde, the world, that is so-called clean. The world that is on the good side of the law, that is "proper," the world of order.
>
> Out there we shall be in the company of swans, storks, and griffons.[8]

What is unclean is expelled, thrown out of the world. By men. By masculine theological, divine law.[9] Law demands that *mund* be *mund*, that law be law. But *CL* says, and *GH* knows, that what is impure is joy.

> what was I afraid of? Being imund? With what? Being imund with joy. (117)[10]

The purpose of the law is to forbid the root, to prohibit joy. Perhaps more than that, it is to make abominable – to abominate – the *imund*, the out-of-this-world, the improper, the deep. Birds, women, and writing. All improper. All strange of and in this world.

In French, *HC*'s language. In Brazilian, *CL*'s and *GH*'s language. Of language I have something to say that cannot wait. On the cover of *HC*'s book, in English, *JD* is quoted as saying something extraordinary – *immonde*.

> Hélène Cixous is today, in my view, the greatest writer in what I call my language, the French language if you like. And I am weighing my words as I say that. For a great writer must be a poet-thinker, very much a poet and a very thinking poet.

The cover tells us that he said this in his public introduction to *HC*'s second lecture, *The School of Dreams*. Not the one before us here today. Even so it was an *immonde* thing to say about anyone, wonderful for *HC* to hear. But perhaps a bit too *mundus*. To be great, the greatest writer, is to be great in someone's world.

Greatness is too extravagant for me here, too worldly. I'm more interested in what follows: my language, the French language if you like. *JD*'s language – is that French? Is that French as other French people write and speak? Or is it *immonde*? And the French language, is that *monde*, or something else? Finally, then, if you like, or want, or please, or will: the French language, is it a certain kind of language and not some other? Must one write in words? Must one speak a language with a proper name? If writing and speaking are *imund*, are French and English also *imund*?

CL's thought – I will try to get this straight: *GH*'s thought, in the words of *CL*, as *HC* reads them to us, is that being *imund* is joy. One might imagine that this is what *HC* means to tell us, that the step of roots is back or down to the depths, to un-world, with joy. I would imagine that this step, this joy, to be un-worldly is difficult, frightening, disruptive. That is how *GH* feels it. *Hell*, as *CL* tells it:

There is not a single text by Clarice in which hell does not arise and arise jubilantly. Hell is a place of jouissance, a place of happiness; we might imagine that hell, despite its name, is situated celestially, though it is situated in the lower realms.[11]

This is difficult to feel and difficult to understand. It has something to do with the mysteries of language and writing. Perhaps of a certain kind.

From one day to another, from one page to the other, writing changes languages. I have thought certain mysteries in the French language that I cannot think in English. This loss and this gain are in writing too. (3)

It has something to do with the tradition of hell. Our tradition if you will. I wonder if birds and women have something to do with angels.

They have something to do with animals, who are at the root. Who descend to the roots. *HC* asks us, in her language, the French language if you will, in my language, English perhaps, to think and to whisper certain mysteries of death and dreams and roots that reveal themselves in birds, women, and writing, whose voice and music sing out in writing, women, and birds, however loudly or softly. However cruelly of death.

Let us listen to *HC*'s music and the music she hears.

You may already know the ones whose music I hear. I have brought them with me, I will make them resound. There is Clarice Lispector, whose music is dry, hard, and severe, like Bernhard's. There is the more tender, melodious music of Tsvetaeva, or the more heartrending music of Ingeborg Bachmann. (5)

She will make them sing. Perhaps that is what it means to write – to echo, to resound. Perhaps *HC* and *CL* are among the composers of the music we may hope to hear, and read, at the edges of the familiar world. In my songs and melodies, if you wish. The joyful sound of impure and painful music.

Her work is poiēsis. *She sits in a stone room opening onto the stars, the air, the night, the trees, with two small windows. The birds fly out the windows to the night, the trees, the air. The corner of the room curves down like a beak to create a corner that mirrors the curve of her nose, an aviary room. The floor is tiled in square red-brown tiles that match the colors of the desk. In the back of the room, close to where the ceiling curves down, a chest sits quietly with a metal cup resting on its top. It is a room, a place to work; it is a natural place, a place in nature, a place for creation. For joy.*

To her right, to a spectator's left, is a laboratory instrument, shaped like two ovaries, two eggs, one over the other, joined by a wire, connected in a standing pose. It is unmistakably a scientific, laboratory apparatus, unmistakably feminine, unmistakably organic, unmistakably incomprehensible. The egg shaped receptacles are shaped like ovaries, shaded like ovaries, living body organs. Fluid, energy, colors, pigments flow out of the upper receptacle ... organ onto the palette as pigments for the drawing ... writing, the writingdrawingpainting that emerges as life.

It is a room for the creation of life. It is the room for the creation of the birds. Nothing is unclean in this room. Everything is strange. The room is unworldly, sous-real, in but not of the world, in and out of human and other worlds, birds and women, science and painting, drawing and writing, image and language. All are other, other worlds, otherworldly. Nothing is cruel and nothing can be cruel. All is other. All is joy.

RV sits in the room, writing-drawing-creating birds that fly. She is inspired-facilitated-moved by scientific-organic energies. If this is nature, biology and humanity come together. If this is art, writing and drawing and organic reproduction are inseparable. This is a room for poiēsis *as an image of* mimēsis. *Nature, writing, poetry, science, magic, creation, production, and reproduction, all take place in their mysterious ways in the image, the work, the* mimēsis, *of a mysterious womanbird, the birdwoman who goes by the initials RV. If it is she.*

The joyful sound of painful music. The painfulness of joy. The He-philosopher who speaks most eloquently of joy is Spinoza. And perhaps he means to speak of *imund* when he says that hatred can be changed into love by joy. Certainly as a Jew he knew what the He-bible says of uncleanness and abomination.

> P46: If someone has been affected with Joy or Sadness by someone of a class, or nation, different from his own, and this Joy or Sadness is accompanied by the idea of that person as its cause, under the universal name of the class or nation, he will love or hate, not only that person, but everyone of the same class or nation.

> P43: Hate is increased by being returned, but can be destroyed by Love.

> P44: Hate completely conquered by Love passes into Love, and the Love is therefore greater than if Hate had not preceded it.

> P15: Any thing can be the accidental cause of Joy, Sadness, or Desire. . . .

> Cor.: From this alone – that we have regarded a thing with an affect of Joy or Sadness, of which it is not itself the efficient cause, we can love it or hate it. (Spinoza, *Ethics*, Part 3)

We hate what makes us sad; we love what gives us joy. And we hate or love an entire class or nation, an entire group or kind. We hate birds, animals, other human beings as *imund.* Yet *imund* is joy.

I do not say that Spinoza shares the love of animals, the joy of being *imund* with animal, cockroach, tiger, or bird. To the contrary.

> XXVI. Apart from men we know no singular thing in nature whose Mind we can enjoy, and which we can join to ourselves in friendship, or some kind of association. And so whatever there is in nature apart from men, the principle of seeking our own advantage does not demand that we preserve it. Instead, it teaches us to preserve or destroy it according to its use, or to adapt it to our use in any way whatever. (Spinoza, *Ethics*, Part 4, Appendix)

Even so, nature is in question, singular things in nature who can give us joy, plants and animals who are not of our world in their joy. *GH* discovers, *CL* shows us, *HC* asks us to think of feeling *imund* as joy, living in and out of nature, immanent, un-worldly, strange and unfamiliar and other to the law of this world as joy. With love. *HC* asks us to think and feel and place ourselves on a ladder by writing so that we might feel un-world as joy. Perhaps another joy. But right now, the question, perhaps, is what is *imund*, what is it to be un-worldly, other-to-the-law-of-the-world? What is the un-world of birds, women, and writing that is other, with joy?[12]

So a woman meets a barata, and it becomes the focus for a type of fantastic, total, emotional, spiritual, and intellectual revolution, which, in short, is a crime.[13]

And they call reading a sin, and writing is a crime. And no doubt this is not entirely false.[14]

Those who belong to the birds and their kind (these may include some men), to writings and their kind: they are all to be found – and a fair company it is – outside; in a place that is called by Those Bible, those who are the Bible, abominable.

Elsewhere, outside, birds, women, and writing gather.[15]

Those He-bible decides what is good and what is abominable to eat. *GH* imagines that if she can eat what oozes from the cockroach she will be saved. Eating is divine.

For redemption must be in the thing itself. And redemption in the thing itself would be my putting into my own mouth the white paste from the cockroach.

I knew that I would really have to eat the cockroach mass, and all of me eat it, even my very fear eat it. Only then would I have what suddenly seemed to me to be the anti-sin: to eat the cockroach mass is the anti-sin, sin that would kill myself.

The anti-sin. But at what a price. At the price of my going through the sensation of death.[16]

I dug my fingernails into the wall: now I tasted the bad taste in my mouth, and then I began to spit, to spit out furiously that taste of nothing at all, taste of a nothingness that nonetheless seemed to me almost sweetened with the taste of certain flower petals, taste of myself – I spit myself out, never reaching the point of feeling that I had finally spit out my whole soul.

I only stopped in my fury . . . when I realized that I was betraying myself. And that, poor me, I couldn't get beyond my own life.[17]

In the Christian tradition – perhaps not my tradition, if you will – eating is a passion. *GH*'s passion links body and blood with what is *imund* to eat. If the *barata* is the other, if it is a god, it is an animal with the destiny of animals for humans, to be eaten. To be treated with cruelty. Perhaps it is not so bad to eat an animal as *imund*, with joy instead of cruelty. Perhaps eating itself is *imund*, as are reading and writing. Perhaps *imund* is betrayal.

> We are eating. Reading is eating on the sly.
> Reading is eating the forbidden fruit, making forbidden love. . . .[18]

I am living in my culture, at least *GH*'s, *CL*'s, and *HC*'s culture, the Judeo-Christian culture if you will, where some are eaten and some are unclean, and living is a crime.

> We are criminals and we do not know how to express or prove that we are criminals. The problem is that if, as criminals, we were recognized as such, we would have to pay for the crime. ... How do we save our crime from the punishment and thus the forgiveness that threaten to wipe out our crime? How do we escape the burial of the fault that deprives us of our truth? (45)

This is Judeo-Christian fallenness, *GH*'s, *CL*'s, *HC*'s, perhaps *JD*'s as well. How do we escape the fault that returns? *GH* wants to eat the cockroach, believes that eating god or *barata* or something else will save her. Nothing will save her. Salvation belongs to their culture, to yours if you will. Eating is something everyone must do, but perhaps differently in every culture, every language, different especially toward every animal.

HC says that she chooses not to speak of women. And she does so in the name of exclusion.

> Each one of us – the whole of mankind, irrespective of sexual difference – must deal with the feeling of things being taken away from us. What is interesting is that birds, writing, and many women are considered abominable, threatening, and are rejected, because others, the rejectors, feel something is taken away from them. But let me leave women aside for today, since this is a controversial issue, and keep only birds and writing. Neither birds nor writing take anything away, yet people feel that some forms of writing do take something from us. (115)

Some people feel that birds, animals, life itself take something from us. We live in fear of what may be taken away. We hope to know what may be taken and how to hold it tightly for ourselves. And our kind.

GH loves what she does not know because it does not exclude her. So perhaps what we may seek in love and joy, in impurity and abomination, is not to exclude, especially not to exclude ourselves, not any part of ourselves. *HC* chooses, at least *for today*, to exclude women. Yet perhaps, in not speaking of women but of birds and writing, she speaks of nothing else. In speaking of writing and birds, in writing of birds and writing of writing, she is writing of women. Of women and birds and writing that do not exclude.

Perhaps she is writing of death, of a death that does not exclude. Perhaps of a cruelty not to be excluded.

If we faced a cruel death that did not exclude – for example the unclean and impure – would we eat more, eat more animals, eat and kill more animals, with more joy? If we knew the cruelties with which animals who will be eaten are treated, would we eat less or more? Would we desire to be less cruel?

The passage from those He-bible that speaks of what is unclean, abominable, impure, speaks of cruelty and of death. It may be read as speaking of life, what the Bible says we need to live. That is the death of certain kinds of animals and not others. Death is the condition of life. There does not seem to be an answer to that. Impurity, abomination, uncleanliness are other conditions of life. Birds, women, and writing may offer a joyous answer.

Even so, *HC* begins *Three Steps*, begins to climb up or go down, on the step of death. The school of the dead will teach us to live. It will teach us right in our face.

> We must have death, but young, present, ferocious, fresh death, the death of the day, today's death. The one that comes right up to us so suddenly we don't have time to avoid it, I mean to avoid feeling its breath touching us. Ha! (7)

Its breath touching us, alarming us. This is what I take *HC* to want to teach us, what we want to avoid feeling. We want to avoid feeling breath, want to avoid feeling being touched. By what? By death and cruelty. That is, by life.

> Here is the birth scene of writing for Thomas Bernhard: ... a butcher's shop. Open doors, axes, knives, cleavers, tidily arranged, slaughtering instruments some bloody, others shining and clean, slaughtering pistols, then the noise of the horses collapsing, those huge open bellies vomiting bones, pus, blood. Then past the butcher's, a few steps leading to the cemetery, to the morgue, to the tomb. (8)

The butcher's shop of animal death leads to the cemetery of human death. "Nothing but corpses." Bernhard's writing, with which *HC* begins her school of death, begins with animal deaths, animal slaughters, pus and blood. The death of animals for human life is the beginning of writing, the beginning of humanity, the beginning of women perhaps. And birds. The beginning of writing and humanity is the unworldliness of death. I mean the cruelty of life.

> As future skinned animals, to go to school we must pass before a butcher's shop, through the slaughter, to the cemetery door. Through the cemetery, our hearts beating from so much death, until we reach young life. This is our primary school, the school before school. The school to get to school. (8)

The school of death. The school of the dead. Filled with animals, dead and alive. It is the spring of writing, resistance to death, at least in a man's, Bernhard's hands. In *HC*'s writing it is something else.

I prefer to talk about it in terms of feminine sexuality, as a vital spring brought about and ordered by the disappearance of the one who was the source. (11)

Death is a vital spring that on the side of women – perhaps birds and animals – opens up the world in abundance. One might say *impurely* so long as one kept in mind and body the root.

What would make death pure? What would make life pure? The answer, given by the breath of animals, the touch of animals in our face, is that they are impure. Their impurity is our joy. Our impurity is from the schools of death and dreams and roots. With animals and the earth in mind. Again, roots and dreams and death.

I think we ought to only read the kind of books that wound and stab us. If the book we are reading doesn't wake us up with a blow on the head, what are we reading it for?

But we need the books that affect us like a disaster, that grieve us deeply, like the death of someone we loved more than ourselves, like being banished into forests far from everyone, like a suicide. A book must be the axe for the frozen sea inside us. (17)

This is Kafka speaking of writing and books. *FK*'s and *HC*'s and *CL*'s and *MB*'s writings affect us like a disaster. How, we ask, are we to live after the disaster? How are we to write? With joy. The answer is, with joy. However, that joy is from the disaster. That is, from within the end of the world, at the edge of the world, in the roots of things, death and cruelty. And so we return to plants whose roots are at the depths of things and the wounds of disaster. But perhaps that is just a bit too far to go down, even for *FN*. I keep thinking of the birds. And of animals on the way to slaughter killed by blows on the head. For us to eat. Is it ever time for a blow on the head to take us down to the roots where animals live and die? Can suffering take us down to face God, in the eyes of animals and women? Can we write before the face, of God, and birds, and women, and suffering?

It is worth a pause to reflect upon some of the other animals – living and dead – that inhabit *HC*'s schools of writing: birds of course, swans and storks; griffons and cockroaches; also cows, sheep, horses, pigs; chickens, ducks, geese – the animals of slaughter whose bones, pus, blood are the impurities for the living. With what joy? with what love?

The dead are our masters; the animals we kill are our lovers. We witness a scene, we watch performers on a stage, that oozes with the blood of animals, with unclean, impure blood.

I said that the first dead are our first masters, those who unlock the door for us that opens onto the other side, if only we are willing to bear it. Writing, in its noblest function, is the attempt to unerase, to unearth, to find the primitive picture again, ours, the one that frightens us. Strangely, it concerns a scene. The picture is not there without a reason. Those who have been in contact with this opening door perceived it in the theatrical form of a scene. Why a scene? Why is it a scene? Why will it become the scene of the crime? Because we are the audience of this scene: we are not in the scene; when we go to the theater we are not on stage. We are witnesses to an extraordinary scene whose secret is on the other side. We are not the ones who have the secret. It's a pictorial scene. (9)

I was writing down the names of animals in the schools of writing, beginning with their deaths. Earlier we were fireflies in the world, surrounded by an enormous concert (xxx); later mosquitoes brush up against Bernhard's "Montaigne" who interrupts this zoology, interrupts it by another, reminds us repeatedly that we are at the zoo: death, flight, panting, mosquitoes, the text bounds up 22 stairs like an animal. The reader reads like a body, with a body. If this is human it is human as animal, where the human body flees, climbs, bounds out of its animal body. That is, impure.

> The text flees paragraph by paragraph. "Montaigne" comes to an end in twenty-two steps or paragraphs – twenty-two bounds. Since you read with your body, your body paragraphs. The steps are almost comparable in size. Sometimes a bit shorter or a bit longer. And they are all equally dense and urgent.
>   It is immediately about the essential experiences of our lives. No sooner do we enter than we take flight. In the first paragraph we already have a series of directions. And each one of them will be pursued, none of them will be abandoned by the text. However, for the major part of this text, we run and flee in the dark. (23)
>   Montaigne said philosophizing is learning to die. Writing is learning to die. It's learning not to be afraid, in other words to live at the extremity of life, which is what the dead, death, give us. (9–10)

Philosophizing is learning to die, as are living and writing. This is something animals know, birds and horses. Not knowing by fearing death, but in the cruel impurity of life as death. Perhaps the cruelty of death as life. At the root we do not divide life from death, human from animal, woman from bird, man from woman, love from hate, truth from death, suffering from joy. At the root we are impure, with a cruel joy. Montaigne knew this in his language, the language of *HC* and *JD* if you like. Writing writes to link, to entwine, embrace. *GH* embraces the cockroach with joy.

In my culture, in my tradition, if you will, philosophy lives with death. *FN* asks us to live with life. As animals. *HC* begins with death on the way to roots. I do not know what that would mean for animals.

> To my sincere surprise, which is only the product of a form of blindness, I realized in time that the writers I love above all are of the dying-clairvoyant kind. What also reunites these authors is that they wrote, as I like to say, by the light of the axe: . . . they all dared to crack skulls, their own skulls, and return to the forest. (63)

Hens, ducks, and goats have good reason to fear the cruel axe, know too well whose skulls get cracked.

Writing leads us through the forest where the wild things are. *CL* leads us down into the forest where we are the wild things, where violence and love are wild and impure.

> It happens that I kill. My victim is a fly. It happens that when I write a fly enters: I try to chase it away; a combat begins. It happens that, having been unable to save the fly, I kill it. I admit this, then feel I have increased my share of the crime. I have killed flies and then there is no end to killing. Will I ever admit it? Never really. (42)

> In Clarice Lispector's pitiless works we sometimes measure ourselves and are measured against a being of our species – though one who is violently different from us – sometimes, as a woman, we are measured against a man, sometimes as a woman we are measured against a beggar, or against a blindman, or else against a hen, or against a barata; sometimes, as a man, we are measured against a dog. (43)

Dogs and cats compose the scene of the crime. I mentioned the scene and the crime. It is as if *HC* wished the crime upon us as the avowal of writing, her kind of writing if you will. She does not quite allow herself to say what *GH* and *CL* know explicitly: that animals are *imund*. She does not allow herself to live with a dog, who is *imund*. If *imund* is joy, if I am to love what I do not and cannot know, then animals – birds and horses and dogs and cockroaches – are what I love and cannot know, thereby allowing me to be *imund*. Animals are (at) the root, in and from the root. In death and dreams. With pain and cruelty. The roots are unthinkable, inexperienceable, without other living things. We are impure at the roots by means of them, what we do to them.

> How do we avow the unavowable? This is the problem the narration, the point of enunciation deals with in Edgar Allan Poe's "The Black Cat."
> It's about a man who tells an appalling story.
> His wife, who wishes to please him, brings cats, dogs, fish, etc., into the house ... and a black cat. This cat is called Pluto.
> The man's character alters. He becomes capable of violence and cruelty.
> The narrator ends up killing Pluto.
> A second cat arrives.
> One day the narrator goes down to the cellar with his wife and the cat. The characters cannot be distinguished. The cat slips between the narrator's legs who swings an axe at the cat. The cat is quicker than he is and the axe falls on his wife, cutting her in two.
> Poe wrote "The Black Cat" about this: a cat's love that is so infinite the narrator comes to hate the cat.
> Meeting a dog you suddenly see the abyss of love. Such limitless love doesn't fit our economy. We cannot cope with such an open, superhuman relation. (45–8)

The characters cannot be distinguished: men, women, cats; birds, women, writing; *imund*. It is a question of men and women, of sexual difference. Sexual difference is impure.

> Not only is there a war between people, but this war is produced by sexual difference. And not just by sexual difference. By the wiles, paradoxes, and surprises that sexual difference reserves for us. This is why the man–woman conflict is insufficient for me, in my time, in my place. It is a question of sexual difference, only sexual difference isn't what we think it is. It's both tortuous and complicated. There is sexual difference, and there is what it becomes in its appearances and distributions in each one of us. (50)

Death, cruelty, dreams, roots teach us more than we think, more than we think they are, more than we think we are. The schools we pass through on the ladder of writing are steps on the ladder of life. It is always more than we think it is, always more than it is.

It is always a question of men and women, animals and humans, cats and mice.

> There is something in the title "The School of Dreams" that plays with us: a type of displaced game of cat and mouse. Let's suppose that the mouse has a great desire to be eaten. (58)

> We are all dog-killers of the dog you are, killers of others. (53)

You've got another life to give, another body to be eaten, another desire for life and death. You've got these and you give these as a matter of writing. The body of writing is the dream of roots. In the forest where the wild things are.

> So perhaps dreaming and writing do have to do with traversing the forest, journeying through the world, using all the available means of transport, using your own body as a form of transport. (64)

Living with a cockroach or grub. *HC's* dream.[19] Living cruelly with birds and women in writing.

> [P]rovided they are told by fearless narrators, each human being's story is always the greatest and cruelest of stories. We are the ones who reduce and annihilate them to nothing. (49)

> We are approaching the point where the self bursts apart, the hour of cruelty. In a while we will kill, that is, we will show the ferocity hidden in us. Kill whom? Always the same creature, the figure of our impossible innocence.

> While walking she saw a dog and at the price of a huge effort to come out of close waters as if to come out of what no one can do, she decided to kill him while walking. (71–2)[20]

"My" writers, "my" sisters, "my" guides, what do they have in common? They have all written by the axe's light. They have sought bliss in savage conflict and have found it. (72)

Birds hover at the edges of our cruelty. Owls and eagles soar, cats stalk the streets of our humanity. Insects crawl on our skin. In our language, if you like. In our writing.[21]

Writing's impurity rises and falls on the steps of the ladder. As if its impurity had no world of its own. As if every world and un-world belonged to writing, at last of a certain kind. This returns us to the roots of language, *HC*'s and *CL*'s and *JD*'s language if you like. One can write only in one's language, and it is immensely difficult, perhaps impossible to change one's language. But that language is impure even when one knows no other language. One may say that language stares one in the face, whispers uncleanly in one's ear, echoes of that other language, that other world, over the limit, on the journey, right beside me here. Writing and animals and women are right beside me here. Unclean, impure, worldly and other worldly. Birds fly and I cannot fly like a bird – even if I could fly. Women are women as I cannot be – even after surgery. Writing is always in my language, my one or two or other languages, always confronting me with what I can say or perform, in my language if you like, and with what I cannot. And more, what I cannot say when I write, and what I can say when I do not know how to say it, what I do not know. One might say that in these ways writing is in the feminine, or is animalistic, wild, untamed, too ready to fly off. If there be language, if there be writing, it is given to us in the face of the animal or insect or bird who does not write.

The truth that writing needs is down below and a long way off. It stares us in the face of animals and insects, birds and plants, touches us with skin and fur and scales. Perhaps a snake has no face. Perhaps a cockroach has too much of a face. Perhaps writing is as strange as any animal face.

Who can deny what animals know? Who can deny the call of nature? As language and in writing.

> The natural word, the word *nature*, has a sad fate: it was taken up in the great disputes, aimed in particular at people like myself who work on the sexual scene. ... For a while ... I no longer used the word *nature*, even though I adore it. Then I adopted it again. As soon as I use it in the domain of writing it begins to move, to twist a little, because in *writing* this is what it's all about. As soon as there is writing, it becomes a matter of *passage*, of all kinds of passages, of delimitation, of overflowing. (128–9)

Overflowing in writing, a certain kind of writing if you like. As if nature and writing were impure: moving, twisting, passing, overflowing. We do not know what bodies and writing can do.[22]

> In Clarice's work ... there is nature of all kinds. She designates nature as "supernature," as "supernatural." She stresses that there is nothing more supernatural than nature. (129)

When I began to read Clarice I was enchanted by a tiny sentence in *The Stream of Life* that asked: "*And the turtles?* This is her oriflamme. The forgotten of the forgotten.

What would the two natures be for Clarice? The first, the one I love deeply, is the extraction from the repressed of what we are made of, i.e., matter. Clarice Lispector brings back more than the turtles to our feeble memories – because we notice tortoises from time to time; she returns the ability not to forget matter, which we don't notice: which we live, which we are. (130)

It is a matter of the nature that represses and the nature that transgresses, the nature that bounds and unbounding nature to adore, the marvelous, abundant, superfluent, overflowing, enchanted nature, filled with tiny animals and plants, cruelty and death. Writing is one of these plants. A plant that makes plants move. A name that moves.

As soon as there is writing. . . . As soon as there is *mimēsis*. . . .

If it is she . . . who is sitting in a highbacked chair, her arms resting on the arms of the chair, her hands on the curved wooden hand rests. But no, her hands are not resting, they are curving, are turning into the arms, are becoming wooden, are no longer hands. They are hands . . . wooden arms. The wooden, material arms of the chair are the woman's hands. She is a woman . . . chair; she is calm and peaceful, in repose; her eyes are wary.

Everything in the room is changing. Everything in the room is becoming, turning into something else. Everything is transfiguring, as if it were something else. The room is changing, becoming, imund. Imund is mimēsis. *Imund is* poiēsis. Mimēsis *and* poiēsis *are imund, and imund is joy.*

The woman – is it RV? – does not look joyful. She looks pensive, perhaps with joy. Her arms are changing into chair arms. Her feet are becoming chair feet, mimicking the feet of the chair in which she is sitting. To her left a basin of clothing is rising up behind the chair behind her head. A leg of the stand on which the basin sits is wrapping itself around a leg of the chair, as if it would wrap itself around her leg. In the far left corner the leg of a chair has slyly opened a drawer of a chest, drawing out a cloth. Up above the chest opens onto clouds and sky.

Sitting, becoming, moving, wrapping, transforming, transfiguring. Nature and the woman are mimēsis, *each the other, the other's* mimēsis.

Everything is touching something else. Everything is touching everything else. Nature, matter, bodies touch; transmuting and transforming by reaching, embracing, caressing. The woman's hands embrace the arms of the chair so deeply – and lightly – as to turn themselves over to them. The clothing in the hamper rises up to caress her shoulders. The leg of the stand curls around the leg of the chair as if it were in love, as it were in joy.[23]

As soon as there is language, writing, *mimēsis*. . . . This long excursion began with *JD*'s comment on his language. *Imund* and *immonde* are not words in my language, English if you will. In English we can speak of uncleanness and abomination but not at the limits of our world. *Impurity* may be as close as English can come to *GH*'s joy. For the moment, however, I'm interested in the joy of my language, if you will, not here the English language, not *JD*'s and *HC*'s language

– French or something else, perhaps – not even *GH*'s and *CL*'s language – Brazilian or Portuguese, perhaps.

Could my language, any language, be impure? Could a writer, any writer, know the impurity of writing in a language, the ways in which words cajole us, threaten us, make us unclean, the abominable task of writing, laying down the law, the hateful struggle with words that crawl on all fours on the ground, cockroach, *barata, cafard* words that soar like the hawk or eagle and crawl like a snake, still abominable … in joy? The joy of writing is writing in language, my language if you will, mine and yours, ours and no one's. Never mine alone.

In the wounds of time and space – memory, death, and loss – between one language and another, does the impure, the abominable, face us with hatred – and with love? Do we write – of birds and women; are we women and animals? – in this impure space of writing, not knowing whether we are up or down, ascending or descending, dreaming, dying, returning to and growing from our roots? Do we do these all with joy? Do we live with love?

In the He-bible, certain animals and birds are unclean, impure. In Descartes, animals have no reason at all. In *The Passion according to G. H.*, a cockroach is *barata*, impure with love, being *imund* is joy.

I cannot say this in English. I write in English, read *HC* in English, she who is said to be the greatest writer in her language. I would read her in French, yet here the French has passed over into English, impurely and uncleanly. I read *HC* in English of English and French and Brazilian Portuguese, which is itself impure, composed of colonial traces. As no doubt is *HC*'s and *JD*'s French. What is language but unclean, impure, *imund*? With joy.

The joy that follows sorrow is greater than if sorrow had not preceded it. The love that follows hatred is greater. The *mund* that follows *imund*, that grows from its roots, is greater. The human who is entwined among the roots and leaves and feathers and carapaces of nature is all the more human, all the more joyful and loving.

Not only human, *JD* says. Well beyond humanity.

the processes of difference, trace, iterability, ex-appropriation, and so on. These are at work everywhere, which is to say, well beyond humanity.[24]

I am thinking in particular of the mark in general, of the trace, of iterability, of differance. These possibilities or necessities, without which there would be no language, *are themselves not only human.*[25]

He is speaking of eating. We return to the *imund* of eating.

The moral question is thus not, nor has it ever been: should one eat or not eat, eat this and not that, the living or the nonliving, man or animal, but since *one must* eat in any case and since it is and tastes good to eat, and since there's no other definition of the good [*du bien*], *how* for goodness' sake should one *eat well* [*bien manger*]?[26]

The sublime refinement involved in this respect for the other is also a way of "eating well," in the sense of "good eating" but also "eating the Good" [*le Bien manger*]. The Good can also be eaten. And it, the good, must be eaten and eaten well.[27]

Animals and humans are linked in the *imund* well beyond humanity. By language – reading, writing, speaking; perhaps by drawing, painting, singing, acting. The possibilities of language are not only human and not only language. Animals and humans are linked by eating, by the necessity and the obligation and the goodness and the violence of eating. And eating is not only eating, opening the law to what is clean and what is unclean, to propriety and impropriety, to passion beyond knowledge and world.

Could the *mund* be animal flesh? Could the *imund* be animal bodies? Is there a point at which we may write the animal body without insisting on consuming it?

In *GH*'s and *HC*'s culture eating is the cruelty of the necessity that devours animals for the sake of human beings. Well beyond humanity. Perhaps not *JD*'s or my culture. Language and culture are both my culture, with its laws, and not only that culture, not only those laws. Knowledge and truth and passion and joy are beyond themselves.

As *GH* says: "I can love only the unknown evidence of things and can add myself only to what I do not know."[28] I would understand her to mean that I cannot love what I know, that knowledge, science, philosophy, who knows what, are incompatible with love and joy. Perhaps the unknown, unknowable, are where we need to turn for love and joy, turn to find ourselves.

> And giving myself over with the confidence of belonging to the unknown.
> And such a giving of myself is the only surpassing that doesn't exclude me.[29]

Returning ourselves to God.

> For I can pray only to what I do not know. . . .
> And, therefore, I adore.[30]

I prefer the cockroach, dog, and bird. It is nature that I adore. God is love, and God is law. What I do not know is not what looks down on me but what I look at in the face, what is face to face with mine. The cockroach, *GH*'s *barata*, is right there before her in its incomprehension, her incomprehension, incomprehending her right in the face. Before the face, as Levinas says, except that he did not know if a snake had a face. And he meant that he did not know if the snake called to him beyond humanity, beyond subjectivity. I do not know if the face of the snake is *imund* in my culture, or in *HC*'s and *CL*'s culture if you will.

I do not know if a snake or a cockroach has a face, whether I can know the face of the earth, rivers, mountains, and plants. But I do know that their world is not mine even as it is ours, that the world-poverty of the animal[31] may be the world-richness of ours, that our world is the richer for animal worlds, worlds that make it impure. Impurity is joy. Heterogeneity is abundance. Death and dreams and roots entwine among the impurities of the earth, of writing, of language.

The possibility of meaning, of writing, in my language – *JD*'s, *HC*'s, *GH*'s, and *CL*'s language if you will – is the unmeaning, unwriting, unliteracy, cruelty of language – and well beyond. It is the cacophony of the sound, the silence of the word, the materiality of the medium: the viscosity and smell and sheen of paint, the hardness of the stone, the gestures of bodies that do things our minds wonder at, in love and joy.[32] It is the betrayal of the truth, the revelation of the impurity of truth, in joy and love.

> Insistence is our effort, desistance is the prize. One gets the prize when she has experienced the power of building and, in spite of the taste of power, prefers desistance. Desistance has to be a choice. To desist is a life's most sacred choice. To desist is the true human moment. And it alone is the glory proper to my condition.
> Desistance is a revelation.[33]

Desistance before the law, in the face of necessity, passivity beyond passivity, vulnerability, these are revelations beyond humanity, animality, divinity, and responsibility. In the name of language, well beyond language, beyond reading and writing, beyond words. In the depths of words is something beyond words. In the depths of humanity, in the face of an animal, is the earth beyond any world – our world, if you wish, never only ours.

> We have lost the taste of hands, of the touching of hands. We have lost all the small and great secrets of joy. But the country of exile is not unattainable. It is even easier to go to that country, Exile, than it sometimes is to cross the border of a country like the United States.[34]

My country if you will.

As it were in joy. She is somewhere between becoming transfigured and transfiguring. We cannot tell if this is happening to her or happening with her, even being made to happen by her. The stillness of her body as it becomes something else, as the room turns into other things, is the becoming of her mind. The quietness of her body and her mind do not mean that she is afraid or passive, that she is empty. If she is imund, if she is at the root, if she has ascended by descending to the impure root, she is joyful in her repose and mobile in her stillness.

A cat is under the floor watching through a hole. Perhaps a hole in which a cockroach lives. Perhaps the cat has caught the cockroach. Perhaps the cat is imund. Perhaps the cat is watching the mund from the edge, the crack, where it becomes unworldly. Perhaps animals, cats and dogs and insects especially, animals who live in human worlds, crack the edges of our worlds.

Descartes says the animal, the bird or cat, has no reason at all. Cats do not speak our language, if you like, French or English. But perhaps they speak another language, or practice a language they do not speak, or know a reason we can never know because it knows nothing of our language. In the face, the eyes, the paws, fangs, and claws, the fur and skin, in the touch of animals is joy. The cacophony and mimēsis of the world is strange and impure joy.

My mimēsis if you like.

CHAPTER TEN: IRIGARAY

ANIMAL COMPASSION

Luce Irigaray

How can we talk about them? How can we talk to them? These familiars of our existence inhabit another world, a world that I do not know. Sometimes I can observe something in it, but I do not inhabit it from the inside – it remains foreign to me. The objective signs that appear do not bring me the key to the meaning for them, the meaning among themselves. Not really, unless I project my human imaginary onto them. To make them simple objects of study is not appropriate any more than to make them partners of a universe that they do not share. What to say about them? Except to narrate the signs of themselves that animals have given me? What I have perceived, received from them. To bring together at times what various authors, sages or traditions have already said.

So, at first, to bear witness through relating. Not everything obviously, just a few facts. The most constant companionship of my childhood, its greatest joys are bound to animals. To contemplate a flowering bush covered with fluttering butterflies moved me to ecstasy, or something close. I later learned that the word *papillon* ("butterfly") comes from a Greek word meaning "soul." I would contemplate for hours those souls flying or resting in the empyrean or some terrestrial paradise. Nourishing themselves from the nectar of flowers and giving thanks by beating their wings. That spectacle brought me a perception of what beatitude could be. Alas! I wasn't satisfied with approaching beatitude such as it was offered to me in such a way. I wanted to appropriate it – a naïve gesture to which I devoted any number of hours of my childhood. Impossible to measure the time dedicated to waiting for a butterfly to appear in the garden, the meadow, the forest. Nor the patience spent in waiting for it to alight, fly away, return, depart again and stop finally on a beloved flower where my hand or a net would pluck it. What the butterfly would give me in happiness would vanish with this gesture, or almost. No doubt the flight of a butterfly on the window put a little lightness and joy into the house. But only briefly. How not to under-stand that it would truly be generous only when I contemplated it in a space appropriate to its life? To give thanks for what it let me perceive should have sufficed to perpetuate, indeed amplify, a joy to which capture put an end.

Perhaps I should have wished that the butterfly choose me? It happened – later, it is true – that one of them came to rest on me. I did not, then, retain it. I stayed immobile the time it wanted to stay there, indeed to walk or flutter on me here and there, and I let it go away when it pleased. That happened notably at a difficult moment of my existence. A modest white butterfly seemed thus to assure me of its friendship. Perceiving to what point I needed its friendship? Astonishingly, it lit on me at a moment when I was engaged in a somewhat difficult conversation with a friend. That it did so with me helped me to stay quiet without useless raving. In some way it marked the limits of my territory, reminding me that it was also a part of it, that I was not as alone or as powerless as it might seem.

Are animals sometimes messengers? Come from where? Sent by whom? Or what? By themselves? Or??

The unhoped for support provided by that butterfly other animals have given me at critical moments of my life. I could speak endlessly of the helpful presence of rabbits in my childhood. More than dolls, I loved their company. And, may they forgive me if, there too, I sometimes removed them from their universe to dress them in clothes and walk them in a baby carriage, like dolls. I treated them nevertheless with great gentleness, and they did not seem to suffer from my bustling activity. One of the happy events I hold in my memory is to have shared my room one night with a litter of young rabbits. An exceptional parental indulgence had permitted me to carry them up in a crate, slid under my bed. That sleep accompanied by the beating of their hearts was the sweetest of my childhood. On the other hand, when I learned through a letter my mother sent to the boarding school where secondary studies kept me captive of the death of a cherished rabbit, little Moïse, whom I had rescued from drowning in a washtub, I decided that my urban sojourn had lasted long enough. It was time for me to return to watch over the garden and its inhabitants. How to obtain this impossible parental authorization? I began a hunger strike. The pediatrician's verdict was in my favor. He prescribed freedom as a remedy. He has a claim to my eternal gratitude. Returning "home" somewhat weakened, I was roundly scolded for my resistance to family projects. And they invited me "to go look outside if I must." I thus found myself back in the garden.

I leave the girl in her preferred landscape with her winged and furry friends. Being thus immersed in life was her consolation, her happiness. She demanded nothing more.

But what became of her exiled in "adult life"? In "society"? In the "city"? The risks of the world assailed her, the contrived, technological world, and the pains coming from the world of work, but even more from the community of humans. Lack of understanding dominates there. Compassion is rare. Distress causes flight. Sometimes on their own or thanks to an attentive heart, certain childhood companions rejoined her. They comforted her, healing her, giving her confidence and energy. Thus, after the savage repression which followed her first book, the exclusion from her university teaching and the rejection by various analysts who presumably listened to her, she simply could not recover from a bad case of the flu. A worried friend had the idea to offer her a little rabbit. A few hours sufficed to make her feel like getting on her feet, a day or two for health to return. She had to take care of the livelihood of the rabbit, and to do this to leave the phantasms of death with which humans had infected her. It was a little female rabbit who quickly showed a strong will. As soon as she could, she furiously gnawed the wicker of the basket used to carry her. The spectacle of the sleeper-car that she had shared could only make its occupants flee in the wee hours, fearing some sanction by the railway authorities. It was on a trip to the mountains. During that stay, the jealousy of the rabbit came alive: she became adult. Whenever there was a telephone call too long for her taste, she nibbled pitilessly the text I had just written. If I sat down with some friend on a couch, the latter was subsequently inundated with urine. And I could go on. I found some caretakers during my vacation. From their place she presumably escaped. I rather think they ate her. But a curious event happened several years later which perhaps shows I was mistaken. I had just returned, after many months of absence, to my hermitage – if I dare call it that – in the Forest of Foutainbleau. I was afraid to go back and at the same time wanted to. At first I made short stays with friends. On the first stay, awake before the others, I opened the shutters of my room and espied with emotion my rabbit – or one of her descendants? – gamboling on the terrain. Impossible to confuse her with a wild rabbit, given the color. One brief glance, and she disappeared. She gave me just a sign of welcome.

For many months as soon as I arrived there, scarcely out of the car to raise the barrier, a bird would whistle, one of those birds that imitates a human voice so well you can be fooled. I was tricked each time, turning around to thank whoever was welcoming me. There was no one, if it not the bird, invisible to me but whose greeting I recognized. I was, then, expected. By the squirrels also. More demanding than generous, perhaps. If I filled their feeder as soon as I got in, they would let me sleep in the morning, if not, I couldn't count on it. And if, by mischance, I rose a little abruptly after a siesta on the lawn where they had come to frolic, they reprimanded me violently, from a branch beyond my reach for the fear I had involuntarily caused them. But how could I resent them. They are so entertaining to watch, their rage included?

The most precious and also the most mysterious aid has most often come to me from birds. The most decisive was that brought by a very little bird, probably a sparrow, who had come to perch on the sill of the balcony of my Paris apartment one December day when a storm was raging. How did that baby bird come there in winter and in such weather? I have no explanation, but he was there, a sign of life and friendship which was providential for me. Like the rabbit, he did not dally. The comfort lavished by animals, especially winged, is as timely as grace. And the advent of that little messenger has remained unforgettable like that of certain blessings. Certain other blessings?

Birds are our friends. But also our guides, our scouts. Our angels in some respect. They accompany persons who are alone, comfort them, restoring their health and their courage. Birds do more. Birds lead one's becoming. The bird's song heals many a useless word, it makes the breath virginal again and helps it rise. The birds' song restores silence, delivers silence. The bird consoles, gives back to life, but not to inertia. The bird animates breath while safeguarding its materiality. It is, more than overly logical speech, the pathway to restore but also transsubstaniate the body, the flesh. It is not for naught that the bird appears as the spiritual assistant, even the spiritual master, in many a tradition. Most of the birds love us but want us inhabited by a subtle, divine breath.

At times it is enough to hear them sing for this to happen. Their vocalizings lead our breath from elementary vitality to the most ethereal of the mental, and beyond. Like mantras, they go from the low to the high-pitched and shrill, from the high-pitched to the low, not without pausing on certain tonalities, raising the breath without ever cutting it from its corporeal site, from the intimacy of the flesh. Moreover, their vocal scale changes according to the seasons, the hours of the day, and the weather. Birds celebrate the harmony of nature, they praise the return of the sun, the joy of spring. They transform the energy they then receive into useful activity, games, songs of thanks and love. Does there exist an amorous incantation more moving than that of a nightingale? No word of a human declaration has touched me as much at least in the instant. And the words of seduction of a lover either do not reach the most secret part of our flesh or we cannot perceive them as such at the moment we hear them. Words often fail us human beings, there where birds are capable of rousing us with their song.

How to respond to their call? If not through becoming the delicate friends they want us to be? By listening to their instruction as well. Calling to love by singing: Is that not better than using the eyes or the hand to try to capture the other's desire? It is, however, what our learned philosophers prescribe, imagining themselves very superior to animals. To subdue, to possess, to violate the modesty or intimacy of the other, seems, for them, a proof of virility, rather than learning to sing to invite, at a distance, the other to come much closer. Western reason has led us to forget song and poetry as words permitting an encounter between us. We pass from submission to a language founded on abstract argumentation to mute comportments where there is a dominator and a dominated. It is always the same logic, alien to the sharing of speech, of love, of desire. Birds seem more advanced than we are in the amorous dialogue, and could serve as our guides at least a part of the way, if we keep still to listen to them.

I have evoked little about the animals termed domestic or domesticated. I do not like this relationship to animals very much, and I have only rarely, or briefly, animals at my home, brought there through someone else's initiative, not mine. I like animals in their home, living in their territory, and coming from time to time to offer me freely some testimony of friendship. I like them also in the domain we share; earth. I try never to harm them, even inadvertently, in this common universe. Besides, they reveal themselves generally inoffensive there, unless we ourselves bother them, because of fear which keeps them from approaching us. If so-called domestic animals have become aggressive, it is often by an artificial cultivation of their instincts. As a friend wisely taught me, a satisfied animal does not look for blood. Such a comportment is human. When animals are subjected to people, do they feel constrained to imitate this behavior? I have noticed something interesting in this regard: the fact that I have become vegetarian, which means for me giving up killing to eat, has made certain animals, dogs, for example, more friendly to me. A silent non-aggression pact exists between us. Having less fear, they attack less. And I, for my part, experience less fear toward them.

I cannot yet welcome with enthusiasm, yet, alas, just any animal that gets in my house. Some still provoke my terror, hence my rejection. Let us hope that Buddha will lead me to universal hospitality and that every animal will become, by that fact, a guardian for me. In the meantime, it remains for me to call on

Lord Vishnu, creator and restorer of life, beseeching him to help me not make an attempt on the existence of some invading animal. It has happened that after my plea, the animal has mysteriously disappeared. It happens also that I kill it not without regret or remorse. In hoping that this time will be the last!

Nevertheless I granted hospitality one night to an animal presumed dangerous: a hornet. One summer evening, it came to rest on the inside of a lamp shade in the room where I was reading. It was not disturbing me. Why hurt it? The problems began when it came time to go to bed. The hornet no longer wanted to leave me! It followed the light wherever I went. I was obliged to use a stratagem to shut it away in the kitchen, my courage not going so far as to let him sleep in my bedroom. The next day I opened the window where it was resting, and it flew out peacefully. What message was that hornet bearing? Anyway, it was not hostile to me. Perhaps I had needed that distraction? Or proof that a hornet is not so systematically harmful as we have tended to believe?

What can I say, as a philosopher, about these animal comportments? What do they want to tell us? In all the events narrated, it is always a question of bringing help. It is difficult to impute it simply to chance, especially if all the signs of help received are placed in relation. It would be problematic also to object that I have projected my needs or desire on the random appearance of some animal. Should it accordingly be thought that the help brought by these unhoped for messengers was sent by some superior power? Would not that deny what the animals are themselves? More receptive to certain phenomena than humans who have developed their mental powers to the detriment of the so-called more archaic zones of the brain? Capable of perceiving a call where human beings hear nothing, and of providing a comforting presence where more rational arguments would have neither appeased nor healed the suffering or distress. Where a human body or affectionate gesture would not have been able to have the simplicity of an animal presence. As pure as that of an angel, Rilke claimed. Or that of a child? Who feels, also the danger or the trial that the other is going through.

Where does the extraordinary intuition of these mysterious assistants in our lives come from, of which they sometimes bear witness? Once, during a stay with a friend living on a high floor of an urban tower, I was seized by a disturbing and ambiguous vertigo. I tried not to let any of it show. But the cat of the household perceived my difficulty: he came over to walk between the opened bay window and the place where I had stopped during the time it took for my malaise, my anguish, to dissipate. No question of showing him any gratitude. He was acting as lord of the manor, seeming to know what was suitable for each and to play his role in maintaining order in the world.

Was this cat conscious of his gesture? No doubt. But certainly, differently from us Westerners, or he would not have bothered with a concealed and mute suffering. Certain Eastern masters seem closer than we are to the perception of that sorrow or universal joy, that silently propagating through air, through light … ? Our mythologies themselves speak of gods or angels who come to succor us in distress. They know it without our having had to express it, at least rationally. And they intervene with mediations other than those we use as means of communication considered appropriate for human beings.

Such facts exist: they are not only the fruit of the imagination. At least it is that way for me. The animals I evoked forth were absolutely real, and not imaginary, allegorical or symbolic. Like those of Nietzsche, perhaps? They were truly there, physically present. But not only in the sense in which we understand it. It is not simple matter, vitally animated, surviving in some respect, that came to support me in my difficulties, my abandonment. But rather a living body having at its disposition sense capabilities that we, as humans, have lost. In separating body and mind, matter and thought? In claiming to make of one the dominator of the other, renouncing thereby without knowing or wanting it so all the potentialities resulting from the passage of one to the other, from one into the other. Having developed the perversities or kinds of cancerous mental prolif-erations there where a superior energy would have been able, should have been able, to transform our elementary vitality into more subtle breath. Enjoying thus more extraordinary powers certainly than those of the animal, but that we have left behind for other works where friendship and compassion have less place, retain less attention, have finally less value. We have had thus amputated what we had that was more precious, making animals, angels or gods the figures of humans we have not succeeded in being. At least not yet.

This does not mean that we have totally lost the memory of it and that these messengers cannot put us back on the way. On the condition that we do not use their assistance to pursue our project of arrogant world domination. That we try to stop ourselves and listen to what touches us and helps us through their presence. That we pay attention to the part of us that is then upheld, indeed reanimated, to continue or resume, our course, and how it happens that these animal interventions in my life remain unforgettable? Not as a more or less egocentric memory, even narcissistic memory, of my humanity, but rather as a relational mystery for which above all I wish to give thanks.

How to distinguish this animal assistance from that of humans in similar circumstances? The latter have rarely the same immediacy or simplicity, and the quality of help that an animal can bring us without harming ourselves, our own way and freedom. Human help procures rarely this memory of life, this recall to life accorded by an animal's and sometimes a child's presence. Humans borrow the mediation of a communication code, of personal experience which prevent a simple being-there. They are complex, often passed on through an instru-mental and secretly hierarchical technique, because of an economy of debt, of obligatory gratitude, leaving us less autonomous. Only a few masters are capable of transmitting to us by compassion a little of that free energy we need. This then has a different quality: more subtle than animal help, it leads us more to wonder about our course, even later or indirectly. Most often we let animals offer us their support without asking ourselves too many questions. It is not the same on the part of a human. What this gives makes us interrogate ourselves, includes an obscure form of indication for our becoming, an unconscious problem of imitation. In our dereliction, some spiritual parent would silently point to the road to take. That would not necessarily belong to the visible order. The injunction would rather be confided to listening, feeling. We would perceive the message a little like that of the animal but at another level, the animals themselves touching us moreover at diverse levels of ourselves, according to their species, birds no doubt accompanying us the furthest along our way.

The support a human brings us is more or less than that of the birds. That depends on the timing of their course, of the capacity they have for addressing the entirety of what, or of whom, we are. The dimension of reciprocity there is also more important. The intervention of a master will be all the more decisive in that it does not remain simply hierarchical, parental, but calls for a mutual exchange. Even if the latter is only announced, will happen only later, a possibility or a secret obligation is revealed. We enter there into a proper human assistance on our way. This favor does not often arrive, and an entire life may have no experience of it. It belongs perhaps to a scarcely foreseen future of our human becoming. It is the term which gives us, or will give us, of being truly born into our humanity. And to discover there what can be the amorous exchange, the embrace not only of bodies but also of hearts, of thoughts, of all ourselves, a total embracing at some crossroads of our way. A difficult favor to receive while remaining faithful to our singularity, and which asks us to remember ourselves and to prepare a reciprocity with respect to the other.

To know in this way, the most intimate proximity and to work it out from a distance, in difference, in autonomous space and time but allowing a becoming of the encounter, seems the task to which we are called as human beings. For this unity of ourselves and at that crossroads where the other awaits us we are little prepared. It means learning to meet the other and to welcome them in their difference, to be reborn thus in a fidelity to ourselves and to this other. Towards this accomplishment we must force ourselves along the way with the aid or friendship of animals, of angels, and of gods who agree to accompany us in a course towards the accomplishment of our humanity.

Translated by Marilyn Gaddis Rose

NOTES

PREFACE

1   Charles Magel, *Keyguide to Information Sources in Animal Rights* (Jefferson, NC: McFarland, 1989).
2   *The Animal Rights Crusade: The Growth of a Moral Protest* (New York: Free Press, 1992), p. 90.
3   For further details, see the preface to the Ecco 2001 edition of Peter Singer, *Animal Liberation*.

EDITORS' INTRODUCTION: THE ANIMAL QUESTION IN CONTINENTAL PHILOSOPHY

1   Martin Heidegger, *What Is Called Thinking?*, trans. J. Glenn Gray (New York: Harper & Row, 1968), p. 16.
2   Friedrich Nietzsche, *The Antichrist*, in *The Portable Nietzsche*, trans. Walter Kaufmann (New York: Penguin, 1982), section 14, 580.
3   Ibid.
4   Ibid., 614.
5   Martin Heidegger, *Parmenides*, trans. André Schuwer and Richard Rojcewicz (Bloomington: Indiana University Press, 1992), p. 154.
6   Gilles Deleuze and Félix Guattari, *A Thousand Plateaus: Capitalism and Schizophrenia*, trans. Brian Massumi (Minneapolis: University of Minnesota Press, 1987), p. 11.
7   Ibid., p. 23.
8   Gary L. Francione, *Rain without Thunder: The Ideology of the Animal Rights Movement* (Philadelphia: Temple University Press, 1996).
9   Luce Irigaray, *An Ethics of Sexual Difference*, trans. Carolyn Burke and Gillian C. Gill (Ithaca, NY: Cornell University Press, 1993), p. 5.

CHAPTER ONE: NIETZSCHE

O MY ANIMALS (FRIEDRICH NIETZSCHE)

1   Friedrich Nietzsche, *Thus Spoke Zarathustra*, trans. Walter Kaufmann (New York: Penguin, 1980), III, "The Convalescent," 2.
2   Friedrich Nietzsche, *Human, All too Human*, trans. R. J. Hollingdale (Cambridge: Cambridge University Press, 1986), I, 18.
3   Friedrich Nietzsche, *Daybreak*, trans. R. J. Hollingdale (Cambridge: Cambridge University Press, 1997), 26.
4   Ibid., 108.
5   Friedrich Nietzsche, *On the Genealogy of Morals*, trans. Walter Kaufmann (New York: Vintage, 1969), II, 16.
6   Friedrich Nietzsche, *The Gay Science*, trans. Walter Kaufmann (New York: Vintage, 1974), 294.
7   Ibid., para. 39.

8   Ibid., para. 55.
9   *Thus Spoke Zarathustra*, III, "On Old and New Tablets," 19.
10 *The Gay Science*, para. 10.
11 *Thus Spoke Zarathustra*, IV, "On the Higher Man," 4.
12 *Thus Spoke Zarathustra*, IV, "On Science."
13 *Thus Spoke Zarathustra*, "Prologue," 10.
14 *Thus Spoke Zarathustra*, III, "The Convalescent," 2.

NIETZSCHE AND ANIMALS (ALPHONSO LINGIS)

1   Friedrich Nietzsche, *Thus Spoke Zarathustra*, trans. Walter Kaufmann (New York: Penguin, 1980), IV, "The Drunken Song," 9.
2   Friedrich Nietzsche, *Daybreak*, trans. R. J. Hollingdale (Cambridge: Cambridge University Press, 1997), I, "Animals and Morality," 26.
3   Friedrich Nietzsche, *On the Genealogy of Morals*, trans. Walter Kaufmann (New York: Vintage, 1969), III, 14.
4   Jared Diamond, *Guns, Germs and Steel* (New York: Norton, 1999).
5   Barbara Ehrenreich, *Blood Rites: Origins and History of the Passions of War* (New York: Henry Holt, 1997).
6   Nietzsche, *On the Genealogy of Morals*, II, 1.

CHAPTER TWO: HEIDEGGER

THE ANIMAL IS POOR IN WORLD (MARTIN HEIDEGGER)

1   Martin Heidegger, *The Fundamental Concepts of Metaphysics: World, Finitude, Solitude*, trans. William McNeill and Nicholas Walker (Bloomington: Indiana University Press, 1995), pp. 177, 197, 198.

HEIDEGGER'S ZOONTOLOGY (MATTHEW CALARCO)

1   This charge has been made most notably and most forcefully by Jacques Derrida, in, for example, *Of Spirit: Heidegger and the Question*, trans. Geoffrey Bennington and Rachel Bowlby (Chicago: University of Chicago Press, 1989). See also Jean-Luc Nancy's interview with Derrida, "'Eating Well,' or the Calculation of the Subject," in *Who Comes after the Subject?*, ed. Eduardo Cadava, Peter Connor, and Jean-Luc Nancy (New York: Routledge, 1991), pp. 96–119.
2   Martin Heidegger, *Hölderlins "Germanien" und "Der Rhein"*, ed. S. Ziegler (Frankfurt am Main: Klostermann, 1980), p. 75, quoted in Michel Haar, *The Song of the Earth: Heidegger and the Grounds of the History of Being*, trans. Reginald Lilly (Bloomington: Indiana University Press, 1993), p. 29.
3   Martin Heidegger, "The Nature of Language," in *On the Way to Language*, trans. Peter D. Hertz (San Francisco: Harper, 1971), p. 107. For two contrasting readings of this enigmatic passage, see Giorgio Agamben, *Language and Death: The Place of Negativity*, trans. Karen E. Pinkus with Michael Hardt (Minneapolis: University of Minnesota Press, 1991), and Jacques Derrida, *Aporias: Dying—Awaiting (One Another at) the "Limits of Truth"*, trans. Thomas Dutoit (Stanford: Stanford University Press, 1993).
4   Martin Heidegger, *The Fundamental Concepts of Metaphysics: World, Finitude, Solitude*, trans. William McNeill and Nicholas Walker (Bloomington: Indiana University Press, 1995), p. 267. All parenthetical citations in the text refer to this volume.
5   Martin Heidegger, "Letter on 'Humanism,'" in *Pathmarks*, ed. William McNeill (Cambridge: Cambridge University Press, 1998), p. 247.
6   Ibid., p. 248.
7   Martin Heidegger, *What Is Called Thinking?*, trans. J. Glenn Gray (New York: Harper & Row, 1968), p. 16.

8   Martin Heidegger, *Parmenides*, trans. André Schuwer and Richard Rojcewicz (Bloomington: Indiana University Press, 1992), p. 154.
9   The outlines of this project have been sketched by David Farrell Krell in his impressive volume *Daimon Life: Heidegger and Life-Philosophy* (Bloomington: Indiana University Press, 1992).
10 Heidegger, "Letter on 'Humanism,'" p. 248.
11 Martin Heidegger, *An Introduction to Metaphysics*, trans. Ralph Manheim (New Haven: Yale University Press, 1987), p. 45.
12 Martin Heidegger, "The Origin of the Work of Art," in *Poetry, Language, Thought*, trans. Albert Hofstadter (New York: Harper & Row, 1971), p. 45.
13 See note 4 for full bibliographical information. The secondary literature on this lecture course is quite massive. Some of the more important scholarly and critical commentaries can be found in the following works: Jacques Derrida, *Of Spirit*; David Farrell Krell, *Daimon Life*; William McNeill, "Life beyond the Organism: Animal Being in Heidegger's Freiburg Lectures, 1929–30," in *Animal Others: On Ethics, Ontology, and Animal Life*, ed. H. Peter Steeves (Albany: SUNY, 1999), pp. 197–248; Didier Franck, "Being and the Living," in *Who Comes after the Subject?*, pp. 135–47; Jean-Luc Nancy, *The Sense of the World*, trans. Jeffrey S. Librett (Minneapolis: University of Minnesota Press, 1997); and Giorgio Agamben, *The Open: Man and Animal*, trans. Kevin Attell (Stanford: Stanford University Press, forthcoming).
14 See *Being and Time*, trans. John Macquarrie and Edward Robinson (New York: Harper & Row, 1962), pp. 91–168, and "On the Essence of Ground," in *Pathmarks*, pp. 97–135.
15 As we will see, however, despite his efforts to examine the animal's relation to world on its own terms, Heidegger will in the final analysis be forced partially to retract his thesis on the world poverty of the animal inasmuch as the notions of "poverty" and "deprivation" have a meaning only in relation to something else that has a comparative plenitude in relation to world, namely, the human.
16 The reader might have noticed the slippage from talking about a particular lizard to a generalization about "the animal" in the general singular. The slippage is not mine but Heidegger's, and I will discuss this type of hasty generalization later in the paper.
17 For a useful discussion of Descartes's remarks on animals and awareness, see Tom Regan's *The Case for Animal Rights* (Berkeley: University of California Press, 1983), chapter 1.
18 Recent work on bee cognition (stemming from the seminal investigations of Karl von Frisch) suggests that Heidegger's conclusions might be mistaken. Bees may in fact have cognitive skills that cannot be explained simply in terms of instinctual or "driven" behavior. For a helpful overview of the literature on these debates, see James L. Gould "Can Honey Bees Create Cognitive Maps?," *The Cognitive Animal: Empirical and Theoretical Perspectives on Animal Cognition*, ed. Marc Bekoff, Colin Allen, and Gordon M. Burghardt (Cambridge, MA: MIT Press, 2002).
19 Haar, *Song of the Earth*, p. 29.
20 McNeill, "Life Beyond the Organism," p. 245.
21 See note 13 above.
22 See Martin Heidegger, "Plato's Doctrine of Truth," in *Pathmarks*, pp. 181–2.
23 Although the reader can consult the passages I cited in the opening section of the essay for confirmation of this tendency, the following remark from *The Fundamental Concepts of Metaphysics* serves as further evidence that Heidegger's thinking remains uncritical with regard to traditional oppositional human/animal distinctions: "There belongs to man a being open for ... *of such a kind* that this being open for ... has the character of *apprehending something as something*. This kind of relating to beings we call comportment, as distinct from the behavior of the animal. Thus man is *zoōn logon echon*, whereas the animal is *alogon*. Despite the fact that our interpretation and way of questioning is altogether different from that of antiquity, it is not saying anything substantially new, but – as always and everywhere in philosophy – purely the same" (306).
24 Although I do not have the space to develop this reading here, one might suggest that Heidegger's work is radically non-anthropocentric inasmuch as, for Heidegger, the essence of man is "nothing human," and that every determination of human essence is a "question"

rather than an "answer." On this reading, what is at issue in Heidegger's work is not a recovery of the human but rather an opening onto *Dasein*, which would render Heidegger's texts *Dasein*-centric, if anything. While such a reading is no doubt correct as far as it goes, it is also necessary to counter-balance this aspect of Heidegger's thought with Derrida's critical remarks about *Dasein* being proper to man, and *man alone*: "We can see then that Dasein, though *not* man, is nevertheless *nothing other* than man" (Jacques Derrida, "The Ends of Man," in *Margins of Philosophy*, trans. Alan Bass [Chicago: University of Chicago Press, 1982], p. 127).

25 I thank Steven Vogel for helpful discussions of several of the issues raised in this paper, especially the question of Heidegger's anthropocentrism. I also wish to thank Will McNeill and Lawrence Hatab for their insightful questions and comments on the issue of animals in Heidegger's work at the Heidegger panel at the Central Division meeting of the American Philosophical Association, April 2003.

CHAPTER THREE: BATAILLE

BATAILLE AND THE POETIC FALLACY OF ANIMALITY (JILL MARSDEN)

1 Georges Bataille, *Theory of Religion*, trans. Robert Hurley (New York: Zone Books, 1992), p. 20. Henceforth *TR.*
2 Georges Bataille, *Madame Edwarda*, trans. Austryn Wainhouse (New York: Marion Boyars, 1989), p. 140. Henceforth *ME.*
3 Georges Bataille, *The Tears of Eros*, trans. Peter Connor (San Francisco: City Lights, 1989), p. 41.
4 Georges Bataille, *Inner Experience*, trans. Leslie Anne Boldt (Albany: SUNY, 1988), p. 114.
5 Georges Bataille, *Eroticism*, trans. Mary Dalwood (New York: Marion Boyars, 1987), p. 198.
6 Ibid., p. 15.

CHAPTER FOUR: LEVINAS

THE NAME OF A DOG, OR NATURAL RIGHTS (EMMANUEL LEVINAS)

1 Emmanuel Levinas, "The Paradox of Morality: An Interview with Emmanuel Levinas" (conducted by Tamra Wright, Peter Hughes, Alison Ainley), trans. Andrew Benjamin and Tamra Wright, in *The Provocation of Levinas: Rethinking the Other*, eds. Robert Bernasconi and David Wood (London: Routledge, 1988), pp. 168–80, p. 169.
2 Ibid., pp. 171–2.

ETHICAL CYNICISM (PETER ATTERTON)

1 Emmanuel Levinas, *Difficult Freedom*, trans. Seàn Hand (Baltimore: Johns Hopkins University Press, 1990), pp. 151–3. Henceforth *DF.* It has been necessary to modify Hand's translation on occasion.
2 Emmanuel Levinas, "The Paradox of Morality: An Interview with Emmanuel Levinas" (interview conducted by Tamra Wright, Peter Hughes, Alison Ainley), trans. Andrew Benjamin and Tamra Wright, in *The Provocation of Levinas: Rethinking the Other*, eds. Robert Bernasconi and David Wood (London: Routledge, 1988), pp. 168–80, p. 169. Henceforth *PM.*
3 The first work to appear in English on the subject of Levinas and animals was John Llewelyn, "Am I Obsessed by Bobby (Humanism of the Other Animal?)," in *Re-Reading Levinas*, eds. Robert Bernasconi and Simon Critchley (Bloomington, IN: Indiana University Press, 1991), pp. 234–45, an expanded version of which appears in John Llewelyn, *The Middle Voice of Ecological Conscience: A Chiasmic Reading of Responsibility in the Neighborhood of*

Levinas, Heidegger and Others (New York: St. Martin's Press, 1991), pp. 49–67. It still remains one of the best essays on the topic, and I have learned from it enormously. Llewelyn set up many of the terms of the debate that is being conducted here. This essay is dedicated to him.

For a more recent interrogation of Levinas regarding the animal question, see David Clark, "On Being 'The Last Kantian in Nazi Germany': Dwelling with Animals after Levinas," in *Animal Acts: Configuring the Human in Western History*, eds. Jennifer Ham and Matthew Senior (New York: Routledge, 1997), pp. 165–98.

4   Emmanuel Levinas, *Totality and Infinity: An Essay on Exteriority*, trans. Alphonso Lingis (The Hague: Martinus Nijhoff, 1969). Henceforth *TI*.

5   See Emmanuel Levinas, *Humanisme de l'autre homme* (Montpellier: Fata Morgana, 1972).

6   See Jacques Derrida, "The Animal That Therefore I am (More to Follow)," trans. David Wills, *Critical Inquiry*, 28 (Winter 2002), pp. 369–418. Derrida makes a similar observation concerning the status of his "little cat" (374).

7   Emmanuel Levinas, *Collected Philosophical Writings*, trans. Alphonso Lingis (The Hague: Martinus Nijhoff, 1987), p. 122. Henceforth *CPP*.

8   Ibid.

9   Jean-Jacques Rousseau, *The Basic Political Writings*, trans. Donald A. Cress (Indianapolis: Hackett, 1987), p. 151.

10 Count Leo Tolstoy, *The Kreutzer Sonata*, trans. Benjamin R. Tucker (New York: J. S. Ogilvie, 1890), p. 89.

11 Martin Heidegger, *The Fundamental Concepts of Metaphysics*, trans. William McNeill and Nicholas Walker (Bloomington, IN: Indiana University Press, 1995), p. 194.

12 Ibid., part 2, chaps. 3 and 4.

13 Immanuel Kant, *Critique of Practical Reason*, trans. Lewis White Beck (New York: Macmillan, 1993), p. 91.

14 Immanuel Kant, *The Metaphysics of Morals*, trans. Mary Gregor (Cambridge: Cambridge University Press, 1993), p. 201.

15 See also Hegel, for whom animals have an immediate existence that leaves no time beyond the present moment of "sense-certainty" for consciousness to differentiate "between the 'I' and object." G. W. F. Hegel, *The Phenomenology of Spirit*, trans. A. V. Miller (Oxford: Oxford University Press, 1977), p. 62.

16 I do not know if this is true. Indeed, I doubt very much that it is when we consider the total wealth of the world's 298 billionaires (2002, Forbes) equals more than the combined incomes of the poorest one-third of the world's population – over 1.7 billion people. Some deprivation. But leaving aside the issue of Levinas's shocking and politically debilitating rhetoric, the question is this: If desert is proportional to penury, would that not imply that the millions on millions of animals that are currently being farmed for food or experimented on or exploited for entertainment purposes are entitled to more consideration than many humans are at present?

17 For some discussions of Levinas and ecology, see Llewelyn, *Middle Voice of Ecological Conscience*; Roger Gottlieb, "Levinas, Feminism, Holocaust, Ecocide," in *Artifacts, Representations and Social Practices*, ed. Carol C. Gould (Dordrecht: Kluwer Academic Publishers, 1994), pp. 222–40; and Danne Polke, "Good Infinity/Bad Infinity: *Il y a, Apeiron*, and Environmental Ethics in the Philosophy of Levinas," *Philosophy and the Contemporary World*, 7 (Spring 2000), pp. 35–40.

18 See Peter Singer, *Animal Liberation* (New York: Ecco, 2002); also Jeremy Bentham, *Introduction to the Principles of Morals and Legislation*, chap. 17 (quoted Singer, p. 7).

19 Immanuel Kant, "Duties to Animals and Spirits," in *Lectures on Ethics*, trans. Louis Infield (New York: Harper and Row, 1963), pp. 239–41.

20 Bertrand Russell, *The Problems of Philosophy* (Oxford: Oxford University Press, 1998), p. 48.

21 Emmanuel Levinas, *Of God Who Comes to Mind*, trans. Bettina Bergo (Stanford: Stanford University Press, 1998), p. 171.

22 Friedrich Nietzsche, *Twilight of the Idols*, trans. R. J. Hollingdale (London: Penguin, 1968), p. 45.

CHAPTER FIVE: FOUCAULT

MADNESS AND ANIMALITY IN MICHEL FOUCAULT'S
MADNESS AND CIVILIZATION (CLARE PALMER)

1   I would like to thank Alison Stone, Emily Brady and Matt Calarco for their comments on earlier versions of this paper; and Jeremy Carrette for responding to some textual queries.

2   For further, albeit also controversial, discussion of this whole issue, see Colin Gordon, "*Histoire de la folie:* An Unknown Book by Michel Foucault," in *Rewriting the History of Madness: Studies in Foucault's* Histoire de la folie, eds. Arthur Still and Irving Velody (London: Routledge, 1992), pp. 19–42.

3   See, for instance, Roy Boyne, *Foucault and Derrida: The Other Side of Reason* (London: Unwin Hyman, 1990), and H. C. Erik Midelfort, "Madness and Civilization in Modern Europe: A Reappraisal of Michel Foucault," in *After the Reformation*, ed. Barbara Malament (Manchester: Manchester University Press, 1980), pp. 247–66.

4   Roy Porter, "Foucault's Great Confinement," in *Rewriting the History of Madness*, pp. 119–25, p. 121. Gordon, however, refutes this claim in "*Histoire de la folie*."

5   Derrida raises similar questions about Foucault's view of madness in general. See Jacques Derrida, "Cogito and the History of Madness," in *Writing and Difference*, trans. Alan Bass (London: Routledge, 1978), p. 41.

6   See, for instance, the discussion in Boyne, *Foucault and Derrida*.

7   See Still and Velody, *Rewriting the History of Madness*. In the earliest preface to his book – a preface important to Derrida's critique – Foucault comments that he wants to "write a history of madness itself, in all its vivacity, before its capture by knowledge." He then notes that "no doubt that is a doubly impossible task." How far he tried, nonetheless, to carry out this task is a subject of dispute. See Derrida, "Cogito and the History of Madness," and Gordon "*Histoire de la folie*," pp. 35–7.

8   It should be noted that some critics have suggested that Foucault emphasized the distinctness of these epochs more in *Madness and Civilization* than he did in *Histoire de la folie*, reflecting his later views concerning the discontinuity of epistemes. See H. C. Erik Midelfort, "Reading and Believing," in *Rewriting the History of Madness*, ed. Still and Velody, pp. 104–9. It is also worth noting that these periods are not "slices of calendar time" but particular dominant configurations of discourses and practices. See Mark Cousins and Athar Hussain, *Michel Foucault* (London: Macmillan, 1984).

9   Michel Foucault, *Histoire de la folie à l'âge classique* (Paris: Gallimard, 1972), p. 38; Gary Gutting, *Michel Foucault's Archaeology of Scientific Reason* (Cambridge: Cambridge University Press, 1989), p. 71.

10 Although how harsh this life was, and, indeed, how harshly Foucault intended to portray it, is the subject of much heated debate. The Velody and Still edited volume explores this in some detail. It is not essential to this account to come to a firm view.

11 This is one of Foucault's more controversial claims. Some historical critics argue that confinement was not new to the seventeenth century; that the rapid increase in confinement happened, rather, in the nineteenth century; while others maintain that the confinement in France cannot be generalized to the whole of Europe. See Midelfort, "Madness and Civilization in Modern Europe"; and Porter, "Foucault's Great Confinement."

12 Michel Foucault, *Madness and Civilization: A History of Insanity in an Age of Reason*, trans. Richard Howard (New York: Random House, 1965), p. 46.

13 Ibid., p. 58.

14 Blanchot suggests that Foucault came to reproach himself for thinking of madness as having depth, as constituting "a fundamental experience situated outside history and to which poets (artists) can serve as witnesses, victims or heroes." Again, this seems to be related to Derrida's critique of Foucault's work. See Maurice Blanchot and Michel Foucault, *Foucault/Blanchot* (New York: Zone Books, 1987), p. 67.

15 Foucault, *Madness and Civilization*, p. 288.

16 In *Histoire de la folie*, Foucault suggests that those with venereal disease filled this category for a time. This chapter is omitted in *Madness and Civilization*, and is not essential to the account here.

17   Cousins and Hussain, *Michel Foucault*, p. 106.

18   This may reflect a Nietzschean influence on his work. Nietzsche's scorn for domestication and "the herd," however symbolically understood, is well known. Wildness may be regarded by Foucault as a "truer" state of the animal (and, perhaps, the human too) at this stage in his writing.

19   Foucault, *Madness and Civilization*, p. 17.

20   Ibid., p. 20.

21   Ibid., p. 21

22   The possibility that Foucault might distinguish between "beast" (*bête*) and animal was suggested to me by Jeremy Carrette during personal communication. Chebili also makes a distinction between animality (as part of humanity) and bestiality (as humanity stripped of its humanness in classical ideas of madness). See Saïd Chebili, *Figures de l'animalité dans l'oeuvre de Michel Foucault* (Paris: L'Harmattan, 1999), p. 52. I am not, however, convinced that there is a significant distinction between "beast" and "animal" in the text of *Histoire de la folie*.

23   Senior suggests Renaissance scholars thought that "God had revealed the essences of animals to Adam, who gave them names perfectly expressive of their natures." See Matthew Senior, "When the Beasts Spoke: Animal Speech and Classical Reason in Descartes and La Fontaine," in *Animal Acts: Configuring the Human in Western History*, eds. Jennifer Ham and Matthew Senior (London: Routledge 1997), pp. 61–84, p. 66.

24   See Jennifer Ham, "Taming the Beast: Animality in Wedekind and Nietzsche," in *Animal Acts*, eds. Ham and Senior, pp. 145–65, for a discussion of Nietzsche and wild animals.

25   Foucault, *Madness and Civilization*, p. 95.

26   Ibid., p. 74. In a rather strange passage a few pages later, Foucault claims that "western culture has not considered it evident that animals participate in the plenitude of nature" and that, thus, while man stripped of humanity may reveal his animal nature, the animal was viewed as belonging to an anti-nature that actually threatens order. He only cites one source for this idea, Lautreamont, an author not footnoted even in *Histoire de la folie*. The idea that animals were widely regarded as unnatural and not part of the "plenitude" or "great chain of being" is not supported, for instance, by the work of Lovejoy. See Arthur Lovejoy, *The Great Chain of Being* (Cambridge: Harvard University Press, 1973). The key point, however, Foucault seems to be making is that madness–animality was not regarded as natural in the sense that it was a natural disease, amenable to medical treatment.

27   Foucault, *Madness and Civilization*, p. 106.

28   Foucault, *Histoire de la folie à l'âge classique*, p. 166.

29   Foucault, *Madness and Civilization*, p. 81.

30   Ibid., p. 74.

31   Of course, discourses of this kind have a long history. For instance Aristotle writes in the *Nicomachean Ethics*: "For beasts have neither decision nor rational calculation, but are outside [rational] nature, as the madmen among human beings are." Aristotle, *Nicomachean Ethics*, trans. Terence Irwin (Indianapolis: Hackett, 1999), 10496b 33–6.

32   Derrida, "Cogito and the History of Madness," p. 42.

33   Alan Megill's translation, in *Rewriting the History of Madness*, eds. Still and Velody, p. 95.

34   Marc Hauser, *Wild Minds* (London: Penguin, 2001), p. xx.

35   Reason – or rationality at least – can be interpreted in several different ways. Bermúdez, for instance, argues that non-linguistic forms of rationality can be displayed by animals, involving (at different levels) elements such as adaptive evolutionary behavioral strategies; selection between different possible alternative behaviors; and action grounded in instrumental beliefs about consequences. See José Luis Bermúdez, *Thinking without Words* (New York: Oxford University Press, 2003), ch. 6.

36   Foucault, *Madness and Civilization*, p. 75.

37   See Val Plumwood, *Feminism and the Mastery of Nature* (London: Routledge, 1993) for discussion of homogenization and "hyper-separation."

38   See Clare Palmer, "Taming the Wild Abundance of Existing Things – A Study of Foucault, Power and Animals," *Environmental Ethics*, 23/4 (2001), pp. 339–58.

CHAPTER SIX: DELEUZE AND GUATTARI

BECOMING-ANIMAL (GILLES DELEUZE AND FÉLIX GUATTARI)

1   [Translator's note: H. P. Lovecraft, "Through the Gates of the Silver Key," in *The Dream-Quest of Unknown Kadath* (New York: Ballantine Books, pp. 1970), 191–2.]

2   Hugo von Hofmannsthal, *Lettres du voyageur à son retour*, trans. Jean-Claude Schneider (Paris: Mercure de France, 1969), letter of 9 May 1901.

3   *Anton Reiser* (extracts), in *La légende dispersée: Anthologie du romantisme allemand* (Paris: Union Générale d'Editions, 1976), pp. 36–43.

4   On the man of war, his extrinsic position in relation to the State, the family, and religion, and on the becomings-animal, becomings-wild animal he enters into, see Dumézil, in particular, *Mythes et dieux des Germains* (Paris: E. Leroux, 1939); *Horace et les Curiaces* (Paris: Gallimard, 1942); *The Destiny of the Warrior*, trans. Alf Hiltebeital (Chicago: University of Chicago Press, 1970); *Mythe et épopée* (Paris: Gallimard, 1968–1973), vol. 2. One may also refer to the studies on leopard-man societies, etc., in Black Africa; it is probable that these societies derive from brotherhoods of warriors. But after the colonial State prohibited tribal wars, they turned into crime associations, while still retaining their territorial and political importance. One of the best studies on this subject is Paul Ernest Joset, *Les sociétés secrètes des hommes-léopards en Afrique noire* (Paris: Payot, 1955). The becomings-animal proper to these groups seem to us to be very different from the symbolic relations between human and animal as they appear in State apparatuses, but also in pre-State institutions of the totemism type. Lévi-Strauss clearly demonstrates that totemism already implies a kind of embryonic State, to the extent that it exceeds tribal boundaries (Claude Lévi-Strauss, *The Savage Mind* [Chicago: University of Chicago Press, 1966], pp. 157ff.).

5   Marcel Moré, *Le dieu Mozart et le monde des oiseaux* (Paris: Gallimard, 1971).

6   As we have seen, imitation can be conceived either as a resemblance of terms culminating in an archetype (series), or as a correspondence of relations constituting a symbolic order (structure); but becoming is not reducible to either of these. The concept of mimesis is not only inadequate, it is radically false.

7   Gisèle Brelet, "Musique contemporaine en France," in *Histoire de la musique*, ed. Roland Manuel, "Pléiade" (Paris: Gallimard, 1977), vol. 2, p. 1, 166.

8   A text by Henry Miller for Varèse, *The Air-Conditioned Nightmare* (New York: New Directions, 1945), pp. 176–7.

9   Kafka, *Diaries*, trans. Martin Greenberg (New York: Schocken Books, 1949), 24 January 1922, vol. 2, p. 210.

10 Letter to Brod, in Wagenbach, *Franz Kafka*, p. 156: "Diabolical powers, whatever their message might be, brush up against the doors and rejoice already from the fact that they will arrive soon."

11 Note, for example, Kafka's enduring disdain for Zionism (as a spiritual and physical reterritorialization): Wagenbach, *Franz Kafka*, pp. 164–7.

12 There is another version of the same text where it is a question of a sanitarium: compare, the ape's cough.

13 Kafka commentators are at their worst in their interpretations in this respect when they regulate everything through metaphors: thus, Marthe Robert reminds us that the Jews are *like* dogs or, to take another example, that "since the artist is treated as someone starving to death Kafka makes him into a hunger artist; or since he is treated as a parasite, Kafka makes him into an enormous insect" (*Oeuvres completes* [Paris: Cercle du livre precieux, 1963–5], vol. 5, p. 311). It seems to us that this is a simplistic conception of the literary machine – Robbe-Grillet has insisted on the destruction of all metaphors in Kafka.

14 See, for example, the letter to Pollak in Kafka, *Letters to Friends, Family and Editors*, trans. Richard and Clara Winston (New York: Schocken Books, 1977), 4 February 1902, pp. 1–2.

15 Kafka often contrasts two types of voyage, an extensive and organized one, and one that is intense, in pieces, a sinking or fragmentation. This second voyage takes place in a single place, in "one's bedroom," and is all the more intense for that: "Now you lie against this, now against that wall, so that the window keeps moving around you. ... I must just take my walks

and that must be sufficient, but in compensation there is no place in all the world where I
could not take my walks" (Kafka, *Diaries*, 19 July 1910, vol. 1, pp. 27–8).

ANIMAL BECOMINGS (JAMES URPETH)

1   Gilles Deleuze and Félix Guattari, *Kafka: Toward a Minor Literature*, trans. Dana Polan
(Minneapolis: The University of Minnesota Press, 1986). Henceforth *K*.
2   Gilles Deleuze and Félix Guattari, *A Thousand Plateaus: Capitalism and Schizophrenia*, trans.
Brian Massumi (London: Athlone Press, 1988), p. 237. Henceforth *TP*.
3   A philosophical problematic on such a scale requires, of course, an extensive exposition
beyond the reach of this introduction. Two such attempts at this, both of exceptional quality,
are Michael Hardt, *Gilles Deleuze: An Apprenticeship in Philosophy* (London: UCL Press,
1993), and Brian Massumi, *A User's Guide to Capitalism and Schizophrenia: Deviations from
Deleuze and Guattarri* (Cambridge, MA: MIT Press, 1992).
4   "Introduction: Rhizome" (*TP*, 3–25) provides an invaluable overview of many of Deleuze
and Guattari's basic philosophical concerns, and is especially helpful for an understanding of
the notion of "becoming-animal."
5   An important source of the materialist critique of science (and, even more so, of "scienticism")
at work in the texts on becoming-animal is the extensive discussion of the nature of science
throughout Gilles Deleuze, *Nietzsche and Philosophy*, trans. Hugh Tomlinson (London:
Athlone Press, 1984). Deleuze summarizes his position thus: "the balance sheet of the sciences
is a depressing one: *passive, reactive* and *negative* concepts predominate everywhere" (71).
However, that science per se is not, for Deleuze and Guattari, inherently objectifying and
reductive (a stance taken by, in general terms, the phenomenological "rethinking of the
transcendental") is clear from their own appeal to numerous scientific sources.
6   See *TP*, 275–80, 291–2. "Becoming-animal" as a form of "becoming-minoritarian" is an
important instance of what Deleuze and Guattari term "micropolitics," a politics of desire
that at crucial points departs from the agenda of the "politics of identity," and pursues a more
radical trajectory than that of representation and emancipation that, it is argued, remains a
"molar" or "majoritarian" politics. This theme is also clearly evident in *Kafka* in the guise of
"an entire micropolitics of desire" (*K*, 10). See also *K*, 12–13.
7   For an interesting formulation of Deleuze and Guattari's conception of the "unconscious,"
see *TP*, 284. This contestation of psychoanalysis's Oedipal determination of desire and the
unconscious is, of course, a main theme in Gilles Deleuze and Félix Guattari, *Anti-Oedipus:
Capitalism and Schizophrenia*, trans. R. Hurley, M. Seem, and H. R. Lane (London: Athlone
Press, 1984).
8   A "haecceity" is an impersonal mode of individuation; examples given are "a season, a winter,
a summer, an hour, a date" (*TP*, 261). They consist "entirely of relations of movement and
rest between molecules or particles, capacities to affect and be affected" (*TP*, 261). See also
TP, 253, 261–5, 540, n. 33. The connection between the notions of "haecceity," "rhizome,"
and "becoming" occurs implicitly at *TP*, 263.
9   Deleuze and Guattari state that "schizoanalysis, or pragmatics, has no other meaning: make a
rhizome" (*TP*, 251). There is a further scathing criticism of the reactionary tendencies of the
psychoanalytic interpretation in this case and its negative effect at *TP*, 14.
10 "Becoming-animal," Deleuze and Guattari argue, is of limited radicality in comparison with
other types of "becoming-minoritarian" (e.g., "-woman," "-child"), which they identify on a
scale of intensity that culminates in "becoming-imperceptible" (*TP*, 248, 272, 279). The
merely preliminary character of "becoming-animal" is an important element in Deleuze and
Guattari's claim that Kafka's stories, which are the principal site of the "becoming-animal" of
his writing, are less radical ontological events than his novels (*K*, 14–15). See also *K*, 36–9,
59, 87.
11 Aside from Kafka, a "great author of real becomings-animal" (*TP*, 243), Deleuze and Guattari
appeal among others to Melville (*Moby Dick* is venerated as *the* masterpiece of "becoming-
animal"), Lawrence, Woolf, and, in music, Mozart, Schumann, Messian, and Boulez. For
Deleuze, the painting of Francis Bacon also contains a dimension of "becoming-animal." See
Gilles Deleuze, *Francis Bacon: The Logic of Sensation*, Daniel W. Smith (London: Continuum,

2003), pp. 20–7, 32, 59. All these artists are engaged, in varying degrees, with various "blocks of becoming."

CHAPTER SEVEN: DERRIDA

THE ANIMAL THAT THEREFORE I AM (MORE TO FOLLOW)
(JACQUES DERRIDA)

1 Later the same day, and on the next day, this introduction was followed by four sessions during which I proposed readings of Descartes, Kant, Heidegger, Levinas, and Lacan. Those interpretations, as close and patient as possible, were designed to test the working hypotheses that I am outlining here, on the threshold of a work in progress.

2 Michel de Montaigne, *Apology for Raymond Sebond*, in *Essays*, in *The Complete Works of Montaigne*, trans. Donald M. Frame (Stanford, CA: Stanford University Press, 1957), p. 331; hereafter abbreviated *A*. The *Apology* needs to be examined very closely, especially to the extent that Montaigne doesn't just revive, in its luxuriant richness, a tradition that attributes much to the animal, beginning with a type of language. Most pertinent in this respect, marking a difference from the modern (Cartesian or post-Cartesian) form of a hegemonic tradition is the moment where Montaigne recognizes in the animal more than a right to communication, to the sign, to language as sign (something Descartes will not deny), namely, *a capacity to respond.* For example: "It is not credible that Nature has denied us this resource that she has given to many other animals: for what is it but speech, this faculty we see in them of complaining, rejoicing, calling to each other for help, inviting each other to love, as they do by the use of their voice? How could they not speak to one another? They certainly speak to us, and we to them. In how many ways do we not speak to our dogs? *And they answer us.* We talk to them in another language, with other names, than to birds, hogs, oxen, horses; and we change the idiom according to the species." And following a quotation from Dante concerning the ant: "It seems that Lactantius attributes to beasts not only speech but also laughter" (*A*, 335; my italics).

3 *The Cat* is, as we well know, the title of two poems, but only the first of those directly addresses its subject in the singular, familiar form ("*Viens, mon beau chat*"), before recognizing in it the figure of "the woman I love" [*ma femme*]. Baudelaire even names the cat's gaze ("the image of the woman I love rises before me: her gaze, like yours, dear creature" ["*Je vois ma femme en esprit. Son regard,/Comme le tien, aimable bête*"] and "When my eyes are drawn ... towards my beloved cat ... and find I am looking into myself" ["*Quand mes yeux, vers ce chat que j'aime/ ... Et que je regarde en moi-même*"]; and its voice ("To utter the longest of sentences it has no need of words" ["*Pour dire les plus longues phrases,/Elle n'a pas besoin de mots*"] (Charles Baudelaire, "Le Chat" and "Le Chat," *Les Fleurs du mal*, in *The Complete Verse of Baudelaire*, trans. and ed. Francis Scarfe, 2 vols. [London, 1986], vol. 1, pp. 98, 122, 121).

4 See Rainer Maria Rilke, "Schwarze Katze," in *Neue Gedichte/New Poems*, trans. Stephen Cohn (Manchester: Carcanet, 1992), pp. 202–3. (On another occasion I will have to try to read this poem that I have rediscovered thanks to Werner Hamacher.) The poem is dedicated, if that is the word, to "your gaze" ("*dein Blick*") and to a specter ("*ein Gespenst*") – those are its first words; one could set it into play with the poem he signs concerning "The Panther"; see pp. 60–1 (which again begins by naming the gaze [his gaze this time: "*Sein Blick*" are the first words]) – rediscovered thanks to Richard Macksey, who has also translated it into English. Since the conference at Cerisy, cat lovers and friends the world over have been giving me cats like this. This would also be the moment to salute Jean-Claude Lebensztejn's forthcoming masterpiece entitled *Miaulique (Fantaisie Chromatique).*

A propos, why does one say in French "has the cat got your tongue" ("*donner sa langue au chat*") to mean that one has thrown in the towel?

5 "An animal's eyes have the power to speak a great language. ... Sometimes I look into a cat's eyes" (Martin Buber, *I and Thou*, trans. Ronald Gregor Smith [New York: Scribner, 1958], pp. 96–7). Buber also speaks of "the capacity to turn its glance to us." "The beginning of this cat's glance, lighting up under the touch of my glance, indisputably questioned me: 'Is it

possible that you think of me? ... Do I really exist?' ... ('I' here is a transcription for a word, that we do not have, denoting self without the ego)" (97).

6 Lewis Carroll, *Through the Looking Glass*, in The *Complete Works of Lewis Carroll* (New York: Modern Library, 1936), p. 268. Derrida used Lewis Carroll, "*Les adventures d'Alice au pays des merveilles*" *et "Ce qu'Alice trouva de l'autre côté du miroir*", trans. Jacques Papy, ed. Jean Gattegno (Paris: Gallimard, 1994). – Trans.

7 "Chasser": also "to hunt." – Trans.

8 In modern French the noun, *une bête*, is normally used to mean "animal" with a slightly familiar sense; as adjective *bête* means stupid. *Une bêtise*, which I have taken the liberty of translating below with the neologism *asinanity*, means a "stupid mistake" or "idiocy." – Trans.

9 *Ça*, also "Id." – Trans.

THINKING WITH CATS (DAVID WOOD)

1 See "'Eating Well,' or the Calculation of the Subject," trans. Peter Connor and Avital Ronell [interview with Jean-Luc Nancy], in Derrida's *Points ... Interviews 1974–94* (Stanford, CA: Stanford University Press, 1995). In this paper Derrida notoriously develops the idea of a generalized carnophallogocentrism.

2 For the full details, see the note appended to the selection from Derrida in this book.

3 There is something uncanny, for me at least, in Derrida's pursuing here the theme of following in an autobiographical context. A year before presenting a paper at Essex entitled "Heidegger after Derrida" (1986) I found myself at a Derrida conference in Chicago slated to present the paper just before Derrida's paper. The hall was packed with people making sure they had seats for the following paper. My paper was entitled "Following Derrida." My *Thinking after Heidegger* (Cambridge: Polity Press, 2002) continues the same meditation on the many senses of "follow" in English, including "understand."

4 Jacques Derrida, "The Animal That Therefore I Am (More to Follow)," trans. David Wills, *Critical Inquiry*, 28 (Winter 2002), pp. 369–418.

5 From A. A. Milne, *Winnie-The-Pooh* (New York: Penguin, 1996), chap. 3, p. 32.

6 Derrida's cat first came to my attention in *The Gift of Death*, trans. David Wills (Chicago: University of Chicago Press, 1995), p. 71: "How would you justify the fact that you sacrifice all the cats in the world to the cat that you feed at home every morning for years ... ?" His theme will become most apposite to this paper – Abraham's willingness to sacrifice Isaac illuminates the "aporia of responsibility" that afflicts all of us when we acquire special attachments. We find ourselves infinitely betraying everyone else. On the whole, Derrida argues that the abyss always threatens our complacencies, while I tend to respond that the abyss is always historically and contextually framed.

7 Thomas Nagel, "What Is It Like to Be a Bat?", *Philosophical Review*, 83, no. 4 (October 1974), pp. 435–50.

8 *Being and Nothingness* [1943], trans. Hazel Barnes (London: Methuen, 1986), part III, chap. I, section IV: "The Look," p. 259.

9 Emmanuel Levinas, *Totality and Infinity* [1961], trans. Alphonso Lingis (Pittsburgh: Duquesne University Press, 1969).

10 In *Being and Nothingness* (257) he describes the structure of "Being-seen-by-another." This is the general structure of his play *No Exit*.

11 From "The Paradox of Morality," in *The Provocation of Levinas: Rethinking the Other*, eds. Robert Bernasconi and David Wood (London: Routledge, 1988), pp. 168–80, p. 172.

12 D. H. Lawrence, "The Snake," in *Complete Poems* (Harmondsworth: Penguin, 1994), p. 349.

13 See my "Where Levinas Went Wrong," in *The Step Back: Towards a Negative Capability* (Albany: SUNY Press, 2004 [forthcoming]).

14 *The Animal That Therefore I Am*, p. 379.

15 Though it is clear we would have no cognitive capacity without general terms!

16 Derrida's own words are: "At the risk of being mistaken and of having one day to make honorable amends ... I will venture to say that never, on the part of any great philosophy from Plato to Heidegger, or anyone at all who takes on, *as a philosophical question in and of itself*, the question called that of the animal and of the limit between the animal and the

human, have I noticed a protestation *of principle*, and especially a protestation of consequence against the general singular that is *the animal.*" In fact, in my essay "Comment ne pas manger: Deconstruction and Humanism", in *Animal Others*, ed. H. Peter Steeves (Albany: SUNY, 1999), pp. 15–36, p. 29, a paper originally presented at the conference "The Death of the Animal", University of Warwick, November 1993, I take Derrida himself to task for his unthinking use of the word "animal" and "the animal": "It is instructive ... and yet perhaps as necessary as it is a limitation, that Derrida uses the words 'animal' or 'the animal' – as if this were not already a form of deadening shorthand. Human/animal (or Man/animal), is of course one of a set of oppositions which anaesthetizes and hierarchizes at the very same time as it allows us to continue to order our lives. But ... there are no animals 'as such,' rather only the extraordinary variety that in the animal alphabet would begin with ants, apes, arachnids, aardvarks, anchovies, alligators, Americans, Australians ..." Who is following whom? Derrida and I are perhaps playing leapfrog.

17 Lacan's "symbolic" stage reflects the same ambivalence – the acquisition of language is both a power and a subjugation. See Derrida's discussion of Lacan in his "And Say the Animal Responded," in *Zoontologies: The Question of the Animal*, ed. Cary Wolfe (Minnesota: University of Minnesota Press, 2003), which formed part of the original 1997 Cerisy presentation.

18 The list would include mad, terrorist, criminal, evil.

19 In *On the Genealogy of Morals*, Nietzsche writes that nature set itself the task (with man) of creating a creature with "the right to make promises."

20 The ethological or field studies approach of Niko Tinbergen is a good example here.

21 Ludwig Wittgenstein, *Philosophical Investigations* (Oxford: Blackwell, 1963), p. 223e.

22 What is true for naming appears at another level up, so to speak, in the battle over assigning money values to natural amenities like water, mountains, etc. Sometimes, to have a chance of winning you have to play the game. But what if, ultimately, it were not a game?

23 For this and other similar statistics see *The Earth System*, ed. Lee R. Kump et al. (New Jersey: Prentice-Hall, 2003).

24 The despair evinced by pronouncements about the catastrophe ahead by people like Paul B. Ehrlich has to do not with the fact that there are still some skeptical optimists, but that few people in a position to make a difference have the requisite combination of knowledge, courage, intelligence, and imagination to promote convincingly another path.

25 For a clear account of the legal framework in which giving a voice to those without a voice makes sense, in an even less promising terrain, see Christopher Stone, "Should Trees Have Standing?" [1972], in *Should Trees Have Standing and Other Essays* (Dobbs Ferry, NY: Oceana, 1996).

26 In an extraordinary book, J. M. Coetzee's character Elizabeth Costello expresses at least the empathic part of this achievement in uncompromising terms: "There are no bounds to the sympathetic imagination ... I can think myself into the existence of a bat, a chimpanzee, or an oyster, any being with whom I share the substrate of life" (*The Lives of Animals* [Princeton: Princeton University Press, 1999], p. 35). Costello seems to share Derrida's sense that we are witnessing a war over pity. But as I argue later, much of what we collectively do to animals is made possible by a handful of humans with psychopathic proclivities, while the rest of us cast our eyes away.

27 Vicki Hearne, *Adam's Task: Calling Animals by Name* (New York: Harper, 1994). She argues persuasively against the obvious charge of anthropocentrism. Is she, too, sensitively playing in the abyssal rupture? A reviewer writes: "The author believes that the training relationship is a complex and fragile moral understanding between animal and human" (*Library Journal*).

28 Taken from John Berger's *About Looking* (New York: Pantheon, 1980), p. 26. Cited in Coetzee, *Lives of Animals*, p. 34 n. 11.

29 I argue this point more generally in dialogue with Chris Fynsk at the end of "Heidegger after Derrida," in *Thinking after Heidegger* (Cambridge: Polity Press, 2002), esp. pp. 104–5.

30 I draw heavily here on conversations with Beth Conklin, who has studied this tribe extensively in the field, and on her brilliant *Consuming Grief: Compassionate Cannibalism in an Amazonian Society* (Austin: University of Texas, 2001).

31 Conklin, *Consuming Grief*, pp. 186–7.

32 In *Of Spirit: Heidegger and the Question*, trans. Geoffrey Bennington and Rachel Bowlby (Chicago: University of Chicago Press, 1989), Derrida argues that it is problematic to suggest

(as Heidegger repeats) that humans are distinguishable from animals by their awareness of their own death. What kind of awareness do *we* really have?

33 My first introduction to the jaguar came in a lecture by Claude Lévi-Strauss in the late 1960s. It was held in the Collège de France, and the room was full despite the fact that it was raining ... hard. He got to the part at which the jaguar brings down fire from the heavens. As he said these words, there was a violent lightning flash outside. Lévi-Strauss paused, and repeated the guilty sentence. As he did so, the bulb fell out of the lamp illuminating the lectern, and rolled onto the floor, casting his paper into shadow. He moved away from the lectern into new light, and moved on to the next sentence. Everything was fine. More ammunition for the multifaceted nature of the man/animal abyss?

34 See *Gay Science*, trans. Walter Kaufmann (New York: Vintage, 1974), section 60.

35 *Specters of Marx* (London: Routledge, 1994), *inter alia* a brilliant antidote *avant la lettre* to the doctrine of the pre-emptive strike defense policy thematizes the idea of another kind of following, inheritance, and the presumption of ownership and legality, a theme renewed in "Marx and Sons," in *Ghostly Demarcations*, ed. Michael Sprinker (London: Verso, 1999).

36 At the "Returns to Marx" conference, Paris, March 2003, I presented a paper – "Globalization and Freedom" (to appear in *The Step Back*) – in which I insisted that environmental destruction needed to be included in the list of plagues. Derrida agreed.

37 I take up elsewhere the vexed use of the expression animal holocaust (in "The Philosophy of Violence ... ," see below). My view is that the expression is wholly justified even if politically divisive. The reasons for this are deep, and connected with the difficulty most of us have in coming to see that some social practices we take part in clear-headedly might be utterly contemptible. This contrasts with our *shared* condemnation of all Nazi genocidal activity. The attempt to connect these events produces extreme reactions. J. M. Coetzee's Elizabeth Costello addresses this very issue head on (see *Lives of Animals*). And the comparison, originally made by Isaac Bashevis Singer, is gaining currency. See for example Charles Patterson, *Eternal Treblinka: Our Treatment of Animals and the Holocaust* (New York: Lantern Books, 2002). For a parallel treatment see Marjorie Spiegel, *The Dreaded Comparison: Human and Animal Slavery* (New York: Mirror Books, 1997).

38 I offer a study of the extent of such violence, and the complicity of philosophy in violence, in "The Philosophy of Violence: The Violence of Philosophy," to appear in *The Step Back*.

39 This remark is made by Elizabeth Costello, J. M. Coetzee's central character in *The Lives of Animals*, p. 61. Peter Singer's response to these Tanner lectures, included in the volume, is especially delightful.

40 *Cartesian Meditations*, trans. Dorion Cairns (The Hague: Martinus Nijhoff, 1960).

41 Husserl writes: "Now in case there presents itself, as outstanding in my primordial sphere, a body 'similar' to mine – that is to say, a body with determinations such that it must enter into a phenomenal *pairing* with mine – it *seems* clear without more ado that, with the transfer of sense, this body must forthwith appropriate from mine the sense: *animate organism*" [my emphasis] (*Cartesian Meditations*, p. 113).

42 The point of saying *without translation* is that our capacity to appreciate the other's suffering is not in these cases an anthropocentric projection at all. It is instead a mammalocentric or biocentric projection. It is not as humans that we feel physical pain, but as "animate organisms."

43 Although this section "Calculating Pity" is a *response* to Derrida, it is not in fact a critique of his broader position at all, which has always been to insist on the impossibility of avoiding calculation, and the dangers that arise if we try. The point is, however, that environmental concerns, however, do threaten to turn the scene with the cat into a privileged primal scene *malgré soi.*

44 Aldo Leopold, *A Sand County Almanac* (New York: Oxford University Press, 1949), pp. 224–5.

45 Tom Regan, *The Case for Animal Rights* (Berkeley: University of California Press, 1983), p. 262.

46 Poet Gary Snyder has suggested the earth would be better off with a 90 percent smaller human population (see his *The Practice of the Wild* [San Francisco: North Point, 1990], p. 177). But deriving some political program from this is quite another thing. An excellent response to these charges, arguing for complementarity between animal rights and environmental concerns, can be found in J. Baird Callicott's "Holistic Environmental Ethics and the

Problem of Eco-Fascism," in his *Beyond the Land Ethic* (Albany: SUNY Press, 1999). As I
understand it, complementarity does not imply perfect convergence, but perhaps allows us to
articulate more effectively what Derrida has called the space of the undecidable through which
a decision must go to be responsible.

47   These are the last lines of Foucault's *The Order of Things: An Archaeology of the Human
Sciences* (New York: Vintage Books, 1973), p. 387.

48   We might discover that the whole question of whether values *can* be derived from facts is a
misunderstanding. It could not be itself a normative issue without begging the question.

CHAPTER EIGHT: FERRY

NEITHER MAN NOR STONE (LUC FERRY)

1   See Maurice Aguilhon, "Le sang des bêtes," *Romantisme*, 31 (1981), p. 83.
2   "L'animal, l'homme," *Alliage*, 7/8 (Spring/Summer 1991).
3   Alain Renaut, "L'esprit de la corrida," *La Règle du Jeu*, 6 (Spring 1992).

MANLY VALUES: LUC FERRY'S ETHICAL PHILOSOPHY (VERENA CONLEY)

1   Luc Ferry, *Le nouvel ordre écologique* (Paris: Grasset, 1992); *The New Ecological Order*, trans. Carol
Volk (Chicago: University of Chicago Press, 1995). All quotations are from this translation.
2   Luc Ferry, "Des 'droits de l'homme' pour les grands singes? Non mais des devoirs envers eux,
sans nul doute," *Le Débat*, 108 (January–February 2000), pp. 163–7.
3   N. Katherine Hayles, *How We Became Posthuman* (Chicago: University of Chicago Press,
1999).
4   Claude Lévi-Strauss, "Reflexions sur la liberté," in *Le Regard éloigné* (Paris: Plon, 1983);
"Reflections on Liberty," trans. Joachim Neugroschel and Phoebe Hoss, in *The View from
Afar* (Oxford: Basil Blackwell, 1985), pp. 279–88.
5   Luc Ferry and Jean-Didier Vincent, *Qu'est-ce que l'homme* (Paris: Odile Jacob, 2000), pp.
278–97.
6   Luc Ferry and Claudine Germé, *Des Animaux et des hommes* (Paris: LGF, 1994).

CHAPTER NINE: CIXOUS

BIRDS, WOMEN, AND WRITING (HÉLÈNE CIXOUS)

1   *The Holy Bible*, Revised Standard Version (New York: Thomas Nelson and Sons, 1952), p. 83.
2   Ibid., pp. 22–4.
3   Clarice Lispector, *The Passion according to G. H.*, trans. Ronald W. Sousa (Minneapolis:
University of Minnesota, 1988).
4   Ibid., p. 64.
5   Ibid.
6   Ibid.
7   Hélène Cixous's italics.
8   Clarice Lispector, *A Paixao segundo G. H.* (Rio de Janeiro: Editora Nova Fronteira, 1979),
p. 68.
9   Jean Genet, *The Thief's Journal*, trans. Bernard Frechtman (New York: Grove, 1964), p. 45.
10   Lispector, *Passion according to G. H.*, p. 3.
11   Ibid.
12   Ibid.
13   Ibid.
14   Hélène Cixous's note: The translation reads: "I know," because the translator thinks that "I
was knowing" sounds "unclean," incorrect. But let us keep the "incorrectness" of Clarice
Lispector's text intact.

15   Lispector, *Passion according to G. H.*, pp. 64–5.

16   Ibid., p. 65.

17   Clarice Lispector, *The Stream of Life*, trans. Elizabeth Lowe and Earl Fitz (Minneapolis: University of Minnesota Press, 1989), p. 13.

18   Marina Tsvetaeva, "The Poem of the End," in *Marina Tsvetaeva: Selected Poems* (Newcastle on Tyne: Bloodaxe, 1990), p. 136.

THE WRITING OF THE BIRDS, IN MY LANGUAGE
(STEPHEN DAVID ROSS)

1   I am looking into Remedios Varo's painting *Creation of the Birds – Creación de las aves* in her language. I will have more to say of *RV*'s painting and language and of my language, not to mention *HC*'s and *JD*'s. I will have more to say of language and writing and *mimēsis*, not to mention *poiēsis*. For more on Varo, see Luis-Martin Lozano, *The Magic of Remedios Varo*, trans. Elizabeth Goldson and Liliana Valenzuela (Washington, DC: National Museum of Women in the Arts, 2000). See especially Varo's *La buhita – The Little Owl; Caza nocturna – Nocturnal Hunt; Mimetismo – Mimēsis; Personaje – Personage; Vampiros vegetarianos – Vegetarian Vampires*.

2   Hélène Cixous writes of Clarice Lispector as Clarice, but of Jean Genet as Genet. I do not know either of them well enough to call them by their first names, so I will follow *CL*, who writes of *GH*.

3   Clarice Lispector, *The Passion according to G. H.* Trans. Ronald W. Sousa (Minneapolis: University of Minnesota Press, 1988), p. 169.

4   Hélène Cixous, "Birds, Women, and Writing," in *Three Steps on the Ladder of Writing*, trans. Sarah Cornell and Susan Sellers (New York: Columbia University Press, 1993), p. 114.

5   *HC*'s translation quotes from *The Holy Bible*, Revised Standard Version (New York: Thomas Nelson and Sons, 1952), p. 83. Here is the King James version: "(13) And these are they which ye shall have in abomination among the fowls; they shall not be eaten, they are an abomination: the eagle, and the ossifrage, and the ospray. (14) And the vulture, and the kite after his kind; (15) Every raven after his kind; (16) And the owl, and the night hawk, and the cuckow, and the hawk after his kind; (17) And the little owl, and the cormorant, and the great owl, (18) And the swan, and the pelican, and the gier eagle, (19) And the stork, the heron after her kind, and the lapwing, and the bat. (20) All fowls that creep, going upon all four, shall be an abomination unto you" (Lev. 11). The words that matter to me here are *after their kind.*

6   Lispector, *Passion according to G. H.*, p. 168.

7   Cixous, "Birds, Women, and Writing," p. 116; Lispector, *Passion according to G. H.*, pp. 64, 65. I am quoting *GH* from *HC* rather than from the English translation. *HC*'s reading is *imund.*

8   Cixous, "Birds, Women, and Writing," p. 117.

9   By the Judeo-Christian God, if you will.

10   Again, I am quoting *HC* reading *CL*. The translation says *impure.*

11   Cixous, *Three Steps on the Ladder of Writing*, p. 121.

12   In Spinoza nature itself may be un-worldly, *imund: natura naturans* as the creative powers of nature, naturing and un-naturing the world we know, *natura naturata.*

13   Cixous, "Birds, Women, and Writing," p. 117.

14   Cixous, *Three Steps on the Ladder of Writing*, p. 26.

15   Cixous, "Birds, Women, and Writing," p. 113.

16   Lispector, *Passion according to G. H.*, p. 157.

17   Ibid., p. 160.

18   Cixous, *Three Steps on the Ladder of Writing*, pp. 21–2.

19   *"My son is no bigger than a grub. This is why we almost forget him, we don't really believe in him, my dream and I. Where does he live? At the moment, between the leaves of a book. . . . What is the future for such a grub? Not much hope. He'll vegetate. If he stays this size"* (*Three Steps*, 66).

20   This last sentence is from Lispector's *O Lustro* (Rio de Janeiro: Editora Nova Fronteira, 1982), described by *HC* as "a vast premonitory book written . . . at the age of twenty" (*Three*

Steps, 70), adding: "She dreamt that her strength said very softly at the remotest ends of the world: I want to go beyond the limits of my life, wordlessly, with only obscure strength to guide me.

"I feel moved when I read that. It's already *The Passion according to G. H.* Today she is dreaming it; she will write it thirty years later."

This is what *CL* writes: A cruel and living impulse pushed her, drove her, and she would have liked to die forever if dying had given her one instant of pure pleasure. At that point of gravity which her body had reached, she could give her own heart to bite. She wanted to go beyond the limits of her own life as a means of supreme cruelty. Then she went out of the house and left in search, searching with all the ferociousness she possessed: she was looking for an inspiration, her nostrils were sensitive like those of a delicate and frightened animal, but gentleness was all around her and she already knew gentleness, and henceforth gentleness would be the absence of fear and danger. She was going to do something that would go so far beyond the limits that she would never understand it – but she didn't have the necessary strength, ah! she couldn't go beyond what she could" (*Three Steps*, 86; *O Lustro*, 57–8).

21   Here is an example from another place: "At four in the morning, a bull is set loose in the streets, where he is riddled with darts, first in the eyes and most sensitive parts. Four hours later, the animal is beaten until he dies of his wounds. ... He looks like a pin cushion. ...

"It is simply an enactment, solely for entertainment, of the reality of animal suffering. And people find this suffering captivating" (Luc Ferry, *The New Ecological Order*, trans. Carol Volk [Chicago: University of Chicago Press, 1995], p. 43).

"[S]ince we are more or less covertly aware that in truth animals are not entirely things, that as luck would have it they suffer, the tortures we inflict remain interesting" (Ferry, *New Ecological Order*, p. 47).

Perhaps writing is different, perhaps impurity in writing is different from violence and cruelty in flesh and skin. That seems meager reassurance for suffering.

22   See n. 32.

23   I am gazing at *RV*'s *Mimēsis – Mimetica* in her language. Here is another view where birds and women meet painting: *RV*'s *Caza nocturna – Nocturnal Hunt*. "*It is dark. The owl-woman hunts. Or perhaps she is the hunted. She is a bird, a great owl, dressed or draped in a woman's cloth. She is a bird made woman by a rose-colored cloth that drapes her, coquettishly yet modestly. She is out on a hunt, perhaps to lure men and birds, perhaps to be caught. Those other birds too are on a hunt, are hunting in the streets. Perhaps for her, perhaps with her. Birds and women are painted as if on a hunt, with painters and writers, an ambiguous, uncertain hunt, we do not know for what or whom or what will be done in or at the end of the hunt.*"

24   Jacques Derrida, " 'Eating Well,' or the Calculation of the Subject," trans. Peter Connor and Avital Ronell, in *Points ... : Interviews, 1974–1994*, trans. Peggy Kamuf et al., ed. Elisabeth Weber (Stanford, CA: Stanford University Press, 1995), p. 274.

25   Ibid., p. 284.

26   Ibid., p. 282.

27   Ibid., p. 283.

28   Lispector, *Passion according to G. H.*, p. 173.

29   Ibid.

30   Ibid.

31   As *JD* rebukes Martin Heidegger for insisting upon, with too little desistance.

32   Another memory of Spinoza, who writes: "No one has yet determined what the Body can do. ... The Body ... can do many things which its Mind wonders at" (Spinoza, *Ethics*, 3, P2, Sch).

33   Lispector, *Passion according to G. H.*, p. 170.

34   Cixous, "Birds, Women, and Writing," p. 120.

INDEX